11-14-66

A LIGHT to the CITY

150 Years of the City Missionary Society of Boston

1816–1966

A LIGHT to the CITY

150 Years of the City Missionary Society of Boston, 1816-1966

by J. Leslie Dunstan

JUDSON PROFESSOR OF CHRISTIAN MISSIONS
AND WORLD RELIGIONS
ANDOVER NEWTON THEOLOGICAL SCHOOL

BEACON PRESS : *Boston*

Foreword

THE CITY MISSIONARY SOCIETY OF BOSTON is the second oldest voluntary family welfare agency in our nation. Its organization stemmed directly from the concern of two Boston Congregational Churches (Old South Church and Park Street Church) for the well-being of the disadvantaged city dweller. Under such auspices, a mission to the inner city began one hundred and fifty years ago—long before the inner city and its needs were discovered to be fruitful source material for theologians and social workers. These concerned Congregational churchmen had been active in the formation of the American Board of Commissioners for Foreign Missions—the first foreign missionary society in these United States. That experience prompted them to look at the city in which they lived, and they confessed that they "found the heathen all around them." 1380483

In this sesquicentennial year, Professor J. Leslie Dunstan has written a history of the City Missionary Society of Boston. It is a moving description of the churches' concern for all those whom the city has classified as poor and needy—concern for the lives of sailors, immigrants, foreign language groups, tenement dwellers, landlords, children, parents, widows and factory workers. Beginning with the period just after the War of 1812 and spanning the years to the present (1966), it is presented against a backdrop of the tremendous changes in Boston's face and way of life.

From the earliest days, lay people were actively involved in the Society's work. The family welfare work and the educational work during its first thirty years were largely carried on by the laity.

The evolvement of the Society's contemporary pattern of family welfare agency work is outlined with understanding and appreciation. In this anniversary volume, Dr. Dunstan perceptively portrays welfare work in the city of Boston, the changing patterns of need, and the sturdy, sensitive Christian social conscience of the churches acting through the City Missionary Society, in the inner city during the last century and a half.

Dr. Frederick M. Meek

Contents

Illustrations

Preface

THE INVITATION from the officers of the City Missionary Society to prepare a history of the organization as a part of the sesquicentennial celebration could not be resisted. The opportunity promised to open the doors to a practically unknown part of Boston's story and to the men and women who, through their lives and their work, had written that story. The promise has been more than fulfilled. There can be no more fascinating experience than to find people one has not known coming alive before his eyes through the pages of past records and speaking to his mind through the words they spoke and the thoughts they penned. Yet anyone who attempts to retell a tale that was told years before in human actions runs the serious danger of putting himself as he is into the persons about whom he writes. Those people of an earlier day dealt with the circumstances of their time with the outlook and the beliefs they had; we who live now, live in our day with our ideas and our faith. Thus the person today who attempts an historical work such as this one must transport himself back a century and a half, in mind and heart, and become as those who lived then. Pictures may help his seeing, and print may guide his thoughts and touch his emotions, but even then he may not make the journey successfully. Probably if those whose names dot the following pages were to come back to life, they might not recognize themselves in the descriptions of them, but at least they would have to acknowledge the authorship of words quoted from their writings. However, the story of the past has been told, and even though the hazard in all such efforts may well have intruded itself, the results follow.

Not only is the story of the Society as an organization a fascinat-

ing one, demonstrating again the strange ways in which Christian
enterprises react to their settings and in turn affect those settings,
but the story also shows the extent to which a society is often the
lengthened shadow of men. This is particularly true of the two
men who directed the affairs of the Society for half of its entire history. Before I opened a page of the Society's records I heard a good
deal about Mr. Waldron and I looked forward to learning about
him. I found him to be a far more interesting and impressive person than I had expected. I was not prepared, however, for Mr.
Cushing. He must have been a man of humble, yet unfailing courage, a man who was unshakeably certain of what he was doing
and where he was going, but who was at the same time deeply ap-
preciative of the joys and sorrows of human existence. In mentioning those two men I do not intend any slight to others who
have worked faithfully to carry out the Society's purpose, but simply seek to suggest some of the personal interest that is in the succeeding pages.

A complete set of the annual reports of the Society have been
available. The records of the meetings of the Board of the Society
and of the Executive Committee, in the earlier years in the handwriting of the secretaries, exist for about a third of the history.
Other occasional documents dealing with specific episodes and
events add to the original sources. Files of the *Recorder* and its
successor *The Congregationalist,* although repeating some of the
material in the Annual Reports, provide additional information
about the work of the Society. For the brief sketches of the historical settings in which the Society has worked reference has been
had to works of other authors and appropriate acknowledgment
has been made. The history of the Boston Archdiocese of the
Catholic church has been of special help, not only for the light it
cast on certain happenings, but also for the judgment it makes on
the work of the Society. I have divided the history into eras as
seemed most fitting in light of the story itself; if this device gives
a wrong impression of the trend of events I must be held responsible. From beginning to end the City Missionary Society has been
referred to simply as the "Society," except where the context
seemed to require a more complete title.

I hereby express my indebtedness to Miss Lillian Moeschler, Mr. Carlisle Crosby, and Dr. F. Nelsen Schlegel of the Society's staff, and to Mr. Elliott Grabill and the Rev. Charles Styron for information, advice, and much patient answering of questions. Miss Corinne Nordquist of the Congregational Library and her associates have put themselves out to make the resources of that valuable collection available. Mr. Ellis O'Neill of the Andover Newton Theological School library has been helpful in a number of ways. I have used material in the Widener Library of Harvard University and the Boston Public Library, and have appreciated those facilities. Finally, I am most grateful to Mr. Carl Seaburg from the Beacon Press for his assistance. Though all these people have aided me most generously, I alone must be held responsible for all inadequacies in the book itself.

J. Leslie Dunstan

NEWTON, MASSACHUSETTS
APRIL 1966

A LIGHT to the CITY

150 Years of the City Missionary Society of Boston

1816–1966

CHAPTER I

The Evangelicals Appear

REVOLUTIONARY BOSTON was not the Boston of 1816 when the City Missionary Society was founded. The town changed in startling ways and a different town came to be. Perhaps this was inevitable. A community caught in the turmoil of two wars, the founding of a new nation, and all the varied shifting of fortune consequent upon those events, all in four decades, could hardly be expected to remain unscathed. The important thing, however, is not that the people of the town had to react to an almost continuous series of disruptive happenings, but the manner in which they did react. War may be a disaster which sinks some men; for others it is a challenge which stirs their spirits and sends them on to new achievements. So it was for the citizens of Boston.

The population and the leadership of the town changed. When the British forces, trapped in Boston by the sudden beginning of the rebellion, were forced out, more than a thousand Loyalists went with them. Over four hundred of these were leaders of the community, government officials, clergymen, merchants, and well-to-do residents. Their going left a vacuum in town life which was filled by men from neighboring areas involved in the Revolution on the winning side. By the Act of Confiscation passed in 1779, the property of the departed Loyalists was sold. The new leaders not only took over their positions—many moved into their houses as well.

For a period after the war, these new people prospered. They developed new forms for the economy. Because of their efforts, people from the rural areas and from Europe came to share in the new enterprises and to establish some of their own. Then came the events that led to a second war. Out of that there developed another shift in the leadership of the town and in the condition of the common people. Those who had profited between the wars sought to defend their position by various means but gradually were supplanted by another group. The Federalists, who had sought protection from foreign aggression through the creation of a strong central government, lost control; and the Republican-Democrats, drawn from the ranks of business, trade, banking, and the commercial classes, took over. The rise of this new group, among whom were a few from their predecessors who changed their outlook, effected changes among the laborers and the lower classes, whose numbers increased. From the year before the Revolutionary War to the turn of the century the population of the town almost doubled. More importantly, the composition of the population and of the centers of power changed both politically and economically. All of this brought to the front a substantial group of younger men of creative power and liberal vision, men intent upon building a new society instead of trying to preserve the one that had been.

The economy of the town changed. The Revolutionary War practically wiped out the fishing and shipbuilding industries which had been the main sources of income for the people. After the war men had to start again. Trade with the Orient developed. From 1786 on, vessels made the long journey to China with increasing frequency, bringing new wealth to Boston. "The great fortunes acquired before the beginning of the nineteenth century had been mainly gained by merchants in the conduct of foreign commerce."[1] Reliable estimates indicate that nearly half of the million tons of American shipping done around the world in 1805 sailed from Boston and neighboring Massachusetts ports. The Embargo Act of 1807 and the War of 1812 severely curtailed that trade. The owners and operators, however, found themselves with a large sum of available capital. This was turned into manufacturing enterprises. What little industry there had been was done in the homes or small shops. With this new capital factories were built and large-scale operations started. After peace came in 1815 and shipping could be openly resumed, Boston found itself with two bases for its economic life.

To the crippling of the merchant marine, Boston owed a new phase of its development—the rapid growth of manufactures in the first and second decades of the century. The capital and energy which commerce had engaged could not be inactive and here was their natural outlet.[2]

This made Boston a great center of wealth, gained and increased by trade and industry.

The topography of Boston changed. Until after the close of the Revolutionary War the land area of the town remained nearly what it had been since the early days of the colony. The town appeared much like a doubled-up fist placed palm side down on a table, with the wrist shrunk almost to the point of disappearance, the wrist being the narrow causeway joining the town with the mainland, and the knuckles of the fist being the hills on the peninsula. Such a constricted setting was hardly auspicious for any kind of development except shipping, and there were limits set to that by the difficulty of transporting goods into other sections of the country. A visitor to the town wrote:

Boston is not a thriving town, that is, not an increasing town. It wants a fertile back country, and it is too far removed from the western states to be engaged in the supply of that new and vast emporium.[3]

However, the men of Boston set to work to transform the small hill-dotted peninsula into a larger, more accessible area and to develop easier connections with the hinterland. The three hills from which the town had taken its first name, "Tri-Mountain," were trimmed down. The Mill Pond was filled in to provide more land area. Bridges were built connecting Boston with Charlestown and Cambridge. Land across the narrows on the east part of town in Dorchester Neck was annexed and a bridge built to facilitate travel for those who purchased real estate there. And the narrow bar of earth which joined the peninsula to the land was widened. These enterprises increased the trade potential of the town and drew people from the rural areas.

One way in which Boston did not change was in its governmental structure. The town had never been incorporated and all matters of community concern were decided in public meetings. As the population increased, this became a most inefficient way of doing business. Said Josiah Quincy:

> In the constitution of town government there had resulted in the course of time a complexity little adapted to produce harmony in action, and an irresponsibility irreconcilable with a wise and efficient conduct of its affairs.[4]

Yet all attempts to change the form of government, and there were a number, were voted down. "The name and character of town became identified with the idea of popular power and civil liberty." Yet in this the citizens showed the same spirit of independence and determination to manage their own affairs for their own welfare as they showed in the changes they made in other aspects of the town's life.

Boston changed religiously. When the Puritans settled the town, they thought of themselves as being "a city set on a hill," as Governor Winthrop Biblically phrased it, and religious the town remained. To be a citizen was to be a churchman. The Revolutionary War disrupted church affairs, as it did other activities. Some church buildings were used as barracks for British soldiers, as storage places for military supplies, as barns for horses, and as training grounds for cavalry practice. The three Anglican churches benefited by the presence of the British in the town as the soldiers increased the size of the congregations, added to the financial resources, and protected the buildings from damage. But when the British forces left, members of those churches and two of the pastors were among those who departed too. The other congregations, those of Puritan heritage, set about repairing the damage that had been done to their property and resuming their customary activities. Church life quickly took on the appearance of normalcy.

But a subtle change had begun to take place.

> Into the ministry of this order [Calvinistic Congregationalism] gradually crept during the closing years of the eighteenth century many doubts regarding the doctrines hitherto accepted without question; especially the doctrine of the Trinity and that of Total De-

pravity. It is declared that by the year 1800 there was hardly a single occupant of a Congregational pulpit in Boston where Orthodoxy would have stood unchallenged.[5]

Men who were creating for themselves a new and enterprising town were hardly willing to be told they were depraved sinners or that they depended for their salvation and their hope for the future upon the intervention of the divine into human affairs. The clergy continued to use time-honored language and to follow customary church practices, and the members of the church paid little attention to what was happening. Occasionally in clergy meetings questions were raised which uncovered a growing difference of opinion among them but, since they were linked together in their interests and their associations with the leaders of the community, the appearance of new ideas among them seemed of secondary importance.

Yet it was hardly to be expected that this growing clash of opinion could long remain unacknowledged. The congregation of King's Chapel, unable to secure an ordained minister as pastor, employed Mr. James Freeman to lead their services. He was a personable young man of liberal mind and quickly commended himself to the church members. At their request he sought ordination at the hands of the bishops of the church but was refused on the ground of his heretical beliefs. Thereupon the church members, in 1787, ordained him themselves as their pastor after having approved changes he desired to make in the Prayer Book to bring the wording into conformity with his ideas. The bishops thereupon denied King's Chapel any further place in the Episcopal Communion.

In 1805, the Hollis chair of Divinity at Harvard, endowed under a provision that its occupant should be a man of strict orthodox belief, became vacant. The college overseers elected to the position the pastor of the church in Hingham, an appointment which was academically most suitable. When the announcement of the election was made, the Reverend Jedediah Morse, pastor of the Charlestown Church, himself a candidate for the Harvard chair and an outspoken defender of the orthodox faith, published a pamphlet stating his opposition to the appointment on theological grounds. This drew further attention to the dispute in the churches which was slowly coming to the surface.

The Reverend Henry Kollock of Savannah, Georgia, in 1808, conducted a series of evangelistic services in Boston at the invitation of the Baptist churches, which had, as one of their results, the formation of the Park Street Church, organized with a clearly-worded creed defining the orthodox faith to which all who joined were required to give their assent.

Thus, gradually there came to be a sharp division among the Congregational churches of the town. The Old South Church and the Park Street Church, together with the churches of Charlestown, Dorchester, and Cambridge, stood firm in the "faith of the fathers," while the rest of the congregations, by far the majority, ranged against them. The differences between the two sides did not result in an organizational change for some time and, aside from some minor yet troublesome incidents, affairs went on much as before.

This development was not confined to Boston, for it appeared at other places in New England. Ministers such as Lyman Beecher, Moses Stuart, and Nathaniel Taylor made clear their avowal of the orthodox position. Timothy Dwight, grandson of Jonathan Edwards, and at the time president of Yale College, launched a public attack on the church leaders and ministers who were openly or silently acquiescing in the shift to more liberal doctrines. He insisted on the truth of God's revelation in Jesus Christ, on the teaching that all men are sinners, and on the belief that man's only hope for salvation was in the mercy of God granted through the death and resurrection of His Son. These doctrines he said were the very essence of the Christian faith and anyone who denied them was *ipso facto* denying that faith. On one occasion he interpreted the events that had taken place since before the Revolutionary War in the following way:

> It ought, here and forever, to be remembered with peculiar gratitude, that God has, during the past half century, often and wonderfully interposed in our behalf, and snatched us from the jaws of approaching destruction. The instances of this interposition are

too numerous to be now recounted, and are happily too extraordinary to be either unknown or forgotten. We have been frequently on the brink of destruction, but although cast down we have not been destroyed. Perhaps we have often been, and are still, suffered to stand on this precipice [between faith and infidelity] that we may see and feel and acknowledge the hand of our preserver.[6]

Thus the company of the orthodox, or the Trinitarians as they came to be called later on, developed. They arose out of a Boston which was continually changing and they were part of the change. But in the midst of the change they chose to hold fast to what they believed to be the traditional teachings of the Christian church. Out of that company came a number of benevolent and missionary organizations. The condition of the widows and orphans of ministers, often left without any resources for their support, came to their attention, and in 1786 the Congregational Charitable Society was organized to provide help. Many of the rural communities in the western part of the state were without pastors and unable to support pastors even if they could get them. When this became known, churchmen in the same evangelical group in 1799 organized the Massachusetts Missionary Society "to diffuse the knowledge of the Gospel . . . in the remote parts of our country where Christ is seldom or never preached."[7] In 1803 they started the Massachusetts Society for Promoting Christian Knowledge, "for the benevolent purpose of promoting evangelical truth and piety by a charitable distribution of religious books among poor and pious christians."[8]

As they reflected on the possible results of the new appointment which had been made at Harvard they foresaw a dearth of ministers to serve the orthodox churches, so in 1807 there came the founding of the Andover Theological School to educate men in their way of thinking. Their vision was not limited to Boston and their immediate homeland but extended to lands overseas. Businessmen in their churches who had traveled to the Orient brought back word of conditions they found. When, therefore, some young men, under the inspiration of information they had received about the work one or two Christian men were doing in India, suggested that their knowledge of the larger world and the contacts they had around the globe were not solely for their benefit and the increase of their wealth, these orthodox leaders recognized the claim made upon them and in 1810 secured a charter from the state legislature to organize the American Board of Commissioners for Foreign Missions.

Not only did that orthodox company found and conduct organizations to carry out the humanitarian and evangelical interests they had, they also established printed media for the dissemination of information about their activities, trusting by such means not only to share with others news of what they were doing but also to win some to their support. *The Missionary Magazine* began in 1803, and *The Panoplist* in 1805, both with ostensibly the same purpose. Dr. Morse effected a union between the two publications, calling the new magazine the *Missionary Herald.* In 1816 *The Recorder,* a bi-weekly newspaper, began publication. In its pages were combined stories of missionary work gathered from sources all over the world, accounts of missionary efforts at home, official reports of state and national legislatures, lists of ship movements in and out of the port of Boston, and items of domestic trade, all designed to catch the interest of a wide circle of readers.

By 1816 the citizens of Boston had lived through two wars, bearing the suffering, the hardship, and the changes that came as the inevitable accompaniments to the struggles. They had turned what might well have been a disastrous situation into one of great possibilities. They were enlarging the living space of their native town. They had established a viable economy and provided their community with educational and cultural institutions. Theirs was no mean achievement. "Nineteenth century Bostonians [assumed that] man not only could, but actually was raising the world to an ever loftier level. . . .Every aspect of existence confirmed an already deep-rooted conviction of progress." Generally speaking the majority of the citizens of the town, those of the upper and middle classes who directed the affairs of the town and managed its business, were churchmen who believed in the present reality of a living God whose purpose and will they could know, and in the furtherance of which they were assisting. But just as they had tried to understand what their religion meant to them and how they

were to interpret their experiences and their responsibilities there
arose a division among them.

Some were sure that God had given them abilities of mind and
body which they were to use for the conduct of their affairs, heed-
ing as best they could the influence of the wise and the righteous
through the ages. In all they did the responsibility for thinking
and planning and acting was theirs, and the results would be the
product of their efforts. Others, however, believed firmly that God
had saved them from serious disaster and freed them from the
burdens and dangers of limited existence, and that out of gratitude they should serve God by undertaking those tasks which they
learned had to be done. While they used all the powers they possessed to carry out their work wisely, they felt that responsibility
for the outcome rested with God. Their job was to do what God
required. John Morley is quoted as saying, "a great wave of humanity, benevolence, of desire for improvement, in short, a great
wave of social sentiment, poured itself out from among all who
had the faculty of large and disinterested thinking."[9]

Out of that company of orthodox, missionary-minded citizens
of Boston there came in the year 1816 one such wave of benevolence and social sentiment—the City Missionary Society.

CHAPTER II

Birth of a Heritage

I N THE YEAR 1806 dissension arose among the members of the Old South Church, ostensibly over the decision of the proprietors of the pews to tear down the parsonage belonging to the church and build stores on the land. Committees were appointed by both sides in the dispute and asked to meet and work out an agreeable solution. When the two groups met, the matter that had brought them together was quickly and easily settled, but in the discussion it was discovered that behind the ostensible reason for the protest there was a growing dissatisfaction with the pastor of the church, the Reverend Joseph Eckley (pastor 1779–1811), on account, so it was averred, of his doctrine. The congregation met, listened to the report of the meeting of the two committees and a recommendation which was made that steps be taken to secure an additional minister, approved the idea in principle, and instructed the deacons to make an investigation as to possible candidates for the proposed position. The doctrinal differences between the churches in the town having become quite clear by then, and the deacons being aware of the inadvisability of talking with any of the neighboring ministers, consulted the Reverend Jedidiah Morse in Charlestown. He told them of Mr. Joshua Huntington, a young man who, he said, was admirably prepared to fill the role of Colleague Pastor with Dr. Eckley.

Huntington was the son of General Jedidiah Huntington, who was graduated from Harvard in the same class as Josiah Quincy, had served with distinction during the Revolutionary War, and had been appointed by President Washington as Collector of Customs in New London, Connecticut. The General was a devout man, deeply interested in church affairs, one of the group who founded the A.B.C.F.M. The son, Joshua Huntington, was graduated from Yale College and then studied theology, under the direction of President Timothy Dwight and Dr. Morse, both ardent evangelicals.

Huntington came to Boston in 1807 at the invitation of the deacons of the Old South Church and for a number of months did some of the preaching. The congregation, thoroughly satisfied with the impression they received, called him to be the Colleague Pastor. He was twenty-two years old at the time. When Dr. Eckley died in 1811, Huntington became the sole pastor, continuing until his death eight years later.

> The attendants on public worship steadily and rapidly increased. The church was gaining strength, both as to the decision of its members in regard to doctrine and piety, and the increase of members.[1]

Huntington was an ardent defender of the Trinitarian faith. Some of his actions undoubtedly widened the breach between the Orthodox churches and those leaning toward Unitarianism.

When the Foreign Mission Society of Boston was organized, Joshua Huntington was made the secretary, a post he held to the day of his death. As young men presented themselves to the A.B.C.F.M. as candidates for missionary service and were ordained, Huntington took a leading part in the services. He was the recording secretary of the Society for the Suppression of Intemperance. The Society for Educating Pious Youths for the Gospel Ministry was organized by a group of people at Huntington's house, and one of the deacons of the Old South Church became its first president. It was said of Huntington at his funeral service by the minister of the Park Street Church:

> The doctrines he taught you are the doctrines of the Reformation. They have long and deservedly been distinguished as the doctrines of grace. They are the doctrines which in every age have been embraced by that portion of the Church of Christ to which, as your departed minister fully believed, we are especially indebted for the existence of evangelical religion. These doctrines he clearly explained and successfully defended. He loved them as the truth of God, and made them the foundation of every instruction and exhor-

tation. On them rested every hope which he indulged, of heaven
and eternal life . . .²

It was therefore inevitable that when the Reverend Ward Staf-
ford, a missionary in New York City, visited Boston and, at meetings in the Old South and the Park Street Churches, spoke of conditions in New York, of "children growing up as ignorant as the
heathen themselves of the first principles of our Christian religion"
that Joshua Huntington would reflect that what was true of New
York City might also be true of Boston. At least Huntington saw
that possibility clearly enough to invite a few friends, strong church
members, to meet with him to consider the matter. Attending were
William Thurston, Pliny Cutler, Samuel Armstrong, Charles
Cleveland, and Henry Homes. After talking a bit, they discovered
that none of them really knew what the situation was, and they
agreed to find out by doing some visiting in the town, "to examine
into the state of the poor and the destitute, ascertain facts and adjust such a plan for their instruction and relief, as may be thought
expedient."³

Who were these men involved in the informal conversation in
Huntington's study? Two of them, Thurston and Homes, were
members of Park Street Church. Thurston had been a member of
the Old South Church when Huntington came, but subsequently
had asked for his dismissal in order to join in the formation of a
new congregation. That Huntington invited him to join in the
conversation about the poor indicates that he must not have been
too upset when a man "who had assisted in the proceedings which
led to his settlement should now be leading a movement for the
formation of a church whose minister would stand doctrinally
where he stood."⁴ A lawyer, Thurston was a man of considerable
wealth. He was a trustee for the property on which the Park
Street Church building was erected, and he prepared the deed
which gave the church title to the property. When he did so he
carefully wrote into the document a paragraph linking the land
to a particular theological position. Henry Homes was the son of
a member of the Old South Church. His father was among the protesters whose action brought Huntington to the church. The son

was not a member of the church and had not made any profession of Christian belief, but when the Park Street Church was formed he took an active part in the proceedings and joined that church.

Pliny Cutler was a merchant, a manufacturer, and a deacon of the Old South Church having been one of the incorporators when the church was incorporated in 1845. Samuel Armstrong, another incorporator and deacon of the Old South, was a printer, publisher, bookseller, and was one of those responsible for starting *The Panoplist*. Daniel Webster took note of him, calling him, with a touch of snobbery, "a self made man of the common people." Charles Cleveland was the son of a clergyman. In his late teens he had, for a few years, lived with his uncle in Salem. While there he shipped on a vessel going to the Cape of Good Hope. After his return he secured a position in the Salem customs house. In 1802 he moved to Boston, entering the employ of Henry Higginson. From there he launched out on his own business, and at the time of the meeting at Huntington's study he was in the process of forming the firm of Cleveland and Dane to handle various kinds of brokerage and exchange business. He was a member of the Old South Church and was chosen for minor responsibilities from time to time. His brother married the sister of Josiah Salisbury, an Old South deacon, and the two men, Cleveland and Salisbury, were active together in the leadership of a number of missionary organizations.

Such were the men who met with Huntington. Ten days later they met again at the home of Charles Cleveland. They had visited some five hundred homes and had found that at least a quarter of them had no Bible; that there were children who had never been to school and were completely illiterate; and that there were individuals, young and old, who knew nothing of the Christian faith.

They reported on their experiences and their observations; then talked of what might be done about the situation. Naturally, given their outlook, they would be a bit disturbed by their discovery of poor, ignorant, religious illiterates. Yet it would have been easy for them, busy men as they were, to have bemoaned the fact that such a condition existed, to have said that someone surely ought to do something about it, and then after some delicious refreshments provided by their host, to have gone home and forgotten the matter. But these men were evangelicals. They believed that God had put them into His church for His purpose and that He would make clear to them the work He wanted them to do. God— they felt—had led them to see that many of their fellow citizens were being led astray in their churches, departing from the faith which had been handed down to them from their forefathers; and they had determined to hold fast to that faith even at the cost of becoming a minority and perhaps of being looked down upon. It was God, they felt, who had brought to their attention the towns and villages of the hinterland and the new settlements farther west, and they had responded by making it possible for clergymen to be sent to such places and spread the faith. God had made them hear of the heathen in lands across the seas and they had answered by giving their support to men who would carry the Gospel to those lands. And now they had discovered heathen right in their own town. The claim of God upon them came just as clearly through that discovery as God's claims had come earlier. Having heard the claim they set out to obey.

One could wish that there had been a tape recorder hidden away somewhere in the parlor of Charles Cleveland's home that evening to catch all the conversation. After each one had spoken of what he had seen and learned while visiting in the homes of the town, they began to talk of what might be done.

They mentioned the possibility of conducting schools on Sunday for the children of the poor. There were no Sunday Schools included as part of church programs then, for the children of church members were assumed to receive their religious instruction from their parents and their attendance at the church services. The idea of such schools was not new, however, although it had not elicited much general interest. In England, Robert Raikes, a church layman of strong evangelical convictions, had started in 1780 a school which met on Sundays to teach children who, the rest of the week, were at work in the industrial establishments of the city.

Similar work was soon being done in this country. Samuel Slater was an Englishman who set himself to learn the method of cotton spinning invented by Richard Arkwright. Even though every effort was being made to keep the invention a secret, Slater was able to do this because his father was the land agent for Arkwright's partner. When Slater was sure he had memorized Arkwright's invention he came to America and joined with Moses Brown in Pawtucket to build and operate a mill. That enterprise is thought of as the beginning of industrial cotton spinning and the beginning of the manufacture of textile machinery in America.[5] Children were employed in the Pawtucket mill, the number running up over a hundred at times. By 1799 Slater had "established a Sabbath School for them, and it has been claimed that he treated them well."[6]

In Boston also there were schools for the poor. In 1814 some ladies of the Old South Church opened a Charity School. They hired a room and employed a teacher. "The children are taken from a class of people who usually employ them in begging from house to house, and it has been only by personal applications to the parents of these children that they have been induced to permit them to attend the School."[7] The purpose of the ladies was to fit the children for the town schools; they were able to show the effectiveness of their work by the results which followed.

Also, there is to be found a reference to a "school for the instruction of children on the Sabbath Day opened not long since by two young men." The brief statement of this effort does not give the names of the young men. They conducted their school in a private room for a time, a gentleman of the town giving them enough firewood to keep the place warm. The number of children attending increased and the young men were forced to shift their enterprise to larger quarters.

The men gathered in Cleveland's home must have been aware of these activities, which may well account for their interest in the possibility of starting Sabbath Schools.

Then they talked of the possibility of establishing weekday schools for the children of the poor. They had heard of the Lancastrian plan of education, which had met with considerable success in England. A person of their close acquaintanceship, whose name is not known, was in London at the time and he had written of the experience the British and Foreign School Society had with that plan. He undertook to send along a complete set of the books that were being used. Huntington's group of men thought that plan to be admirably adapted to Boston and to the needs which they had discovered. All they needed to do, as they quickly saw, was to find someone who knew how to operate schools on that particular plan.

Next they turned their attention to the nonattendance of the poor at the services of public worship. Making some rapid calculations they concluded that if all the people in town wanted to attend church on any given Sunday more than fourteen thousand would not be able to find seats. They were quite aware that their figuring was somewhat meaningless since so many of the "respectable" absented themselves from worship. But they went on to observe that while there were actually a fair number of empty seats in the churches of the town on Sunday mornings, none of those seats were available for the poor, since all of them were rented by the church members. The churches had neglected to make any kind of provision for the poor. As far as the group who were meeting were concerned, they saw that the solution to this situation rested with the wealthy who might be induced to provide free pews "for the relief of this neglected class of their fellow immortals, who are fast wasting in thoughtless irreligion the day of their probation; and heedlessly travelling towards the awful retributions of eternity."[8]

Another matter of concern was the sailors. As a major port, Boston was constantly crowded with seamen. Some of these men had wives and families in town; others were transients. No provision was being made for their spiritual interests and needs. They should have "a house of worship where they might receive religious instruction, which alone can guide them to a haven secure from the storms of Divine wrath, which we are assured, will overtake the finally impenitent."

A review of the various ideas the group at Cleveland's talked over and the many activities they thought they might undertake shows the breadth of their vision. They were quite clear about the beliefs and the faith that motivated their interest and their intentions. For them the Christian Gospel was the Good News that God had acted in Jesus Christ to save men from perdition and therefore men had to hear that Good News and be induced to respond to it. Discovering that hundreds of their fellow citizens either had never heard the Gospel or had failed to respond to it, they were sure that the knowledge of that Gospel they possessed pointed out their line of duty. As a man on the seashore will dash into the waves to rescue one who is drowning and do so with a spontaneous response to a human need, so those men responded to the needs they had seen. They proposed, "to rescue hundreds of your immortals from the paths of perdition, who may now perhaps be insensibly laying the foundation of their eternal ruin."[9]

But who were these poor? And why were their children not in school?

"The poor you have always with you"; the text was repeated with some frequency, both by the town fathers and the church leaders. From the very beginning of the colony there had been poor among the population. However, when the total number of the people was small the poor were known and their needs were met by those who had the means and the readiness to do so. As numbers increased this personal method no longer sufficed; other procedures had to be devised. Not that the flow of freely given funds in aid of the poor was stopped, for such did not happen. Among the interesting evidences of continued individual benevolence are the endowment funds for the poor which were put into the hands of ecclesiastical and government agencies. Under the pressure of the situation which had developed, the town adopted two practices. First, it made every effort to place a restriction on the people who came to live within its borders, by requiring "the constable to keep a good lookout that no strangers were allowed to gain a settlement by lack of being warned out, and that none of the inhabitants were idle or unthrifty,"[10] by demanding bonds of newcomers against their becoming dependent upon the town, and by actually sending back to the places from which they came individuals who showed themselves to be indigent. Secondly, late in the seventeenth century, the town established the Overseers of the Poor, who were given responsibility for the poor and were charged to do whatever seemed best for their welfare. Early in the eighteenth century an almshouse and workhouse were built where some of the poor were housed and made to work.

The Revolution and the continuing troublesome relationships with England which followed, culminating in the War of 1812, aggravated the problem. The number of poor increased; some living in town when the war broke out had not the means to leave; some came during and for the conflicts and were left behind when peace was finally declared; still others were thrown out of work when the economy shifted to new patterns for which they were not prepared. A letter written near the close of the eighteenth century said:

> Boston affords nothing new but complaints and complaints. I have been credibly informed that a person who used to live well has been obliged to take the feathers out of his bed and sell them to an upholsterer to get money to buy bread.[11]

If that happened to a person once fairly well off, the conditions of those who were poor to begin with can well be imagined.

There was no doubt that by the close of the War of 1812 there was a substantial population of poor people in Boston. In the almshouse were four hundred individuals of whom three hundred were aged, invalids, or children, and twenty insane. The Overseers of the Poor, who gave out relief funds to those who applied, dispensed more than $35,000 in 1823 (the first year for which a figure is readily available).

One result of this poverty was the illiteracy of the children and, in some cases, of the adults as well; and once started, the condition intensified, being largely self-perpetuating. After the Revolutionary War the town appointed a committee to consider the state of the schools and to make recommendations for their improvement. There was the lament "that so many children should be found playing and gaming in school hours, owing either to the too fond indulgence of parents or the too lax government of the schools."[12] As a result of the work of the town committee a system of schools was developed which included schools already in existence and added new ones. "The Latin School" fitted students for the university, admitting children at ten years of age if they were qualified and continuing them for four years. There were six common schools, three reading schools and three writing schools, which admitted children at seven and continued them to sixteen. An applicant was required to be able to read and write to gain entrance into those schools, however. And such abilities had to be acquired through private instruction, at the cost of parents or friends, for the town did not provide them. Consequently, while the town had a system of free schools, there were many children unable to make use of it. A letter in *The Daily Advertiser* in 1818 noted that

> In the report of the School Committee we are told that the number of children between the ages of 4 and 14 who go to no school is 526. . . . Have they not the right to a common school education?[13]

Furthermore, there was no compulsory school attendance law, so that children who had started school were frequently withdrawn and put to work when the fortunes of their parents changed.

After the group at Cleveland's house had talked over the situation they found in Boston, they agreed on another meeting to take whatever action seemed best. So a few days afterwards they met again, bringing with them some of their friends. And all in good order they proceeded to form an organization. They named their new group, "The Boston Society for the Moral and Religious Instruction of the Poor." As officers they chose: the Rev. Joshua Huntington, president; William Thurston, vice-president; Josiah Salisbury, treasurer; and Thomas Vose, secretary. Salisbury, a deacon of Old South, was connected with the Sewall family, and thus had considerable standing in town. His father wanted him to be a minister and had sent him to Edinburgh to study. From there he went to London, visited with the men of that city who were engaged in charitable work, and became a close friend of John Newton. Returning to Boston he was licensed to preach, but gave up the ministry. When he was a student at Harvard College one of his classmates was William Ellery Channing, the great leader of the Unitarian cause. Although Salisbury had joined the Old South Church in his youth, apparently under the influence of his father, who was a deacon, and of a heritage of church leadership which went back some five generations, he changed his membership on his return from England to the Federal Street Church where Dr. Channing was the pastor. Later he returned to Old South, "sacrificing an early and cherished friendship to his convictions of what he owed to truth."[14] When still a young man, Thomas Vose became a member of the First Church in Dorchester. He soon moved to Baltimore where he went into business and became a successful merchant. He had returned to Boston a little more than a year before the meeting at which he was chosen to be treasurer of the new Society. Chosen as members of the Board of Directors of the Society were Samuel Armstrong, Charles Cleveland, Pliny Cutler, Henry Homes, John Hopkins, John Proctor, Samuel Train, and Josiah Vinton, Jr. "The object of this Society includes the exercise of duties the most immediately incumbent upon us all, and that its labors cannot but terminate in effects of the most vital importance to the community in general"[15] was the way they saw the work they were about to undertake. So the City Missionary Society was launched. The date was October 9, 1816.

CHAPTER III

Conscience of the Community 1816–1820

T HE NEW GROUP proceeded at once to carry out the purposes they had outlined for themselves. Meeting together from time to time to consider the progress they were making, they carried out tasks which seemed to them best suited to achieve their ends. Each year a committee prepared a report which was printed and distributed to all the people in town whom they could interest in their efforts. "The committee, to whom was assigned the office of reporting to the Society the operations of the last year, congratulate their brethren upon the auspicious circumstances attending this anniversary."[1] So they wrote in 1818. What had they done these first years?

First and importantly they had raised money. They fixed upon classes of supporters: Life Subscribers, who gave twenty dollars toward the work, and Annual Subscribers who gave smaller amounts each year. In addition, a few individuals made donations. A man by the name of John Hopkins went among his friends and collected a fairly substantial sum which he gave to the Society. The churches helped. At one of the anniversaries, Mr. Huntington preached a sermon in behalf of the Society and asked for a special collection. The contributions of the Life Subscribers were to be a "Permanent Fund," in effect an endowment; those of the Annual Subscribers were to pay the cost of the program. At the beginning, a number of individuals were both Life and Annual members, Thomas Vose and Samuel Armstrong for example. Furthermore, the Society made it possible for generous individuals to provide support for particular activities in which they had a special interest, such as a gift toward the salary of the preacher to the seamen or a gift toward the purchase of land for a chapel.

Within three years of the formation of the Society, forms for bequests were appended to the annual reports, one form for individuals desiring to leave, at their death, funds for current use, and another for those who would "give and bequeath X dollars in sacred trust, to be added to the permanent fund, the interest or annual income to be applied to the uses and purposes of the Society." Such was the financial planning of the Society at its beginning. Bills for current expenses each year were met, although it is somewhat difficult to discover from the financial reports just how the permanent fund was managed. It is clear, however, that the Society operated solvently during its early years. Even more important, it is obvious that members of the Society were so convinced of the divine necessity of their plans that they this early sought to establish their work on a permanent foundation.

Having learned through their investigations of the numbers of children unable to attend school, they thought of the possibility of starting their own schools to deal with the situation. The Lancastrian plan of education, mentioned earlier, seemed to them to meet their desires. They sought, but they could not find, a man who knew enough about the plan to start operations. This did not deter them from taking some action to remedy the condition they had found. To them, every child had the right to a basic education. They believed that only if such were supplied could individuals develop in a wholesome manner, and society be free from destructive elements within it. A committee of Board members was appointed—William Thurston, Josiah Salisbury, Samuel Armstrong, Pliny Cutler, and John Hopkins—to see what could be done. Two, or perhaps three of these men made a trip to Philadelphia to learn what the people there were doing for the younger children of poor families. On their return they drew up a report of their findings and the Society added some recommendations for the officials in Boston. Before approaching the selectmen, however, the Society elicited the interest of a substantial number of the leading citizens. The result was

> that at a legal meeting of the inhabitants of the town of Boston, assembled in Fanueil Hall, June 11, 1818, notified for the purpose of considering the subject of establishing Primary Schools, the fol-

lowing vote was passed and $5000 appropriated for the first year's support of these schools: voted, that the School Committee be instructed . . . to nominate and appoint three gentlemen in each ward, whose duty collectively shall be to provide instruction for children between four and seven years of age, and apportion the expenses among the several schools.[2]

The Society quickly discovered that although this action by the town did much to alleviate the condition, they had found it did not completely solve the problem. There remained those children too old for the newly formed Primary Schools and too ignorant to be admitted to the Common Schools, and whose parents could not pay for them to go to private schools. One of the workers employed by the Society wrote:

> The number of boys of this description is between three and four hundred. Many of these boys, both whites and blacks, spend their time in a manner most calculated to ensure their ruin for this world and the next.

The remedy for that was readily seen to be the establishment of charity schools, and the officials were memorialized to that effect. Some years passed before action was taken. In the meanwhile, work undertaken by the Society began to care for some of the neglected children and young people. When, later on, the city decided to undertake a more inclusive program of education, one, and perhaps more, of the schools conducted by the Society were transferred to public support.

A second concern of the New Society were those people who could not afford to attend worship services. No places were provided for them and, as the members of the Society were clear-eyed enough to see, they would not have been welcomed had they tried to attend. A strong plea was made by the Society that churches consider the situation seriously and make it possible for poor people to join in divine service. There appears to have been no immediate response to that appeal; and it is clear why there should not have been, given the arrangements that prevailed in the church buildings of the day.

So the Society undertook to do something about the religious needs of the poor, the needs of "those, whom ignorance and vice have debarred from the blessings of that Christian community in which a kind Providence has placed their lot."[3] Clergymen were employed who visited in the homes, talked with the people, conducted services for small groups whenever possible and in other ways worked for the "spiritual improvement of the poor." At the outset, that activity was spasmodic, for there was difficulty securing anyone to undertake the task on a full-time basis, nor were there sufficient funds. Yet, the pastor of a church in Bridgeport, Connecticut, visiting in Boston, was prevailed upon to see what could be done and for three weeks he visited the parents of the children enrolled in the Sabbath Schools and spoke at the assemblies of the Schools. Another pastor, an older man who because of his poor health could not serve a church, did some visiting for a time. The Reverend Mr. Sabine of St. John, Newfoundland, moved to Boston on the advice of some of the town's businessmen who had heard of him. On his arrival he worked for the Society for three months after which he became the pastor of the Essex Street Church. The Reverend Mr. Rossiter, who had been employed by the Female Missionary Society one or two years before the formation of the City Missionary Society, was then secured. That was the start of the Society's efforts to deal with the unchurched poor.

Shortly after the beginning of that work, the use of a hall was obtained. The market house in the west part of town had an upstairs room; that was rented and fixed up a bit. Services of worship were held on Sunday afternoons, and on Wednesday evenings, what was then called "a lecture," but now would be called a prayer meeting with Bible study. Those meetings quickly took on "the appearance almost of a regular congregation." The only trouble was with the hall. That was known as "Harry's Hall" and was actually, when the Society was not using it, a low-class dance hall. Even worse, in rainy weather the roof and walls leaked, which made the interior rather uncomfortable for people trying to listen to a talk. While those involved in the work were much encouraged by the response they received, they realized that different arrangements had to be made if the effort was to be really useful. Both the ministers who conducted the meetings and the people of the neighborhood who attended found it difficult to associate the message of God's redeeming activity with a place such as Harry's Hall.

Aware of this, the Society moved to do something about it. They found a piece of land in the West End which was for sale. Among themselves and their friends they raised two-thirds of the sum needed to purchase the land. Next, they raised additional money for the purchase of inexpensive building materials. This done, they secured the promises of free work from some friendly artisans who agreed to build a structure when final arrangements for the land were completed. Finally they made a public announcement of their purpose and the steps they had taken, in full expectation "that the remaining three hundred dollars will [not] long be wanting."

The efforts to reach the poor and unchurched were not left to paid professional clergymen. Laymen, or as the reports call them, private Christians, volunteered to serve. They visited in the homes, found living rooms that were large enough to hold a number of individuals, and with the approval and help of the occupants, who themselves wanted the privilege of attending Christian worship, gathered groups for prayer and Bible study. The outcome of that was the meeting of "several attentive audiences in private homes." This work of the laymen met with an immediate response and a plea on the part of those who attended the meetings that they be continued and their number increased, "that others might avail themselves of the opportunities."

During this work, those engaged in it discovered a number of adults who were illiterate. Members of the Society immediately realized the futility of putting Bibles into the hands of people unable to read, or of commending a study of the Bible to such folk. At once the Society made known this state of affairs to the wider community and asked for funds so that some kind of schooling might be provided.

A third area of concern was the provision of spiritual leadership for the seamen. For a short while nothing was done, primarily because neither funds nor personnel were available. But then both lacks were remedied and work was started.

The Reverend William Jenks was selected as the Society's agent in its work with seamen. He was born in Newton in 1778, entered Harvard College and was graduated in 1797. During the years he spent at Harvard he was a member of Christ Church in Cambridge, but afterwards was ordained in the First Church, Congregational, in Bath, Maine, of which he had been elected the pastor. From 1805 to 1812 he continued in the Bath pastorate. Granted a leave of absence to serve as chaplain in the army, he returned to his charge when mustered out at the end of the war. He then received an invitation to the church in Portsmouth, New Hampshire, but declined, for about the same time Bowdoin College asked him to become Professor of Oriental and English Literature. After some years at Bowdoin he moved to Boston, where he opened a private school. This put him in touch with the members of the Society who, after some time, urged upon him the needs of the seamen in the town.

There are references to other things Jenks did, and events in which he took part, which give a fairly clear glimpse of the character of the man. After the death of Josiah Huntington, he was asked by Old South Church to lead the public devotions regularly held in the Vestry, which he did with great acceptability. But he never bothered to make any agreement with the church as to pay for his services. When he was through, the church voted him "a complete suit of clothes or the value thereof in money, at his option, as compensation." At the ordination of the Reverend Benjamin Wisner, chosen successor to Mr. Huntington, the Council called for the occasion fell into such a lengthy and acrimonious discussion that all available time was used up so "the address to the Church and Congregation, assigned to the Reverend William Jenks, owing to the late hour of the day, was dispensed with."[4] There is no indication that Jenks was aggrieved at this unseemly slight. Shortly after that, he was asked to preside at a meeting of the congregation at the Essex Street Church when an attempt was made to settle a disagreement between the pastor of the church and a leading deacon which threatened a division among the membership. While the church eventually separated into two groups because of the issue that had arisen, there is an indication that the meeting was a fairly calm one under Jenks' chairmanship. "In the latter part of his life, Dr. Jenks worshipped at the Old South Church, and occupied a seat in the capacious pulpit. His venerable appearance—white hair, benignant face, and scholarly bearing—as he sat there, with the ear trumpet opening towards the preacher, is vividly remembered. . . ."[5]

Such was the man who became the agent of the Society in its work for seamen. The owners of Central Wharf loaned the room over the Wharf for the use of the Society. "On Sunday, August 9 [1818] Divine Service was performed for the first time at the Long Room over the centre-arch on Central Wharf by the Reverend Mr. Jenks, in the presence of a large concourse of the mariners of Boston and those attached to coasting vessels now lying in our port."[6] Not long after that opening service congregations of between three and four hundred people were attending regularly. Among that number were strangers visiting in the town who did not feel themselves welcomed at the established churches. Occasionally one or more of the businessmen of the town, owners of vessels, proprietors of wharves, and merchants who dealt in the goods carried in the vessels came to these services. Usually Jenks conducted the service and preached the sermon. Occasionally he was able to get a ship's captain who was a Christian to lead. He commented on the helpfulness of such leadership.

Jenks observed that there was one drawback to the meeting place on the Wharf, adequate though it was in so many ways: it was not a suitable place for women and children. He was sure that a Christian church had to be based on family relationships and thus must have people of both sexes as members. He saw, therefore, that whatever results might follow from his work among the seamen, the formation of a church could not be one of them as long as the meetings and services were held at the Wharf. Other than that, however, Jenks was quite clear as to the purpose for which he labored. He sought to bring about "the union of a correct faith with a holy and useful life, as indispensible to the Christian character."[7] What he wished to do was to create or sustain in the seamen, lives of responsible moral behavior through committed trust in Jesus Christ. He wanted to see a company of Christian men scattered here and there on the vessels sailing from Boston who, in the midst of temptations and difficulties, would maintain high standards of behavior and regular devotional practices. Jenks was not one to report in glowing terms any success attending his work. On the contrary he discounted the signs pointing to his personal effectiveness and, instead, praised God for the unmistakable evidences of Christian faith firmly held.

He secured Religious Tracts prepared especially for seamen from the Society for Promoting Christian Knowledge and distributed them freely. From the comments made to him by those who received the tracts, he judged they were a useful means of instructing men in the meaning and obligations of Christianity. The Massachusetts Bible Society made available to him, at the start of his work, about two hundred copies of the Scriptures. Some of them he gave away when he thought that to do so would be helpful, others he sold, using the proceeds to buy more copies. A man dropped in to a service of worship one day and found no hymn books available. He put a notice in one of the town's daily newspapers, describing the need and asking for subscriptions. Sufficient money came in to pay for five dozen Psalm Books. Jenks believed that one of the most effective ways of dealing with men was through personal interviews, and he made himself available for those who sought him out, as much as he possibly could. He expressed to the Society his unhappiness that other duties kept him from having more time to give to such individual conferences. He made regular calls at the hospital for seamen because no chaplain was assigned to the institution and no religious services were held. He approached the deacons of the Old South Church with the request that seamen who were church members in good standing in their home churches might be permitted to attend the celebration of the Lord's Supper when it was held. They approved the plan and Jenks saw to it that eligible seamen took advantage of the opportunity.

Jenk's vision was as large as the world of the seamen he knew. He rejoiced that in New York and Philadelphia work similar to his was going on for the seamen there. Through careful attention to a letter of inquiry that came to him by way of the treasurer of the

Massachusetts Bible Society, he was instrumental in getting a benevolent gentleman in Philadelphia to help meet the religious needs of the seamen there.

The year following the beginning of his service with the Society, Jenks was made its secretary. From that time on he wrote the annual reports, becoming, in a very simple sense of the term, a kind of executive head for the Society. Not that he gave orders to others who from time to time were employed, but that he saw the work of the Society in its entirety, tried to interpret meaningfully all that was going on, and set before the members of the Society conditions and needs to which, in his judgment, they should give due heed.

Almost immediately after the organization of the Society, one of their principal interests was put into practical expression: Sabbath Schools were started. The Society was established in October 1816; the first Sabbath School opened on the 11th of May, 1817, and the second School on the 15th of June following. The former School met in the town school house on Mason Street and the other in the school house on School Street. The location of the two schools indicates clearly the area of the town which had attracted the attention of the Society's members. Both schools were on the same side of the town as the Old South Church, one to the north of it and the other to the south. The Sabbath School on Mason Street was subsequently divided into two sections which were conducted independently of each other, one for girls and the other for boys, and was counted as two schools. During the second year of the Society's existence two additional Schools were opened, making five Schools under the direction of the Society at the time of incorporation. The two new Schools were on North Bennett Street and Hawkins Street, both to the north of the church and north of School Street.

Children were admitted to the Schools when and as they came. They were gathered by members and workers of the Society who visited in parts of the town near the church and told parents of the plan, inviting them to send their children. After the Schools were started the children became recruiters and the teachers also did a good bit of visiting. As a general rule the children had to be five years of age or over. On being admitted they were put into classes on the basis of age and of ability to read. The children attended when they saw fit, although other devices were used to encourage more regularity. Aside from such devices, however, the children came and went as they pleased; this resulted in a fairly large number of different children enrolled in the schools, a relatively low average attendance, and a still lower number who were present regularly. Given the fact that there was no compulsory attendance at any school in town and that children were allowed freedom in their activity if they were not put to work by their parents, it is rather remarkable that the Schools set up by the Society attracted as many children as they did. Over two thousand different children enrolled in the Schools during the early years. The average attendance ran to about five hundred. In ages the children were between five and the middle teens. Members of the Society were greatly surprised when at the start there were among the enrollees a fairly large number of children whose parents were members of the established churches. "Some of the children are the off-spring of Christian parents, and are therefore not dependent on our exertions for their moral and religious culture. We only cooperate with those who are the Heaven-appointed guardians of their tender minds, in forming them to glory and virtue." These children dropped out of the Society's Schools when the regular churches opened Sabbath Schools of their own. Before long the children attending the Society's schools were, in the main, those for whom the schools were designed.

They came from poor families; some had to be provided with clothes before they could come to the schools. They lived in crowded lanes and run-down houses. Some of them worked on weekdays, others were sent out begging by their parents, and still others were idle. Over a quarter of them were unable to read, and those who could do so were so lacking in proficiency that their ability was of no use in advancing their education or stimulating them to further effort. Many of them were ignorant of the Christian religion and, generally speaking, none of them had been inside a church. They were almost wholly neglected by their parents, and had grown up with little or no restraint put upon them nor any instruction in decent behavior given them. Profane and vulgar language was almost their natural way of speaking. They had developed some evil, destructive habits, and knew no moral standards by which they should be guided. They were disturbers of the more ordered life in parts of the town beyond the area where they lived. "Placed in situations where they had nothing to check but everything to quicken the growth of vicious habits, they were advancing as rapidly as the enemy of righteousness could desire, in preparation for his wretched service, of which the wages is death."[8]

The members of the Society were deeply concerned over the condition of these children, and as the work in their behalf continued they began to think out the meaning of that condition. They appreciated, in some measure at least, that the children were living in a terribly impoverished environment, for they had seen the contrast between the part of the town in which the children lived and their own district, but they did not think of the environment as being the final determining factor in the behavior and the character of the children. They quickly learned that the children lacked some of the more basic necessities of civilized life, clothes and shoes and the ready means of keeping clean, and they took steps immediately, by enlisting the help of some of the ladies in the town, to supply those necessities, but they did not believe that those lacks inevitably created evil children. They understood that wretched living conditions were not the best surroundings in which to bring up children, for they were quite aware of the effect conditions have upon the development of human beings, and as time went on they used the influence they had with the government leaders to change the unsavory aspects of the town, but they were convinced that the basic cause of villainous life was other than environment.

The members of the Society believed that the trouble arose because the children had grown up under the control of their own godless, sinful selves expressed through the elementary forces of their own physical natures. They had not been brought up under any kind of control, and certainly had not learned self-control, but were wholly at the mercy of their momentary impulses and inner drives. Their minds had not raised any questions for them about life; they had no purposes or ends toward which they might direct their behavior. The children were neither "inner directed" nor "outer directed," to use modern phraseology. They were unaware of who they were, of the powers they possessed, and of what they might and ought to become. While the members of the Society were aware of the conditions in which the children lived and knew that something had to be done about these, they believed that fundamentally the trouble was spiritual, that the inner reality of the children's lives had never been given any nurture appropriate to their nature.

> Our 'poor laws' are happily adapted to prevent extreme bodily suffering. Associations are formed to relieve the daily wants of the sick, unfortunate, infirm or aged—but there are, we know, other wants than those of food, clothing and shelter—other calamities besides such as strip us of our temporal wealth, and infirmities of mind and heart which time in its progress brings. . . . In the formation of a Society for the Moral and Religious Instruction of the Poor [we] have aimed to establish an influence of the most salutary kind; and, without interfering in the labors of others, to impress on the minds and hearts of the rising and risen generations the great truth, *that godliness is profitable unto all things, having promise of the life that now is, as well as, of that which is to come.*[9]

Such was the diagnosis the Society made of the ills they discovered in the body politic of Boston. Those ills arose, they felt, through a lack of the knowledge of God and a failure to live by the laws of God. The cure for those ills was to impress the mind with divine things, the filling of the mind with subjects of importance, the establishing of patterns of moral control, the "exciting of a state of sin" (which we may take to mean making the children aware of themselves and what they were like as opposed to an ideal example of a human being), and the gradual development of a moral conscience. They believed a man must acknowledge the authority of a divine power, must know of the nature and will of that power, and must so manage his life that he will respond to the reality and will of that power. Since to them the cause of the children's wickedness was spiritual, the cure had to be spiritual, and that cure, the Society believed, lay in leading the children by means of education and Christian nurture into the realms of moral and spiritual reality.

A superintendent was recruited for each of the schools and a sufficient number of teachers so that not more than fifteen children would be in a class. In most cases, as it turned out, there were ten or less children in each class. The teachers were not all church members, nor were they all "pious" as the reports say. But evidently they had sufficient concern for the children of the town to give up their Sundays for them. The Schools met all Sunday long, with a brief noontime recess. The day's sessions began with hymn singing and prayer and closed with hymn singing and the recitation of the Lord's Prayer. The children were to be taught the hymns and the prayers. The curricula material consisted of the Bible, Catechetical books (Emerson: "Evangelical and Familiar," "The Mother's Catechism," "The Assembly's Catechism; Watts: "Biblical Catechism"; Williams: "Biblical Catechism"), prayers and hymns. The Hawkins Street School reported:

> The instructions are principally lessons from the Bible, the New Testament and hymns. The smaller children use the spelling book only. All are, however, taught the Lord's Prayer, and the morning and evening prayers and hymns.[10]

The teaching was mainly by rote and the learning by memory. Teachers and superintendents, almost from the start of the schools, reported on the amount of material mastered in that way by the children. "One of our scholars here, within the year, committed to memory 3429 verses of the Bible. . . . In this school there have been committed to memory during the past year 158 prayers, 54,561 verses of scripture, 6218 verses of hymns and 6387 answers in the Catechisms." These figures apparently refer to material learned by the total number of students. "But the great object in view, we hope, has been, not merely to exercise, much less to burden the memory, but to inform the understanding and affect the heart with the truths of God's holy word."[11] Another superintendent put this in his report:

> Their minds are led to reflect on their contents, while they commit the precious truths to their tenacious memories, and doubtless,

we may look forward to periods in their lives, when these precious truths will *return not void* to Him who gave them in mercy, and shall deter them from sin, or prompt them to repentance, faith, piety and virtue, if blest of God.[12]

Occasionally a clergyman visited the Schools and spoke. The Reverend Hiram Bingham, before he sailed for the Sandwich [Hawaiian] Islands, spent time at the Hawkins Street School. In all the Schools, mission boxes were provided and the children were taught to bring gifts, no matter how meagre, for Christian work overseas. Much time was spent teaching the children to read and write. Parents were invited to attend on a stated Sunday each month, at which time there were special exercises and an address by a clergyman. The teachers visited in the homes of the children. Regular meetings of the teachers were held. "Tickets for punctual attendance, and certificates of merit are used; and once in two weeks the proficiency of the children is read aloud, which serves as a considerable stimulus to diligence."

The Society was not content to establish Sabbath Schools only in Boston. During the first year of its existence the Board of the Society appointed a committee to prepare and send a communication to all the large towns of the state, reporting their activity, urging the establishment of Sabbath Schools, and offering to supply books and materials to those who would see fit to follow that suggestion. Within a year letters had come from Hingham and Pembroke giving the details of the schools that had been started in those towns; and another letter came from Randolph, Vermont, telling of the establishment of a school there.

The third annual report, after the financial statement, which noted an income of $3,673.66 and an expenditure of $2,449.32, balance $1,224.34, ended as follows:

> You have seen what has been attempted for different classes of your townsmen: for seaman, for children of the poor, and for those 'debarred from the blessings of the Christian Community' . . . let it be presumed that the spontaneous and abundant liberality of the people of this ancient and opulant town will furnish ample means for carrying the benefit of instruction into every destitute neighborhood, and the comforts of industry, peace and virtue to every fireside.

CHAPTER IV

Putting Themselves out of Business 1820–1834

THE SOCIETY'S INCORPORATION was in 1820 and 1834 was the year of a marked change in the Society's operations. During these 15 years the work of the Society was mainly a continuation and expansion of the activities which had been devised during the starting years. The Society had determined upon its purpose, the Moral and Religious Instruction of the Poor, and had evolved programs by which they believed that purpose might be achieved. A group of men had come to feel a God-given obligation resting on them, of being responsible for the spiritual well-being of the poor in their town, and they had implemented that understanding in various practical ways. But changing times brought modifications and developments in those programs.

The Society did not carry on its work in a vacuum, nor with utter disregard for the setting of its labors. It reacted to the impact of the changes that occurred in Boston and in its turn it had an impact upon those changes, although the former was much more weighty than the latter. With its clearly defined purpose, the Society sought nevertheless to keep its work relevant to the life of the community, and, at least for a time, the community was conscious of the existence and the efforts of the Society.

In 1820 the population of Boston was 43,298; in 1830, 61,393; and in 1840, 107,437; roughly a fifty per cent growth in each of the two decades. Because of the size and shape of the town, this meant an increasing pressure of population upon the available land area with a consequent crowding of people in the existing housing, particularly in those parts of the town occupied by the poor. It also gave rise to further efforts to enlarge the area of Boston by making new land. It caused the beginning of the exodus of people from Boston to the surrounding towns, a movement which continued with increasing rapidity in the following years. By 1826 horse-drawn coaches ran hourly in both directions from outside the Old South Church to the Town House in Roxbury. Six years later, Tremont Street was built from Boston into Roxbury, paralleling Washington Street, in order to relieve the traffic congestion.

In 1822, Boston officially became a city. Through a deft bit of political maneuvering the year before, when the citizens in town meeting were dealing with a committee report about improvements in the conducting of town business, the decision was made to change the government and the name of the town, the latter, to the "City of Boston." The decision was reported to the State and by an act of the legislature the city was chartered in 1822. The citizens expected that with the formation of a municipal government, with a more centralized and united structure than the town, their needs would be met more expeditiously and the problems of the community dealt with more effectively. In the minds of those who led in the movement to secure a city government, the change would result in substituting for unorganized public services provided by boards or committees responsible only to the town itself, a unified organization under an executive officer with authority.

As noted earlier, the care of the poor in Boston was the responsibility of the Overseers of the Poor. The Overseers fulfilled their task in two ways: by providing funds to the needy directly, through grants in aid; and by maintaining the new town Almshouse on Leverett Street, to which were sent those unable to care for themselves in their own homes and those who by reason of their poverty or their slovenly or offensive ways were "nauseous in the community." Those arrangements had served with a considerable measure of effectiveness when the town was small and the population somewhat homogeneous, especially since the Overseers favored the giving of grants in aid as the better means of carrying out their duties. But as the number of people in the town increased, and the events before and after the turn of the century added greatly to the numbers of poor and needy, serious problems arose. Reforms were suggested from time to time but nothing was done by the town. The situation grew worse. The Overseers of the Poor reported that in 1820 the Almshouse, a building of thirty-six rooms, held four hundred individuals, a mixed company of aged, infirm, ill, insane, indolent, criminal, and children.

About that time the State Legislature took cognizance of the growing numbers of paupers within the Commonwealth and the need to provide directions to communities for the best ways of helping the poor. A committee appointed by the Legislature to study the problem recommended, among other things, the establishment of a House of Industry or a workhouse in communities where the number of idle poor had become large, for, as the committee said, the "most wasteful and injurious mode of providing for the poor" is the giving of direct relief. The Overseers of the Poor in Boston, with the report of the committee of the Legislature in their hands recommended the building of a House of Correction where those able to work could be sent. The upshot of all this was the purchase by the town of an extensive piece of land in South Boston, and the erection of a substantial building as a House of Industry. Here the inmates might occupy their time and provide for their support by the cultivation of land which the town had acquired.

With the organization of the city government a quarrel ensued between the Overseers of the Poor, who were elected by the people, and the Committee of the House of Industry, responsible to the City Council. That quarrel kept the House of Industry empty for more than a year. The outcome, however, was that the buildings on Leverett Street were used by the courts for the reception of individuals under sentence, and for a temporary lodging place for people who came under the care of the Overseers of the Poor. The House of Industry became the place for the respectable poor, while a House of Correction was built on land near the House of Industry. This concentration of institutions in South Boston brought loud protests from the citizens there who said that their area was being turned into a regular Botany Bay by the city fathers. The House of Correction was not used immediately as such, and eventually came to be used as a place for the treatment of juvenile offenders.

Those arrangements were significant for the work of the City Missionary Society for they involved the very people in whom the Society had a special interest. Yet, even with all the provisions that had been made, the problems and needs of the poor were not fully met. That became very clear to the city government before many years went by. Harrison Gray Otis, in his inaugural address as Mayor in 1830, observed:

> The affairs of the Houses of Industry, Reformation, Correction and the Jail, have been conducted in the most meritorious manner by their respective Overseers and superintendents, according to their means. But so much is wanted to place them on a footing commensurate with the claims of humanity and the feelings of the age —so much beyond our present resources—that I refrain from enlarging upon the subject; expressing merely the hope that some cheap provision may be made . . . for the effectual separation of the insane from the children of vice, and the least atrocious of those from the hardened offenders; and that the time is approaching when the unfortunate debtors will not be domiciled or confounded with either of these classes.[1]

But this observation brought no action from the City Council.

Shortly after the formation of the Society, the attention of the members was drawn to conditions in the West End of the town. West Boston, or the Hill, as the area was often called, was that portion of the town on the lower west slope of Beacon Hill, the side of the hill away from the Common and extending along the waterfront to the edge of the former Mill Pond. It included what is now Pinckney Street, and what was, until the new West End Development Project changed the terrain, Leverett Street. Into that area, as the Society saw it, there was concentrated all the vice and evil imaginable. The section was crowded with people. Most of the houses were completely run-down or disintegrating. Nothing had been done to improve the area or to provide its residents with some of the amenities of civilized life supplied in other parts of the town. There were some hundreds of shops licensed by the town fathers for the sale of liquor, and an unknown number of places, not licensed, where liquor could be purchased. So, of course, drunkenness was prevalent. Gambling houses were open day and night. Houses of prostitution abounded; some of them held public dances designed to lure customers. It was estimated that about two thousand women and girls were involved in the business, some as young as fourteen and many who had been enticed from rural homes by procuresses on the promise of remunerative employment in Boston. Crime was rampant. The Society learned, on inquiry of the county officers, that around six hundred serious offenses were committed in the area each year.

> Whoever wishes to see the worst part of the worst cities on earth has only to pass through a single street in the sixth ward of Boston. He will see all the facilities and the fascinations of crime, which are found in any other place, or which the genius of the wicked can invent. The drunkard and the glutton have their board spread in profusion. The comparatively innocent as well as the debauched are assailed with the hottest temptations. The gaming houses are fitted up with imposing splendor. The dancing halls are ablaze with light, and blaring forth noise five nights a week. . . [all this] dazzles the bold and allures the timid, and paves the way for every species of iniquity that can be named or thought of in human society.[2]

Shortly after he took office as the second mayor of the city, Josiah Quincy turned his attention to the West End. Previous to that time, Quincy had been a representative of Boston in the State Legislature, and had raised, in that body, the subject of pauperism. He was made chairman of a committee to study the situation. Subsequently, he was appointed chairman of a committee in Boston to investigate the condition of the poor in the town and make recommendations for their better treatment. Through those activities he had become conversant with the state of affairs in the West End. Serving on the Boston committee with Quincy was William Thurston, the vice-president of the Society. It is easy to picture the two men with their deep mutual concern talking together of plans for dealing with the situation of which they had common knowledge.

Mayor Quincy consulted with the man who had been police chief while Boston was a town and got from him a report on the West End. That report was substantially a corroboration of the information the Society had gained, except that the chief went even further. He told of unsolved murders, of the impossibility of a decent citizen's walking through the area at night without being molested, robbed and perchance killed, of a concentration of "highbinders, jail-birds, known thieves, miscreants, and women of the worst description" who brazenly and openly pursued their evil ways. The police chief said that no attempt had been made to control the area because the police were not strong enough to face the power against order; and he was convinced that only military force could remedy the condition. His advice to Quincy was to let the place alone, "not to meddle with those haunts, their reformation being a task altogether impracticable." In other words, cordon off the moral cesspool existing in the city and leave it to rot in its own evil.

But Quincy decided otherwise. He gave leadership to the City Council as provision was made for suitable places for the incarceration of prisoners, and the care of the poor and indigent, so that individuals taken into custody in an attack on the area could be cared for. He reorganized the police force and brought in as city marshall a police officer of courage and audacity, thoroughly unimpeachable in his activity, and he gave that individual firm assurance of his complete backing. He revoked and denied licenses. He closed houses of prostitution, and he "kept the light and terrors of the law directed upon the resorts of the lawless, thereby preventing any place becoming dangerous by their concentration, or they and their associates becoming insolent through sense of strength and numbers."[3] There were some among the leaders of the city, and some among the members of the Society who feared that the drastic actions of the Mayor would drive the evil out of the West End and spread it into other parts of the city, and they said as much in public print. But the Mayor trusted the moral sensibility and the integrity of the citizens to see to it that such did not happen, and in this the Mayor was correct.

He took a further step to make clear to everybody his intention to clean out the West End and to win the support of others in his efforts. For a time there had been the need for a new school of secondary education. Boston Latin School had become over-crowded, and it was clear that not all boys wanted to or should go on to college, but that a proportion of them should be trained for business. From this came the decision of the town to establish an English High School. An appropriation was made and the school was started in temporary quarters. After the city government was inaugurated the question of erecting a permanent building for the school was raised. Under Quincy's leadership the building was erected right in the midst of the West End. It stood as a guarantee that the area would be kept in the kind of condition that would be a suitable influence for the young men as they came and went from classes.

Mr. Quincy ran for mayor again in 1828, after serving from 1822 to that time, but was unable to secure enough votes to win. After two ballots had failed to elect any candidate Quincy withdrew. Many people who were aggrieved by the reforms he had instituted, especially those who had profited from gambling, prostitution and the sale of liquor had combined in a campaign of insult, false accusation, and invidious rumors that succeeded in keeping him from office. Yet his reforms had changed the city and the lives of its citizens.

During this period, the Front Street Corporation constructed a roadway parallel to Washington Street on the east side of the town and the people who owned the land bordering on the flats which were enclosed arranged to fill in the newly-created area. The Mill Dam, with its roadway, going from the end of Beacon Street at the foot of the Common to what was then Sewall's Point in Brookline (a spot west of the present Kenmore Square) was completed in 1821. The construction of Bunker Hill monument was begun in 1825, for which a railway was built from the quarry in Quincy to the water's edge in order to transport the granite needed. That was the first railway in the area. During these years three other railroads were chartered by the legislature, the Boston and Lowell, the Boston and Worcester, the Boston and Providence, and construction began on all three.

All these enterprises called for a large number of laborers, since most of the work had to be done by men with picks and shovels. Heavy demands were made upon the available supply of workers.

At the same time, the movement of population from the east into lands farther west had begun, and was draining off many of the more responsible, dependable workers, which greatly accentuated the need. The demand was met, in part, by immigrants. A line of packet ships began running between Boston and Liverpool early in the 1820's and they brought people on every journey. So began the change in the composition of Boston's population which was destined to continue at an accelerated pace in the following years. It is estimated that 100,000 foreigners came into New England during the twenty years after 1820. How many of these settled in Boston is not known. Without doubt many moved down the coast to New York, others went west, and still others found homes elsewhere in New England. But many got jobs in Boston on the various enterprises, supplying the much needed labor, and at the same time becoming a new element in the population with which all agencies and societies dealing with people had to reckon.

William Lloyd Garrison, a young man of twenty-four at the time, came to Boston in 1829. Starting his career as an editor and publisher in Burlington, Vermont, he had moved to Baltimore and was a partner in the publication of the 'Genius of Universal Emancipation,' an early anti-slavery paper. Then he moved to Boston. In 1830 he gave a public lecture. He had difficulty finding a place in which to speak and finally was made welcome by the group of men who owned Julien Hall, a building on Milk Street; the group was a company of avowed and well-known infidels.[4] In 1831 Garrison brought out the first number of the 'Liberator'.

> I determined at every hazard to lift up the standard of emancipation in the eyes of the nation, within the sight of Bunker Hill and in the birthplace of liberty. The standard is now unfurled . . . I shall strenuously contend for the immediate enfranchisement of our slave population.[5]

Slavery had been outlawed in effect in Massachusetts under the state constitution adopted in 1780. A court decision of 1783 substantiated this. There were, however, a number who could recall the days before they were made free. In the population were between 1500 and 1700 Negroes. Some of them worked in the homes and on the estates of the wealthy, most of them having living quarters provided for them where they were employed. By far the majority of them were concentrated in a relatively small area on the lower north side of Beacon Hill in the vicinity of what is now Joy Street. The town had been slow to treat them as the rest of the citizens and rather generally ignored them. They had started a school for their own children in 1798 and the selectmen gave them permission to use one of the halls owned by the town. A few clergymen, among whom were Dr. Morse of Charlestown and the Reverend John Kirkland, subsequently president of Harvard College, contributed the funds necessary to carry on the school. A bit later, a public subscription conducted by the ministers raised sufficient money to purchase a piece of land and build a meeting house on Belknap Street. That was the African Baptist Church. The school was moved to the basement room of the church where it continued under the earlier financial arrangements.

> In 1812 the town first took notice of it, granting $200 annually. In 1815 Abel Smith, Esq., died, and left a legacy of about $5,000, the income of which is to be appropriated 'for the free instruction of colored children in reading, writing and arithmetic.' A schoolhouse was built in 1833-1835 and was named for its benefactor.[6]

That schoolhouse was on the land next to the African church.

There is no evidence that it was part of Garrison's purpose to bring about changes in the condition of the Negroes in Boston. His mind was fixed on the institution of slavery itself, and he sought to awaken the people of the country, including New England, to the terrible evils involved in it, and the need to act at once for its abolition. But his efforts aroused the deepest of feelings among the people of Boston. Not many condoned or defended slavery, but most of the leaders of the city were in favor of a program of gradual emancipation. Economically and socially they had strong ties with the Southern planters and they did not want to upset the arrangements which were both profitable and pleasant. Garrison sounded to them as a disruptive force of a particularly offensive kind, and they set out to silence him. The riot which ensued occurred later than the time under consideration, but the ground was being prepared for it.

The new immigrants were a different problem. Some of them

had been driven out of Europe by changing conditions there; some were people who heard of the opportunities in the New World and chose to seek those opportunities for themselves; and some were people recruited by agents for work in America. "For the construction of this road [the Mill Dam] Irish laborers were for the first time expressly imported into this country." Before that time the Catholic population of Boston was small. Some French people had come, and then Spaniards and a few Irish. The Reverend Francis Matignon arrived in 1792. Four years later the Reverend John de Cheverus joined him. When Father Matignon came the Catholics were holding services in a small leased chapel, a congregation of French Protestants who had been using the place having vacated it. Beginning in 1799 a sum of money was raised, land purchased, and in 1803 the Church of the Holy Cross was built. Many Protestants contributed to the building fund and attended the dedication. By 1817 the number of those receiving communion in Boston was about four hundred. They were very poor, "the offerings of the faithful and the small payments made for the pews in the church hardly suffice for food and clothing to the body of the clergy . . ."[7] In 1820 a school building was completed and a small group of Ursulines had come from Canada to conduct the work and by the end of that year a parochial school for the education of poor Catholic children was in operation. The Reverend Benedict Fenwick, a member of the Society of Jesus, arrived in Boston in 1825, having been consecrated bishop of the New England diocese just previous to his coming.

The growing number of Catholics in Boston created a good deal of misgiving in the minds of the rest of the citizens. Much misinformation was abroad as to the nature of the Catholic church and fears were aroused by the apparent hold which the church had over its members. The awareness of the presence of Catholics in the population increased when it became known that numbers of them had become public charges.

In 1832 the South Boston Almshouse held 340 natives as against 613 immigrants. In the same year the Free Dispensary in Boston treated 854 Americans and 1331 immigrants, of whom 1234 were Irish. . .[8]

Gradually an attack against the Catholics developed.

> Popery was a false religion . . . Catholicism was an immoral sys-
> tem . . . The Romish church was a vast political machine . . . utterly
> incompatible with social, intellectual or political progress.[9]

The popular feeling was increased by a series of lectures which
the Reverend Lyman Beecher, father of Henry Ward Beecher, and
at the time pastor of Hanover Street Church, gave in the Park
Street Church. He set out to show that Trinitarian Protestantism
and American free democracy were linked inextricably together. In
the course of the lectures he indicated most forcibly that Catholics, Unitarians and infidels were to be lumped together as dangerous to the safe future of the nation. His presentation, delivered
in the flamboyant oratorical style of which he was a master, had
a marked effect not only upon the people who heard him, but upon others in Boston and the surrounding towns who were told
what he said. When the lectures were finished, in order to answer
Dr. Beecher's allegations, and to confirm in the minds of the
Catholic people the truth of the beliefs they had been taught,
Bishop Fenwick and the Reverend Thomas O'Flaherty, the Vicar
General of the diocese, and associated with the bishop in the edi-
torship of a weekly paper, called at first, *The Jesuit,* gave a series of
lectures at the Cathedral which were open to the public. These
were well attended by both Catholics and Protestants, the former,
pleased that their leaders had seen fit to respond to the things said
about their faith, and the latter, at least some of them, surprised
to learn the falsity of the understanding they held of the Catholic
Church.

Feelings ran deep on both sides. *The Jesuit* put it this
way, "The unholy alliance of mendacious tract-mongers, merce-
nary Bible-mongers, peculating missionaries, and modern Phari-
sees, (that) host of foul libelers, scurrilous scribblers and unprin-
cipled calumniators, who exhaust the armory of falsehood to in-
jure [the church]."[10] Finally events came to a climax when a mob
set fire in 1834 to the Ursuline Convent in Charlestown, after days
of wholly unjustifiable harassment of the Sisters and the students
in their care, some of whom were the daughters of Protestant fam-

ilies. This event so aroused the common people, both Catholic
and Protestant, that troops were called out to forestall a possible
battle in the streets. A series of brawls between Catholics and
Protestants erupted from time to time beginning about 1823,
among the more serious of which was the Broad Street riot in
1826. A resolution passed by the General Association of Congregational Churches in 1830 was typical:

> The man of sin . . . has commenced the work of spreading the
> delusions of popery . . . and is even seeking to bring the heritage of
> the Pilgrims under the influence of that system, which shuts up the
> Book of Life, and would bind the human mind in chains, and which
> has always proved more deadly hostile than any other, to the interests
> of the true church, and the souls of men.

All this points to the rapid growth of a strong anti-Catholic feeling on the part of the native born inhabitants of Boston.

One other matter must be mentioned. In 1832 the legislature of
the Commonwealth appointed a commission to study the effectiveness of laws dealing with poverty. The Reverend Joseph Tuckerman was appointed chairman of that commission. Dr. Tuckerman had been the pastor of a church in Chelsea from 1801 to
1826. Then he moved to Boston to work among the poor and the
destitute. As he went on with that work he organized "The Benevolent Fraternity of Churches" with representatives from the Unitarian churches of the city. As chairman of the Commonwealth
commission Dr. Tuckerman directed a careful piece of work, dis-
tinguishing the various causes for pauperism and recommending
ways that it might be prevented. As a result two new societies were
formed: The Society for the Prevention of Pauperism, and The
Society for the Employment of the Poor. Those Societies carried
on activities in line with their purposes. In 1850 the two merged
into a single Society.

Those were some of the developments which took place in Boston during the years now under consideration which bore upon
the work of the City Missionary Society. They brought about strik-
ing changes in the society of the period, changes which altered
the structure of that society, introduced new elements into it, set
up conditions which had to be dealt with by public agencies, and

brought into existence numerous private agencies, created by those who felt moved to take some responsibility for the state of affairs that arose. But much more significant than the observable changes which took place in the life of the city and the overt responses which were made, were the emotional and deep seated changes in the lives of the people. There were those who had to face the disruption of their accustomed ways, and were shaken in spirit by the experience; and there were those who were reaching out from lowly, impoverished, debased existence to a larger life which they sensed belonged to them. On one hand, turmoil, fear and defensiveness of soul; on the other, vision, determination and readiness to suffer in order to gain desired ends. As James Truslow Adams described it:

> The vast economic changes which occurred in the quarter of a century from 1825 to 1850 upset the equilibrium of the old social structure of New England, and brought in a period of seething unrest. . . . Almost all the movements [which arose from this unrest] in reality express forms of a single contest—that of the common man against the privileged classes for a greater share in the good things of life.[12]

But even more was involved than man's economic interest. Life itself, in the fullest meaning of that word, was involved; some people striving to retain the life they had in the face of forces that threatened to destroy it, and others dissatisfied and seeking a fuller, larger life.

The men of the City Missionary Society were participants in that changing society. They belonged in it and knew within themselves the feelings and emotions that moved their contemporaries. They were of the more privileged section of the community and shared the experiences, the hopes, the fears and the reactions of that group. Yet they were Christian men, with a sincere dedication to God and loyalty to His will. Theirs was a living faith, worked out in the Boston of the early nineteenth century.

Late in the year 1819 Josiah Salisbury invited a number of those who were interested in the work undertaken by the Society to meet at his home. The names of all those attending are not known, but William Thurston and Samuel Armstrong were there. The

Reverend Joshua Huntington had died earlier in the year. The Reverend William Jenks was the secretary of the Society at the time but there is no indication he was present at the gathering. The group, that evening, decided that the time had come to give the Society an official status, so a petition of incorporation was addressed to the State Legislature. In the petition a change was made in the name of the Society, in order that the purpose of the Society might be clarified. As a result, on the 21st of February, 1820, the governor of the Commonwealth signed an act incorporating "The Boston Society for the Religious and Moral Instruction of the Poor," and granting the Society the right to frame its own rules and to hold property up to the value of $20,000.

After the incorporation new officers were chosen. Mr. Samuel Hubbard became the president; he was a member of the Park Street Church. Mr. John Tappan was the vice-president; he was a businessman in the town who, at the time, had no known church connection, but who subsequently joined the Union (Essex Street) Church. The secretary was the Reverend William Jenks. Those three men continued in their respective offices during the period of time under review. The treasurer's office was held by a number of men in succession: Deacon Josiah Vinton, Jr. (Old South Church); Mr. Andrew Bradshaw, who had an office on Long Wharf; Deacon Thomas Vose (Old South Church); Mr. Horatio Willis, and Mr. Albert Hobart.

Looking briefly at the finances of the Society, the reports are sketchy and the information they give quite inadequate. For a few years there are no reports at all; and with the year 1825 the reports cease. From the information available, however, it appears that from $3,200 to $3,700 was raised and spent annually. A good portion of the money was itemized, "cash received from sundry persons." There were collections taken at the annual Anniversary services and at meetings conducted by the Society, such as the seamen's meetings. Miscellaneous amounts were credited as, "cash received for the use of the African School, $21.59; cash received from Hon. William Gray, the bequest of a seaman on board the *Galatea,* $48.99." The income was spent for salaries, for rent and light for halls and wood for heat, for printing the annual reports,

Reverend William Jenks
Secretary of the Society, 1818–1833

Reverend Charles Cleveland putting a loaf of bread
into a poor girl's basket

and for such things as erecting a flagpole over the seamen's meeting, and shoes for needy scholars. In 1821 over $1,600 was spent for the building of the Mission House. That amount was more than the Society possessed at the time, and the report for that year ends, "balance due the treasurer, $178.91."

Previously, mention was made of the plan to establish a permanent endowment fund for the Society. A mystery of the financial reports is the fate of that fund. It appears and disappears in alarming fashion, much like a jack-in-the-box. When last seen it had risen to $746. Then it disappears completely. Certainly the officers of the Society felt free to use the funds given them as they saw fit. Since the idea of a permanent fund was their own, it could, therefore, be forgotten in the face of legitimate needs.

Too little is known of Josiah Vinton, Jr., who was treasurer for two years. He was a member of Old South Church. When the proprietors of the pews at the church held a meeting without the members of the church being present and decided to tear down the minister's house and build some rental property on the land, he was a leader of a group of church members who protested the decision. He wrote and sent the written protest to the deacons stating the case of the protesters. A glimpse of his character can be seen in the argument he prepared on that occasion. It was meticulously worked out and covered all the legal and monetary grounds involved in the action. His financial reports for the Society are completely accurate; income and expenditures are the same; the balance at the end of one year correctly carried over to the next year; the funds remaining in his hands at each year's end itemized in detail. Of no other financial report of the Society during that era can that be said. Vinton must have been one of those careful, painstaking, annoyingly precise individuals so absolutely necessary for the right conduct of an institution, yet so irritating to those who tend to disregard the niceties of financing in the interests of a program involving people.

During the fifteen year period following the incorporation of the Society the work was financed in any and every way the Directors could devise. The work itself was a response to human needs by those who felt a responsibility for those needs; and the finances came, in large measure, through gifts from those who felt that same responsibility. Most of the work of the Society was done as a free service. The entire enterprise was the combined efforts of individuals who gave time and effort as well as money to a cause that elicited their interest. A good number of individuals worked in the program of the Society without pay; they were the backbone of the whole enterprise.

The Society had decided at the outset that its purpose could be realized in part by Sabbath Schools for children who had no religious training and no contact with any church. At the time of its incorporation the Society had under its care and direction eight schools, six of which it had started and two it had been asked to take responsibility for after they had been started by others. One was at the newly formed Essex Street Church, which had been undertaken by the men of the church, and the other a school that was started by the Negro people in the African church. New schools continued to be established from time to time, and those already in existence were maintained until in 1828, when the Sabbath Schools were turned over to the Massachusetts Branch of the American Sabbath School Union, there were eighteen schools. Present at the annual examination in those schools one year were 1,551 pupils and 295 teachers. There is no way of learning the number of different individuals enrolled in the schools through the years.

Shortly after its incorporation the Society appointed a special committee to superintend the schools and make regular visitations to observe the work being done. "The duties of such visitation and superintendence were justly deemed arduous, requiring that acquaintance with the subject in detail, which no one could obtain without a special direction of his mind and pursuits, in this interesting channel."[13] Thomas Vose of the Old South Church was the chairman of the committee, and Charles Cleveland, also of Old South was the secretary. Sometimes the committee prepared their own report to the Society after they had completed their annual visitation, and sometimes they put together excerpts from the reports of the superintendents of the schools and used that.

One of the tasks of the superintending committee was to enlist the superintendents of the schools and occasionally to help in re-cruiting teachers. Nearly forty different individuals served as school superintendents, some of them only for short periods of time. Some were faithful through the years, and a few must have been men of great dedication, carrying the leadership of a school in addition to other responsibilities in the work of the Society. Thomas Vose was an example. Chairman of the Society's committee on the schools, he was also treasurer of the Society for two years; then when a vacancy occurred, because of some emergency, he stepped into the superintendency of a school and would have retained the position had he not been stricken with a serious illness. John Proctor was another, a deacon of Park Street Church, and a member of the Board of Managers of the Society. Superintendent of one of the original schools opened by the Society, he held that office for six years. Colonel Joseph Jenkins was an alderman of the city, and a charter member of Park Street Church to which he had transferred from the First Church. He served as superintendent of the school at the Essex Street Church, taking that position when dissension in the church threatened to put an end to the work which had been started. Ezra Haskell and John Gulliver are two unidentified saints who served as superintendents, one for ten years and the other for twelve, and who through their leadership won the support of both teachers and pupils; the attendance at their schools maintained a remarkably high average during their incumbencies. One of them was lost to the work through ill-health and the other through death. David Hale, Jr., a member of the Union Church, which was formed by some former members of the Essex Street Church after the dissension, was a kind of roving substitute. The Society transferred him from one superintendency to another as need arose; and he continued to serve in that way until he moved to New York to live. Charles Scudder, Pliny Cutler, Daniel Noyes were superintendents of schools and also members of the Board of Managers of the Society. Cutler was a deacon of Old South Church and was active in the affairs of that congregation; Noyes and Scudder were members of Union Church. The evangelical orthodox Congregational churches of the city and the Society were intimately related, although not officially, through men such as these who gave expression to the faith they professed by their leadership in the schools of the Society.

Little is known about the teachers in the schools. Only very occasionally does a name appear and then because of some significant event in which the individual was involved. It is not known how many different individuals served as teachers during the years the schools were under the care of the Society, but there must have been hundreds of them.

> To supply these various schools with able and devoted teachers, demands must be made principally upon our churches. To them we look for firmness of material sufficient for this laborious service. No merely slight impressions of public utility, it has been found, will sustain the continual draft on the patience and self-denial of a sabbath school teacher. And although we must welcome to this field of labour all such who profess a willingness to toil in it; yet it becomes the members of the Society to pray the Lord of the harvest. . . .[14]

One teacher had a most unusual background, tieing together the old world and the new. The reports tell the story:

> Soon after the establishment of Sabbath Schools by Robert Raikes, a school was gathered in the town of Dorchester, England. While searching for scholars, a poor youth was found in one of the manufacturing establishments, who could neither read nor write. His situation and employment were such as rendered any improvement of his condition altogether hopeless. He was invited, and freely accepted the invitation, to enter the Sabbath School. His proficiency was such, that he was soon able to read the Bible and other books. As soon as it was known that he had learned to read, a group of colliers and workmen in the manufactories collected around him, on every leisure evening, and hired him to read to them. After a short time in the Sabbath School, serious impressions were produced on his mind, which eventuated, as he trusts, in the surrender of his heart to God. Not long since he left England for America, and is now active as a devoted teacher in our [Green Street] school.[15]

Occasionally in the reports of the superintendents appear complaints about the lack of teachers or their laxity. "Others [teachers] engage with some degree of reluctance—are not punctual or regular in their attendance." ". . .but the teachers during the year have not been permanent; many changes have taken place."[16] However, by far the preponderance of the comments about the teachers speak of their faithfulness and their interest in the work.

> They "sow the seed of the Word with diligence and labour with cheerfulness . . . our teachers are punctual in their attendance and devoted to this great and good work . . . [we are] furnished with able teachers who are heartily engaged in the great work of communicating religious instruction . . . the teachers have continued to manifest an increasing interest in the religious improvement of their pupils."[17]

There is no way accurately to determine the teacher/pupil ratio in the schools, but from the figures available it must have been lower than one teacher for ten pupils. In some of the schools the ratio dropped to one teacher for five pupils; only rarely did it rise higher than one to ten. Of significance is the fact that as the years went by, individuals who had been pupils in the schools became teachers; the notation that this occurred appears with increasing frequency. Not all the teachers were professed Christians or church members when they entered the work, but as they went on a substantial number were led to make such profession. This came to be seen as one of the significant evangelical results of the enterprise. "Two of the teachers have been hopefully pious during the past year."[18] "Three of the teachers have within the year made a public profession of their faith in Christ."[19] Such statements appear in almost every report. The importance given to this was stated thus, "It is an acknowledged fact, to which it may be useful to advert, that the faithful teacher, like the merciful man, *doeth good to his own soul.* While he is leading the mind of his pupils to the consideration of momentous truth, his own heart cannot but be in some way affected by it: and experience has already shown us that many, who had begun the work without any evidence in themselves of their personal interest in Christ, have in the course of their instructions found Him precious to their souls."[20]

A number of the teachers grew to be greatly beloved by their pupils and respected by the parents. One teacher, Miss Cynthia Farrar, who served in the Hawkins Street School, went as a missionary to Bombay, India. A young man who was a student in one of the schools for a time, left to enter Amherst College with the avowed intention of becoming a Christian minister.

The analogy of an army has from the beginning years of the church been used to describe Christian people, and it serves to describe the work of the Sabbath Schools. An army of people, recruited and organized, trained and directed, were carrying out an attack upon the ignorance, the immorality, the hopelessness, and the paganism in which the children of Boston were living. The eighteen schools from which the attack was carried out were located in all the needy, crowded parts of the city, including South Boston. Some of them met in public school buildings, others in halls loaned or rented, and a few in church buildings. Thus the points of attack were strategically located where the evil to be met was the greatest.

Pupils were recruited in various ways. Some children came, brought by those already in the schools. But the main dependence for securing students was placed on home visits by the teachers. They went from house to house in the districts where their schools were located, and invited parents to send their children. They met rebuffs, a good deal of indifference, but they found students. And having found them, they continued to visit the homes in order to maintain the interest of both parents and children. In that work the teachers were helped, at times, by others. The Female Bible Society had a group within its membership which called in the homes of poor people to see if they had Bibles. They also took the opportunity to recruit children for the Society's schools. Students from Andover Theological Seminary, excused from classes by their professors for the purpose, did some visiting on occasion. Once in a while others got involved, "two gentlemen have been engaged every Sabbath in looking up absentees, or collecting new scholars."[21] When, in one of the schools, pupils enrolled, came a few weeks and then disappeared, so that it became difficult to do any systematic, orderly work, "we [the teachers] adopted the plan of admitting no child as a member of the school until the teacher, in whose class he was intended to be placed, should have visited the parents or guardian and obtained a promise that the child would attend regularly and punctually for at least one quarter."²² In their visiting the teachers saw at first hand the conditions under which the children lived. They went, as one of them said, into abodes of poverty and wretchedness and guilt; they witnessed, as another said, scenes of moral degradation; and during the hot summer, as a superintendent reported, the teachers had to stop visiting because they could not stand the smell of the garrets and cellars where the children lived. But the visiting went on; it was an agreed and an accepted part of the program.

The schools were in session both morning and afternoon every Sabbath day. In one school the experiment was tried of having one group of teachers for the morning session and another group for the afternoon, but it proved to be quite unsatisfactory. Neither children nor teachers were happy with the arrangement, even though it appeared to offer a varied leadership for the children and less of a responsibility for the teachers. Both, however, found value in continuity of relationships, and the experiment was dropped. There were regular meetings of the teachers in all the schools for mutual consultation on the program and discussion of the pupils. These meetings culminated in the organization of a Teachers Union.

Each school day opened and closed with worship consisting of hymn singing, reading from the scriptures, and prayers. Primary reliance for instruction material was placed upon the Bible, and a number of plans were devised to help the children master and understand its contents. In 1826 a series of lesson books were prepared by the American Sabbath School Union, and Mr. Aaron Russell was made the agent of that organization in Boston. Some of the schools made use of those lessons. But most of the time the Bible was the basic and practically the only textbook.

The teachers were quite clear as to what they were after. Whatever method they used in teaching, they sought to awaken the childrens' minds to questions about God and life, and to stir up within them an awareness of themselves and a concern for their ultimate destinies. The reports expressed this in various ways which sound strange to us, but there can be no doubt as to their meaning. Even when the teachers got the children to memorize large sections of scripture, and showed a measure of satisfaction in the achievements of the children, they cared more for the understanding the children had of what they had memorized than for the amount of material they were able to repeat.

> These instructions, happily adapted to the capacities of children, . . . comprehending the eternal interests of intelligent beings, and unfolding the design and issue of creation and providence, and the awful responsibilities of every individual at the bar of final retribution, awaken the attention and fill the minds of the young with reflections of the most salutary . . . and promote a behaviour uniformally decent and respectful.[23]

> . . . many of the larger pupils manifested a solicitude respecting their eternal welfare; but, with respect to the greater part of them, their impressions were like the morning cloud; however, others by their deportment and conversation have given pleasing evidence that Divine Truth has obtained permanent influence over their hearts and conduct.[24]

Some of the reports use the word "conversion" to describe the experience in the lives of the children for which the teachers looked. What they meant was that they hoped for the time when a youngster, who had been behaving under the power of his own basic drives, the habits acquired from his environment, and the influences that had borne in upon him, would begin to raise questions about himself and his conduct. The teachers trusted that such a change would take place, if God willed it so, as the child came to know the Scripture.

> They [the scholars] listened with serious and silent attention to the instructions and addresses which were publically and privately given them, and united in the devotional exercises with a reverence, which indicated a becoming sense of the awful presence of Jehovah, Nor were these impressions transient, as is often the case when produced by some powerful excitement, but continued to hold sway over the feelings and affections of the heart, and in some instances, we have reason to believe, will never suffer the subjects of them to relapse into their former state of giddiness and levity.[25]

For a time the instruction was by memorization. Teachers reported in this manner: committed 38,396 verses of scripture, 3,513 verses of hymns, and 1,488 answers to the catechism! That was the result of a year's work. But gradually the teachers stopped that way of teaching. "It has become more and more evident to us that the good we do to the souls of our children is not to be measured by the number of thousand verses we report at the end of the year, but by the number of truths we convey to their minds."[26] Other methods were used. A question of religious significance was distributed to all the children in a school on one Sunday. The following week they were to bring back all the answers to that question they could find in the Bible. The children were encouraged to enlist the help of their parents and other children in their search. In some schools a particular subject was chosen, such as, the nature of God, or love, or justice, or revelation, and the pupils were asked to find some passages in the Bible dealing with the subject and commit them to memory. In other schools the assigned subject was of a more practical nature, such as, lying, or stealing, and short texts were used to help the children start their search for additional Biblical material. In some places books were given as rewards for meritorious performance. Quarterly examination days were held to which parents and members of the Society were invited. An honorary class was formed in some schools of those students who did exceptionally well in their assigned work, and they were accorded special treatment. Libraries were set up, books bought through gifts of interested people, and loaned out to serious students at two week intervals.

Some teachers made use of unexpected happenings, such as the death of the father of a pupil by a fall from a staging, or the drowning of two pupils who absented themselves from school to go swimming, to awaken the concern of the children for their own lives. In some schools there were charity boxes, the proceeds of which were sent in support of missions. That part of the program served to introduce a number of subjects for discussion, in the hope that interest in other children and perhaps in human relationships might be aroused.

The reports are very indefinite about results. There was no counting of converts or tabulation of the number who became Christians. From time to time there is a notation of a period of marked seriousness that had settled on a school or of a few youngsters who appeared to have undergone a change in their attitude and behavior. There is a good deal of "trusting" that conversion has occurred, and much "expectation" that efforts put forth are not in vain. But beyond that, nothing. Clearly, the teachers were content to do their work and leave the outcome in God's hands.

Two other matters are important in connection with the work of the Sabbath Schools. First, during the period under consideration the workers in the schools met, for the first time, an unpleasant reaction by the Catholic authorities to the participation of Catholic children in their programs. This seems to have come as somewhat of a surprise to all connected with the schools. Apparently, they were so sure of the truth of the faith they avowed and so certain of their God-given duty to spread that faith among all people, since unless people held that faith they were doomed, that it had not occurred to them that individuals whom they considered to be in the grip of the devil would oppose their activity in the name of the Christian religion. During this era, even though the superintendents and the teachers were within the community that was thoroughly aware of the growth of the Catholic church in their midst, they expected parents and children of that church to welcome their efforts and heed the Gospel as they presented it. In the report for 1826, "There have been a considerable number of Irish children who have attended this school [Southack Street School] until within a short time, when the Bishop of the Roman Church stopped them. I called on him to enquire the reason. He informed me he was about establishing a school himself. . . ." In the report of the following year, "About this time a great diminution in our number was perceived [Central School], which we were informed had been effected by the influence of the Bishop of the Catholic Church, who had determined to establish a Sabbath School in his own congregation. . . ." Yet in that same report, in the section which came from the Broad Street School, "On Christmas, it being a holiday with the Catholics, sixty children and several parents attended [our exercises]." In the report for 1828 in noting the loss of pupils at the school in the Mission House, "Catholic children have been taken from the school 'by order of the Bishop.' "

The second matter requiring special notice is that of the Sabbath School for Negroes. At the beginning of this period the African school on Belknap Street had just re-opened. It had been closed for some months. At its re-opening a few individuals appeared, some children and a few adults. The superintendent of the school noted a laxness among them: irregularity of attendance, lateness in coming to school, and no interest in the church which was meeting in the neighborhood. But slowly the numbers in the school increased, and in 1825 a separate school for the adults was started. Only the poorest kind of place could be found at first in which to hold the school, but later on the city officials allowed the Society to use one of the rooms in the new English High School. Most of the adults who came were unable to read and write, so instruction was given in those subjects. In 1825 another school for Negro children was started in Southack Street, reported to be "the most wretched part of the city, where idleness and drunkeness abound, and where wickedness in almost every form is continually exhibited." More than two thirds of the children enrolled in that school could not read, only a few were in weekday school, some had been in the House of Correction. The Sabbath School superintendent observed, "I have no faith in the efficacy of that institution to reclaim vicious youth. . . ."[27]

The workers of the Society were directly in touch with the conditions under which the Negro people lived, and realized how terribly difficult it was for them to overcome the effects of those conditions on their lives. The Society, out of its experience, made the following statement, in published form, to the citizens of Boston in 1827.

> Those who have taken pains to acquaint themselves with the habits and conditions of the colored population of this city believe that they have among themselves sufficient moral strength, which if brought into action would renovate the whole of that community. It is for Christians to set in motion that power. Other means are soon to be employed which will elevate their affections toward God, who has made them to differ in outward appearance, but *has formed of one blood all nations of men* . . . .

In 1829, the Sabbath Schools were turned over to the Massachusetts branch of the American Sabbath School Union. By that time, having seen the effectiveness of the work done by the City Missionary Society, many churches had started Sabbath Schools for the children of members, and other schools for unevangelized children were undertaken by the churches, so that it seemed quite unwise to keep separate the Society's schools. Moreover, as mentioned earlier, the teachers had united to form a Teachers Union, which included workers from all the schools in the city. Thus the Sabbath School movement in Boston was united under a single organization whose sole purpose was the conduct of activities designed to be of benefit to the schools.

The work of the Society for seamen continued in the hands of the Reverend William Jenks. A neglected lot, the seamen were looked down upon by the respectable part of the population. There were ruffians and criminals and vicious men among them, with the result that all of them were put in the same class. Being for long periods of time so closely associated with evil, those who were decent when they went to sea, found it exceedingly difficult to maintain their standards. Some of the seamen had families and they were treated much as the men. These men and their families became objects of concern to the Society. Jenks described the situation of the men as follows: "The merchant too frequently seems satisfied if his voyage is successfully completed, and the crew he employed is paid. That closes his concern with the sailors—and they, their morals and their souls are then forever vanished from his thoughts."

Jenks continued his work until in October 1826 he became the pastor of the Green Street Church. That church had been gathered a few years earlier by Mr. Jenks, and organized with the aid of the Old South Church. Funds for a building were solicited and when the building was completed Jenks resigned his post with the City Missionary Society. The Reverend Stephen Bailey, who had come to Boston from a pastorate on Nantucket Island, was then employed by the Society to continue the work with the seamen.

Services of worship for seamen were held through the years in the hall on Central Wharf. Usually they were on Sunday mornings. Other special services were held from time to time. In 1823 suggestions were made that the seamen should have a church building of their own. One reason advanced for this was that the area around Central Wharf was of such character that women and children should not go through it. This made it difficult for the families to join with their seamen at these services. The first contribution toward a building fund came in a unique way. A sailor who had attended the meetings while in town died at sea when his vessel was nearing the Cape of Good Hope. Before he died he expressed the wish that the money he had might be given to the seamen's meeting in Boston. The sailor who was with him at the time did as he desired. In that way the Society received nearly fifty dollars and "voted, that the legacy bequeathed to this Society by William Bender, late a seaman on board the Galatea, be appropriated as the commencement of a permanent fund for the support of the Seamen's meeting; and for the erection of a church whenever it is deemed expedient."

Two years later Jenks received a letter from the Reverend W. H. Angus, a clergyman completely unknown to him. Angus was a minister to seamen in Europe, moving from Britian to the continent as he felt led. He had read in *The American Sailor's Magazine* of the work Jenks was doing, and having had his interest aroused made inquiry of the captain of a Boston vessel which had stopped at Hamburg where he happened to be at the time. Learning of the desire for a church building for the seamen in Boston he wrote a letter to Jenks and enclosed a gift, "also five Napoleons towards the erection of your new chapel, which I understand is already underweigh." The Society added this money to the Bender gift. By 1830, enough money was in hand and a building was erected on the east side of Fort Hill, near the docks. Called "The Mariners Church," the Reverend Jonathan Greenleaf, from Wells, Maine, came to be the pastor.

In 1821, the pastor of the Old South Church, the Reverend Benjamin Wisner, received a letter from a friend in New York engaged in work with seamen reporting the holding of services on board vessels in port. This practice, the letter said, was followed in London, Liverpool, and Philadelphia with great acceptability by captains and seamen alike. Accompanying the letter was a flag, which was flown from the masthead of a vessel when a worship service was to be held. It was called "The Bethel Flag." The letter urged the adoption of the practice in Boston. When this information was passed on to Jenks he set about arranging for the suggested services. Obviously, it was impossible to hold them during the winter months, but from May to October each year services were conducted each Wednesday evening on vessels and the Bethel Flag was flown. During the winter months the Wednesday services were held in a private chapel on Charter Street, owned by Henry J. Oliver. Those services were continued until 1825.

Tracts were distributed among the seamen. These were supplied to the Society by other organizations which paid for them. Seamen were encouraged to take as many copies as they wanted and distribute them to their shipmates, especially to those who did not attend the services of worship. Bibles and Books of Prayers were also made available to those men who asked for them.

Sailors taken ill or injured could go to the Marine Hospital in Charlestown. That institution was part of the naval base, but was open to seamen not in the navy. Jenks, the Reverend A. Bingham, and sometimes the students of Andover Theological Seminary visited the men in the hospital. A library was put there and as often as finances permitted books were added to it.

Jenks visited the harbors on the Cape, Wellfleet, Harwich, and Truro, conducted services in each place and arranged for some of the local people to continue the work. He entered into correspondence with a Boston merchant who was representing his firm in Canton, China, about the possibility of locating a seaman's chaplain in that port; and he become interested in a similiar enterprise in Buenos Aires. He sent a Bethel Flag to the missionaries in Honolulu and described its purpose. This resulted in the formation of a seaman's church in that place. And he took a leading part in 1820 in the organization of the Marine Bible Society of Boston and vicinity, getting a Christian ship's captain to act as the treasurer. That Society became an auxiliary to the American Bible Society and for a time received help from the national organization.

In 1824 Jenks became concerned over the treatment seamen received in Boston when they got off their vessels. He and Bingham did a bit of investigating. They discovered that men were being systematically victimized by keepers of boarding houses and saloons.

The moment a ship arrives at the wharf, landlords are to be seen, like vultures round a carcass, each engaged to secure his part of the prey. The sailor, with his baggage, is escorted home, where, if he has money, the round of intemperance is kept up until all is absorbed by it, when he is again shoved off [to sea].[28]

Jenks and Bingham found some landlords who were interested in the welfare of the seamen, and they promised to do what they could about the condition. They also agreed to introduce Christian literature and influences into their establishments. Then, the two men found a vacant house, which they agreed to rent proposing to call it the "Bethel Boarding House." Needed support for it, over and above the rent which the transient seamen would pay, they obtained in gifts from the owners and masters of vessels. They changed the location of the Wednesday evening meetings from the harbor to the new house. Then they asked the Reverend John Turner of Biddeford, Maine, to come and manage the house and direct the activities in it. But the enterprise languished. Jenks recorded that much good had been done, because the house was a center from which the distribution of tracts and other religious literature went on, but he granted that "the house has not been the resort of many seamen." He thought that the cause of the failure was that other boarding houses had licenses to sell liquor, which the Bethel Boarding House did not and would not have.

In 1828, the Seaman's Friend Society was organized through the efforts and with the approval of the Board of the City Missionary Society. A Woman's Auxiliary was formed at the same time. Then the work which the Society had been doing, the funds for seamen in its possession, the lease on the Bethel Boarding House, and responsibility for the support of the minister in charge, were turned over to the new organization.

A number of different individuals served as agents of the Society during this era. The Reverend A. Bingham came to Boston with his brother, the Reverend Hiram Bingham, who was preparing to leave for the Sandwich Islands as a missionary of the A.B.C.F.M. The Reverend A. Bingham's salary was paid, partly, by the Female Missionary Society. A Baptist minister who was the agent for the Boston Society for Religious Purposes, the Reverend William Collier, was involved in the work of the Society for a time. The Reverend Mr. Gamble, a Presbyterian minister from Ireland, had come to Boston by way of Nova Scotia and worked for the Society for a brief period. The Reverend D. D. Rossiter, whose support was also provided by the Female Missionary Society, was assigned by the ladies to work with the Society. The ladies employed other ministers: the Reverend Thomas Pillsbury, the Reverend Henry J. Lamb, and Mr. J. Turner and turned them over to this Society. In addition the Society had the services of Andover Theological Seminary students during vacation time.

Centers were soon acquired from which to work. In 1821, a building was erected on the land that had been bought in the West End. This came to be called The Mission House. On weekdays the city used the building to house one of its primary schools. At the time the city made some improvements in the area, repairing the street, paving the sidewalks and putting in street lamps, which greatly increased the usability of the place. Before that, it had not been possible to hold evening meetings because of the character of the neighborhood and the unlighted location of the house. Near the Mission House, the Society rented a tenement— it had previously been a house of prostitution—and made the lower floor into a meeting room, and the upper floor into an apartment for a missionary or a reputable Christian family.

It was learned by 1823 that a considerable number of Protestant Irish people were living on the east side of the city and were unable to find a place where they could attend Christian worship. A vacant room in a building on Broad Street was found, rented, and fitted out so that it could be used for church and Sabbath School. The chapel building of the seamen on Charter Street began to be used also by the other workers of the Society for more general services and activities. A small building on Sea Street, on the lower part of the east side of the city, was secured. And, as work proceeded on the Mill Dam and laborers went to live in that district the city erected a school house to accommodate their children; the Society, with the approval of the city officials, added an additional story to the building while it was being erected, as another center for their activities. The Society made plans to work in South Boston where the brick yards, recently opened, had drawn a number of workmen and their families. But the Baptists undertook a program in that area, so there was no reason to duplicate their efforts.

With these facilities, the Society had provided itself with buildings or meeting places in every needy part of the city, and thus was in a position to reach many of the poor. Almost without being aware of what they were actually doing or where they were being led they had opened a new line of work, different from that which they had envisioned at the start of the Society's history. At these centers, the workers of the Society conducted services of worship and classes for Bible study. Since the number of paid workers was always relatively small, laymen of the churches helped, serving with great acceptability. From those centers the workers visited homes in the nearby streets. With them they took tracts, copies of the Scriptures, and other religious material, distributing it as people expressed a desire for it. They extended invitations to the services and other meetings in the centers. In their visiting, the workers of the Society sought to awaken in people a concern for their spiritual welfare and to attack the customs and habits which led to spiritual degradation.

> It is the intention in every visit to the families of the poor, to converse with each person upon religion, and to bring home to the heart and conscience the important doctrines of the Gospel in such a manner as to shew the person, if he was impenitent, that he was guilty and undone, unless he fled from the wrath to come to the stronghold of hope in Christ.[29]

The workers encountered degradation and evil in all its forms. "We have entered the abodes of ignorance and infamy ... we have visited the sick and the afflicted ... we have found backsliders ... we have met drunkenness and dissipation ... we have faced poverty and wretchedness." The reports carry a number of accounts of individuals who were restored to orderly life through the work of the visitors. And there are accounts of failures, of people who refused to listen or denied the right of the visitor to speak. And always the visitor sought to relate the persons whom they met to the religious meetings being held in their neighborhood.

Visits were made by the workers to the various institutions in the city: the jail, the prison, the general hospital, the House of Correction, the Almshouse, the Penitent Females Refuge, and the Marine Hospital. The Penitent Females Refuge deserves mention. Members of the Society, concerned over the fate of prostitutes in the West End, thought that some of them might be saved if they were taken from the places where they were living and put in a wholesome environment. The Society enlisted the interest of other individuals in the city, a Board of Directors was formed, and a home for girls who might be drawn away from their evil ways was opened. That Board, after encountering a great deal of opposition by those who felt that prostitutes were not subjects for reformation, finally secured a Christian couple to manage the home and made public their intention. During the first year the house was opened twenty-seven girls were admitted.

> One died, six went to places of honest service, two eloped and were married, one was restored to friends, the rest remain. In addition, seventy other girls were rescued and returned to their homes.[30]

It had been the practice of the city, because of lack of facilities to do otherwise, to mix the prisoners in the jail quite indiscriminately, young and old, male and female, hardened criminal and first offender. But when new buildings were built all that changed. Then the women of the churches began to visit the women in prison and to provide them with pieces of work to keep them busy. The church women, under the leadership of the widow of Dr. Huntington, formed "The Distributing Bible Association of Boston" to carry on that work. Then in addition to the responsibilities they assumed in the prison they did some visiting in the homes of the poor in company with the workers of the Society. The work of the Society at the city institutions invariably consisted of the conduct of worship services, personal conversations with the inmates, and the arrangements for libraries so that reading material would be available.

By 1830, the Society had turned over its Sabbath School work to another agency, and had done the same with its work for seamen. That left the Society with the work being done from the centers which it had established. "Now it stands forth with the avowed and simple aim to give the glorious Gospel of the Blessed God to all the destitute whom the city may be found to contain, and who may be willing to receive it at their hands."[31] Under the control of the Society were three chapels or mission houses; on Buttolph Street in the West End (The Mission House), the upstairs hall over the city school house at the Mill Dam, and the chapel on South Street. The Society was also using the seamen's meeting house. In the employ of the Society were a few missionaries, the large part of whose salaries were being paid through the generosity and the industry of the Female Missionary Society.

Mr. David Naismith of Glasgow, Scotland, an evangelist with much experience in his own country and Ireland, visited Boston and aroused renewed interest in religion among the citizens through a series of meetings which he conducted. Among other things he did while he was here was to recommend publicly that all the Societies working for the evangelization of pagans in the city join their efforts under one Association. At the time a number of organizations, similiar in form and purpose to the City Missionary Society had come into existence. Consultations were held with those organizations, proposals made, considered, and then the whole matter dropped as each Society decided to go its own way.

About this time the City Missionary Society worked out a plan for the more effective prosecution of the work which remained as its chief responsibility. Dividing the city into four districts, one missionary was assigned to each district: Reverend Mr. Sheldon to the Western district; Charles Cleveland to the Northern district; the Reverend D. D. Rossiter to the Eastern district, and the Reverend James Kimball to the Southern district. A well-to-do parishioner of the church in South Boston, learning of the plans of the Society, volunteered to pay the salary of another man to work in that area, and Mr. Samuel Gale was appointed. As the missionaries went about their work they did not necessarily stay within the districts to which they had been assigned, but moved rather freely about the entire city. Each had particular responsibility for his own district, however, and when he went elsewhere he reported his findings to the man who was in charge there. For a period of four months the worship services at the Mill Dam Hall were led by clergymen from the churches in the city, under a schedule arranged by a woman in the neighborhood, Mrs. Ann Fisher, who was anxious that the services be held. Otherwise, the services of worship that had been taking place and the visits to the city institutions were assumed by the missionaries. Each missionary made a report to the Managers of the Society regularly, noting the services he had conducted, describing the conditions he had encountered while visiting, and giving some estimate of his accomplishments.

There are no reports of the Society for the following two years, but the missionaries continued their work. The Society was in financial straits in 1831. In 1832, through a special effort by the churches, finances improved. The report for 1834 is an analysis of the troubles that had beset the Society and contained some recommendations for the future. That report was written by the Reverend Isaac R. Barbour, who signed himself, "secretary." With the advent of Mr. Barbour, the first period of the Society came to a close. An unsettled period loomed ahead.

CHAPTER V

Finding the Way

AT A MEETING of the Directors of the Society held on February 14, 1828, Col. Joseph Jenkins, Deacon Eliphalet Kimball, and Deacon John C. Proctor were appointed a committee to "ascertain by what means this Society may be more efficient in its operations." Col. Jenkins had been a member of the First Church, but transferred to Park Street Church when that was formed as one of the charter members. Kimball was a member of Hanover Church, which had been gathered by the people who had been dismissed from the orthodox Congregational churches for the purpose of establishing an additional orthodox church in the city, and had once been a member of the Old South Church.[1] John C. Proctor was a member of Central Church, or as it was then known, Franklin Street Church. They were three men of strong orthodox leanings, men who had taken part in deliberate efforts to spread orthodox doctrine throughout the city after most of the Congregational churches had gone over to Unitarianism. Inevitably, the report they drew up expressed the religious beliefs they held.

Their report was lengthy and carefully reasoned. It began with the statement that the Society must be thought of as among the "favourable means" for the prosperity of the church and the coming of God's kingdom. The Society was not a kind of opportunistic religious organization, always on the lookout for little jobs that might be done, but an important agency in the spread of the Christian Gospel. The men in the Society should never be so overcome by discouragement or so satisfied with past achievements as to give up their interest. They were called to a task when they joined the Society, and while, at the moment and because of the work they had done, they most surely had to create new ways of fulfilling their task, they must never put it aside. The report went on to make some discerning observations about the growth of cities and the significance that had, both for the people who lived in them and the Christian churches established in them. Cities, the report said, are bound to set the moral tone for the entire country, since the more important functions sustaining the national life are located in the cities. Moreover, the cities draw people from the countryside, who stay for a time and then return to their homes taking with them the influences of the city. But cities are ever in danger of becoming, because of the concentration of people in them and their impersonality, "seats of vice and irreligion." Boston, the committee pointed out, demonstrates both those characteristics, since it is a great center for all New England, the place to which New Englanders gravitate and from which moral power radiates back into the more remote areas. The conclusion was clear. If the nation is to be made ready "for the coming of the Millenium, be prepared for God's kingdom, the cities must be cleansed of all moral pollution." The Society, the committee stated, was one of the organizations especially responsible for engaging in that task.

After presenting the reason for the Society's existence, the Committee made some specific recommendations for action. They noted that several of the orthodox Congregational churches in the city (there were eight such churches at the time, although not all were engaged in the kind of activity to which the committee referred) had created organizations among their members for the purpose of doing evangelistic work, or as they put it, "for the purpose of doing good." The first recommendation was that the Society invite the presidents or moderators or some other official of those congregations to meet and under the leadership of the Society to evolve a plan for united action. Instead of each local church organization carrying on work as and where it saw fit with little or no regard for what others were doing, let all join in a completely coordinated program that would reach the entire city. The Committee then went on to speak of the young people from the towns of New England who came to Boston for work. In this they were dealing with one evidence of the basic principles they had laid down. They recommended that the Society find "some pious man in every town in the state, and perhaps in many of the towns in Vermont and New Hampshire" who would serve as correspondents for the Society. The correspondents would notify the Society when individuals in their towns left for Boston, giving the Society all the information they could about the means by which the individuals were traveling and their probable destinations when they got to the city. The Society would then meet those individuals on arrival, help them to find suitable places to live, introduce them to a church, and do all possible to keep them away from those people in the city who would have evil designs on them.

The Committee were thinking of the Society as doing two main jobs: being the coordinating agency for the evangelistic work already being carried on by the churches, and being a kind of intermediary between the churches in the city and the churches in the hinterland to make sure that committed Christians were not lost when they moved to the city. The work of the churches and the Society was thus to bring and keep everyone under the power of the Gospel because "the Truth of God is alone sufficient to bring conviction to the soul and lead to the Saviour." But after the report was presented nothing happened.

For nearly ten years after that—from 1828 to 1837—there followed a strange period in the life of the Society. The Board of Managers met with regularity, during part of the time with considerable frequency. A line of action would be determined upon, tried, and then given up. Another course would be tried with the same result. The Board kept on attempting to interest other people in the Society, but most of those efforts ended in rebuffs or refusals. Through those years there is a strange sense of the relationship between the Society and the life of the city. Quite in contrast to the previous years, when the affairs of the city were reflected in the work of the Society, and the work of the Society was addressed to the conditions of people in the city, during the years now under review the city becomes a kind of amorphous, intangible atmosphere within which the Society lived, while the Society itself comes to occupy the center of interest and concern. Not that

concern for the city was lost and the Society became completely engrossed in its own preservation; such was not quite
the case. The Society sought its own life that it might carry forward the task it was sure it had been given to do. But the Society
had to discover how to perform that task and at the same time
save itself from dissolution while the process of discovery went
on. And it was precisely the business of finding out how to relate
the Society to the life of the city, given all the other organizations
that were at work, that was the problem. What effect the period
of speculation, in which large sections of the population were involved from 1833 to 1837, and the bank failures and public panic
which followed, had upon the Society is not known. The records
of that time do not so much as mention those events.

Yet if the relation of the Society to its setting became blurred,
the dedication of some of the men in the Society to God was not
substantially weakened. Each meeting of the Board during those
years, and there were many of them, sometimes two and three in
a month, was opened and closed with prayer. This was far more
than a perfunctory performance of an established custom. Even
when an insufficient number of Board members appeared to con-
stitute a quorum, the men who were present opened the meeting
with prayer, agreed to adjourn for lack of power to do business,
and closed with prayer. Again and again there is in the record reference to a search for God's will or an understanding of God's
action when some upsetting event occurred; and when suddenly
the way was made clear the words, "in the all wise providence of
God" appear in the account. Here then is a group of men, so committed to the service of God that they remained faithful through
a decade of wearisome, unrewarding labor and almost unbroken
failure.

A good number of different individuals were members of the
Board through those years. Some served one year, some for two
or three. Other men were elected, then declined to serve. Still
others agreed to serve, then dropped out and had to be replaced.
Towards the end of the period the number of those on the Board
had dwindled to a bare minimum. Through all the changes there
were five men around whom all appears to have revolved. Two of

them, Deacon Eliphalet Kimball and Deacon John Proctor were members of the Board in 1830, and were on the committee to make recommendations for the future of the Society. Charles Scudder Esq., Deacon Daniel Safford, and George Crockett came on the Board a bit later. Scudder was a member of Union Church, organized by part of the membership of the Essex Street Church when that congregation was rent by dissension. Safford was a deacon of the Park Street Church and later became one of the charter members and a deacon of the Mt. Vernon Church. George Crockett was a member of the Bowdoin Street Church (Hanover Street).

Proctor was the vice-president of the Board of the Society and from 1836 on was president; Scudder was vice-president when Proctor was president. Kimball did not hold office. Occasionally, an interesting but obscure indication of the devotion of these five men appears in the record. A committee would be appointed to do an assigned piece of work and some of the newer men on the Board would be named to the committee, obviously to give them a chance to make their influence felt. During a following meeting when reports of committees were called for, there would be no report. Then at the next meeting the members of the committee would be absent. Finally the Board would discharge the committee, appoint another one to do the work which was needed, and on the new committee would inevitably be one or more of the active quintet. One further indication of the character of those men is that when an arrangement was finally worked out which gave the churches a direct part in choosing the Board of the Society, they resigned their offices and their membership on the Board in order that the proposed plan might be carried out unhindered. That they did not resign in anger over the changes that were made is shown by the fact that three of them, Safford, Scudder, and Proctor returned to the Board, two of them, later on, to hold the office of president.

In 1831, the Reverend D. D. Rossiter and Mr. Samuel Gale were employed as missionaries, the former on an appointment for three months and the latter on a more permanent basis since his salary was being paid by a generous member of Phillips Church, South Boston. The Society was, however, in financial difficulties. Two members of the Board were deputed "to wait on the Ladies and suggest to them that the money they have in their treasury can be usefully appropriated to City Missions." Whether the men did as they were instructed or not, there is no record of a report from them, but in any case nothing came of the idea. Previously, the ladies had most generously supported the agents of the Society. A letter was then addressed to the churches describing the plight of the Society and asking that special collections be taken up "in our aid." That letter brought in a substantial sum of money, but not enough to enable the Society to get on with any new work. The indebtedness of the Society was reduced. But two months later the treasurer was authorized to borrow $500 from the bank for four months.

Then followed a series of conversations between the Board of the Society and representatives of the churches, quite evidently with no tangible results. At some of the meetings encouraging resolutions were passed, often introduced by the ministers. On one occasion the Reverend Justin Edwards, pastor of the Salem Street Church, made this motion: "Resolved, that in view of the poverty and wretchedness of many in the city, it is the duty of all the friends of God and man, to make strenuous and persevering efforts to remove the cause, that the destructive effects may be done away." That resolution was passed without a dissenting vote, and the Society was none the wiser and none the richer.

Gradually, the Board became convinced that the way to proceed was to employ a General Agent who "would devote his whole time, mind and effort to the objects of the Society." That meant, in practical terms, to raise the money for the expenses of the Society, including his own salary, and to direct the program. That seemed like an excellent idea, and since the terms of the two missionaries then employed were about to end, the Board cast about for someone to take the position they had decided upon. Shortly before, the Reverend Isaac Barbour, pastor of the church in Byfield, had resigned and moved to Boston. Employed for brief periods by the Massachusetts Missionary Society, he had not yet found a permanent position. Mr. Barbour was a dedicated, conscientious person who would not countenance any laxity in Christian behavior. A member of the Byfield Church who had been charged with selling liquor in the town moved away and then wrote the Byfield Church asking for a letter of transfer to another church. The Byfield Church voted to issue the letter. Mr. Barbour resigned at once in protest at the action of the church, saying that the church could not, in good conscience, recommend to another church as an acceptable Christian, a man who had been caught in the act of contributing to another's downfall by selling him intoxicating liquor. Barbour began work with the Society in May of 1833. Before that year was out the results of his work began to show, for the expenditures for a six-month period were less than the income. But this did not solve the financial problem of the Society, for they had been forced to borrow $1000, mortgaging the West End property in order to do so. The balance which accrued from Barbour's work was nowhere near enough to retire that debt.

Under Barbour's leadership and advice, the Board set about working out some definite plans for the future. At that time a clear line was drawn between two tasks which all too often are confusedly intermingled; the gathering of converted and unrelated Christians into churches, sustaining those churches long enough to enable them to become independent and self-supporting; and the job of preaching the gospel to the poor and the infidels, doing this by every means which can be devised, getting people to hear the message of what God has done in their behalf and calling them to repent and believe. The former task belongs to the churches of the city, which must be responsible for the establishment and recognition of new churches, while the City Missionary Society would restrict its efforts to getting the pagans in the population to hear and understand the claims of the Gospel. The entire plan was worked out in detail, and the Board of the Society, having approved it, invited the churches to attend a meeting at which the whole matter would be discussed. A series of meetings followed, at the end of which there was an agreement that a new society should be formed as recommended. On March 22, 1834, there was a meeting at the Park Street Church for the adoption of the constitution of the Boston Home Missionary

Society. Barbour spoke at length describing all that had been talked about. Then the organization was voted. "Object: to aid in sustaining a stated ministry for the forming and building up of evangelical churches." Members of the Society were to be those who contributed to its support. Officers elected were: John Proctor, president (vice-president of C.M.S.); Daniel Noyes, vice-president (former Board member of C.M.S.); Scudder, Kimball, Safford and Denny, managers (all members of the Board of C.M.S.). With that distinction made clear, the Boston Home Missionary Society would make grants of money to the City Missionary Society, thus solving the financial problems of the latter.

During this time Barbour prepared a series of articles published in *The Recorder* over a number of weeks. Addressed to "The Evangelical Congregational Churches of Boston," they described the work of city missions in detail. Barbour outlined the way, which, in his judgment, city missions might be conducted. From time to time a few members from each of the evangelical congregations in the city should ask for their letters of dismissal, it being clearly understood why they were doing so, and should unite to form a new congregation. That new congregation should be helped financially by the established churches to secure a piece of property and erect an inexpensive building as a meeting house. The new congregation would then call a pastor and ask the other churches to install him in office. The new congregation should locate itself in a district of the city where no evangelical church existed and should become the center of evangelical effort in its neighborhood. In that way, so Barbour thought, the influence of the orthodox Christian churches would gradually be spread throughout the city. It is worth mentioning, for in setting the idea down on paper Barbour was either describing something which had already been thought of and put into practical form or else he was elucidating a plan which was subsequently followed. This was precisely the way the Hanover Church originated.

In June Barbour resigned. A committee was appointed to sell the Mission House in the West End "on such terms as they deem expedient." At the same meeting the Board, having discussed the matter with the Boston Sabbath School Union, agreed to employ a Reverend Mr. Wright as a city-wide minister to children, the term of his employment to be for three months. Wright came and so commended himself to both children and Board members that he was re-employed for a year. By that time the Reverend J. R. Cushing had been hired and was preaching at the Mission House and acting as the general agent for the Society. Cushing remained on the job for less than a year.

Early in 1835 the financial affairs of the Society were in a serious condition. Again the ministers of the churches were approached with the request that they make a special plea for the Society in their churches and take up special collections. There are no indications the ministers responded to that request. Mr. Wright received an invitation to go to Detroit as missionary and Sabbath School agent and although the Board voted that "it is not expedient for Mr. Wright to leave this city" he went. The Board had made some kind of an agreement to support Infant Schools, and evidently, as appears from a later record, they did this. That year there was no public annual meeting of the Society, as there had been in the past. Notices of the affair were inserted in the newspapers, according to usual practice, but no one from the churches or general public came to the meeting. The year was a most discouraging one. Before it ended an invitation was extended to the Reverend Richard Stores to come as a missionary of the Society, but he declined. The only heartening thing that happened to counterbalance the discouragement, although probably no one thought of it in that light at the time, was the coming of the Reverend William Rogers to be the pastor of Central (Franklin Street) Church, and his acceptance of an invitation to become a member of the Board of the Society. Then the Reverend George Bragdon joined the membership of the Board at the meeting just before New Year's. At the time he was pastor of the Salem Street Church and had been in Brighton and Boston since 1827.

Early in 1836, Deacon Scudder and Deacon Kimball reported to the Board that their respective churches, Pine Street and Union, had decided to employ a missionary jointly to work in their area of the city. When they made that report they spoke in gracious, thoughtful language, for evidently they sensed that their churches were proposing to engage in the very type of work the Society had done and was hoping to start again. They indicated that their churches would be willing to make some arrangement so that their missionary would feel a relationship to the Society. But the Board members, as they listened, saw the point. They were in no position to pay the salary of a missionary, and if the churches chose to act and do so instead of making funds available to the Society, the churches should have the direction of the missionary's work. Recognizing the possibilities and realizing there was nothing they could do, the Board agreed to send a letter to all the churches relating what Pine Street and the Union Church were doing and urging others to do likewise. Old South Church, Salem Street Church, and Central Church then united to employ a missionary. Mr. Thomas Thwing and Mr. Charles Cleveland were the two missionaries who worked in the city under those arrangements.

Cleveland had played a leading role in the history of the Society. The organization meeting had been held at his house. He was a member of the Board of Managers from the very beginning, and a generous giver to the finances of the Society. When the decision was taken to employ district missionaries he was one of the four who accepted a position. When the funds of the Society were not sufficient to continue the support of the missionaries, Cleveland was taken under the care of a few churches. From that time on he operated independently as a city missionary. His many friends among the church people provided him with sufficient money for his needs and his work. He moved about the city as he chose, doing whatever he thought to do. A few of the ministers signed letters of recommendation for him, which put their stamp of approval on his efforts. He was granted a license to preach in 1835; and in 1838 he was ordained. There is a fascinating lithograph extant which shows him, dressed in a Prince Albert coat and wearing a clergy hat in the custom of that day, handing a loaf of bread to a poor woman. Mr. Waldron, when he spoke of Mr. Cleveland at the Centennial Anniversary Celebration of the Society, said that if Cleveland were alive he would be doing the same thing only, "the loaf of bread [would be] wrapped up in a parafin paper, if he was up to modern methods of charity."

Cleveland was a unique individualist. He gave himself wholly
to the poor. His reports to the Directors of the Society, while he
was a missionary, always opened with a sermonette, a testimony
to God's goodness, in highly allegorical phraseology:

> Let the friends of Zion renounce, as the foundation of their hope,
> all dependence on human wisdom, prudence or power; and let them
> go out into the highways and hedges, relying on the sword of the
> Spirit and the shield of faith; and let their prayers be fervent and
> their labor unremitted for the extension of the Messiah's kingdom.[2]

He lived to be fifteen days less than one hundred years, and was
active almost to the end. He had become a familiar and beloved
figure on Boston streets.

In spite of their financial straits, the Board took a number of actions. They repaired a building they controlled on Stillman Street
and loaned it to the Boston Infant School Society for a year. A committee was sent out to Ware to talk with a Mr. Wilder about entering their employ, an invitation which he accepted. Another committee visited East Boston to learn what was happening there. A
day school was started on Purchase Street in the Fort Hill district
and Miss Mary Jones put in charge of it, which gave the Society two
schools for which they were responsible, the other one being superintended by Miss Eaton. Pastors of all the churches were invited
to attend the meetings of the Board. At a meeting in September,
one minister appeared. He was the Reverend W. Bliss, agent of the
Tract Society. During the meeting, probably more out of politeness
than anything else, he was asked to speak. He told of the work of
tract distribution going on in New York City and "suggested the
propriety of adopting some such course in Boston." It appears
quite evident, however, that while the members of the Board gave
seeming attention to Mr. Bliss as he spoke, none of them really
heard what he said. The incident took on significance later. As
soon as Bliss had finished his remarks, the conversation turned to
the plight of the Society. Before the meeting ended it was agreed
that Proctor and Scudder, with the two ministers who were members of the Board, should arrange to meet with the other Congregational ministers and consult with them "respecting the whole
plan of operations of the Society and its pecuniary concerns."

The meeting of that committee and the pastors must have been a fairly serious one. Moses L. Hale, Esq., a member of the Bowdoin Street Church and a layman, was made secretary of the meeting. After the meeting ended he prepared a set of resolutions which were agreed upon, at least by the ministers. When that document was read to the Board of the Society, "it was concluded that the measure recommended by the first resolution had already been anticipated by this Board"; and it was "voted that the document from Mr. M. L. Hale be put in the files of the Society." Then the Board proceeded to vote on another general agent.

The year 1837 passed with invitations being given to Deacon Thomas Thwing and the Reverend David Sutherland to "labour under the direction of this Board for the present," and further, "that the salaries of these persons be fixed at the rate of $600 per annum for such time as they shall remain in the employ of this Society." But while the work of those two men must have been beneficial to those they served, their employment did nothing to bring new life to the Society.

On December 25th of that year, seven men, the faithful three, Proctor, Safford, and Kimball, with four others who had come on the Board more recently (the two ministers who were Board members being detained elsewhere), took a series of actions which bear the marks of finality. The treasurer, James Houghton, was authorized to borrow $2500, giving as security a mortgage on the Mission House property on Buttolph Street; with that money he was to retire the existing mortgage and pay off all other indebtedness of the Society. The secretary was asked to notify Miss Mary Jones that her services would no longer be required by the Society. The owners of the property on Stillman Street were to be told that the Society no longer needed the place and would cease paying the rent forthwith. All the interest of the Society in the Infant Schools, including the services of Miss Mary Jones, were turned over to the Infant School Society. The president of the Society was then given authority to rent the building on Buttolph Street "for religious purposes for such length of time and for such price as he may think for the interest of the Society."

Daniel Safford
President of the Society at its revival in 1850

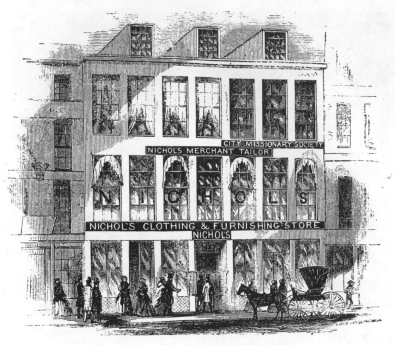

Early office of the Society
96 Washington Street—third floor, right

Minutes of meetings are usually such dry things, and the record just cited is particularly so. Brief, laconic, and matter of fact, written with the customary flourish of the script of the secretary, Mr. R. M. Harvey, the words say all one needs to know about the actions that were agreed upon; yet the words say nothing. The conversation and the feelings of those seven men, especially the three who had worked so hard and so steadily through the years, as they came to the hour when they could not think of any other step to take to carry out the purpose for which the Society had been founded over twenty years earlier, can well be imagined.

But one thing is clear, whether there was any discussion of the possibility or not, the Board did not disband the Society nor vote to bring its history to an end. They might have done this; other Societies at the time which, in the judgment of their officers, lost their reason for being, were dissolved. Such an action was taken by the Board of a Society on which one of the members of the Board of the City Missionary Society sat. Perhaps part of the reason was that the C.M.S. owned property, even though it was mortgaged, and as long as that was the case they remained a living reality in the eyes of the law and of those in the city who knew of their corporate possessions and the work they had done.

The years 1838 and 1839, and half the year 1840 passed. Then a meeting of the Society was called. The same men were present as had been present at the meeting at the end of the year 1837, and John Proctor was in the chair as he had been at that earlier meeting. The Reverend William Rogers, who is not listed in the names of the Board members who were "present," offered the following "preamble and vote: Whereas, Mrs. Ann Lee by her last will and testament constituted the Society for the Moral and Religious Instruction of the Poor the residuary legatee of [her estate]; and whereas twenty-nine hundred and five dollars and ninety-one cents have become available to the purposes of this Society thereby; therefore, be it voted that we accept the Trust for the purpose for which it has been given." This "preamble and vote" was adopted unanimously. The treasurer was authorized to pay all the indebtedness of the Society; a committee was appointed to take charge of the Mission House on Buttolph Street; and the meeting adjourned to reconvene a week later.

The men who made up the Board of the Society were honorable men and they were aware that one does not accept a gift made for a specific purpose without becoming responsible for carrying out that purpose. However impulsively they may have acted when Mr. Rogers announced Mrs. Lee's bequest, they cannot be blamed if under the emotion aroused by that announcement they had voted without due consideration. After a week had elapsed they became aware of the seriousness of what they had done. They saw that they had "to take into consideration the present position of this Society in relation to the obligation imposed upon it by the acceptance of a liberal donation recently given from Mrs. Lee." A committee was appointed to consider the matter and bring in proposals for a course of action.

Some months elapsed before the committee was prepared to report. In October the Board met. The committee read a written statement: Item one: "it is indispensible that the connection and harmony of the Society with our churches should be much closer; to effect this object it is desirable that extensive changes take place in the members constituting the Board." Item two: that men from the Board be appointed to visit each one of the churches to report on the condition of the Society and to ask each church to nominate three persons from whom "one of them be chosen on our part a member of the Board; that thus a new Board will be constituted proceeding directly from the churches." That committee report was adopted and the visits made. Nominations were received from Old South, Park Street, Bowdoin Street, Mission, Green Street, Pine Street, Salem Street and Franklin Street Churches. Then followed a number of meetings of the new Board, some elections, some resignations, some new nominations and appointments. Through it all the old Board was making clear that they were in control of the Society, and that they were going to elect the new members of the Board; and that if they chose to do so, they were going to choose men, other than those nominated by the churches to serve with them, which is what they did. The new arrangement was in no sense to be a complete turning over

of the Society to the churches. When the meeting ended and all
the changes made, there was a Board of thirteen members; Bowdoin Street and Old South Churches had two representatives each
and the other churches one; two men were from the old Board,
and there was one pastor, the Reverend William Rogers. Mr.
Rogers subsequently resigned and the Reverend Joseph Towne,
pastor of the Salem Street Church took his place.

The new Board met, agreed that immediate steps should be
taken to start missionary work in the city, and appointed a committee, "to take the whole matter under consideration, and report a plan of operations, both as respects Missionary labor
among the poor, and the procuring of funds to carry on the operations" and then adjourned. One week later the committee reported that the Society should act as the missionary agency of the
Evangelical Congregational churches of the city to present the
Gospel, in some way or other, to all who do not have it or know
it; that the Society should not do this by means of setting up
permanent chapels for the poor alone and using those as centers
from which to work; that two or three laymen should be employed
who should visit among the poor, urge them to attend church,
enlist their children in Sabbath Schools, distribute tracts, "hold
meetings for Social Worship," [meaning services of worship held
in homes], and help the sick and the needy get in touch with the
established agency, either public or private, which could assist
them; that an ordained minister should be employed to serve as a
general agent of the Society, to supervise the work, keep in close
touch with the churches, and be available for pastoral services
when such were needed; and that numerous laymen be enlisted
to take part in the program. The committee were particularly in-
sistent that chapels for the poor not be established. The issue was
that of segregating the poor from the rest of the population. It
was felt that one of the ways by which the poor might be led to
better lives was through having the opportunity of mingling with
Christian people in the churches, which would not be possible
were chapels especially for the poor to be built. The committee
estimated that $4,000 would be needed to conduct the work as
they had outlined it and if the matter were properly presented the

churches might be willing to contribute that amount. The committee felt that some means should be used to keep the church people in touch with what the Society was doing. They proposed that "Quarterly Concerts" be held at which the General Agent would speak and other demonstrations of the work given to keep alive the interest of those who came. Finally, the committee urged that the name of the Society be changed to "The Boston Society for the Support of City Missions." A new period in the life of the Society was beginning.

CHAPTER VI

Building on a Legacy 1840–1850

BOSTON WAS RAPIDLY CHANGING. It was in the midst of those changes that the City Missionary Society was called on to work when it resumed in 1840. The Boston that existed when the Society was formed was almost gone, and a new setting was coming to be. The massive modification that was taking place was creating chaos and much disorder.

In 1833, the East Boston Company was granted a charter. Largely through the enterprise of General William H. Sumner, the Company gained control of Noddles Island, an outcropping of land, marshes and tidal flats in the bay off the northeast corner of the city. The Company sold the land at auction, realizing a rather high return to the stockholders for their investment. By 1835 the population of the island had grown from one lone settler when the project was started to somewhere in the neighborhood of six hundred people. Thus a whole new area had to be taken into consideration by agencies and societies working within the bounds of the city. In 1836, the terminus of the Eastern Railroad was located on the island and the development of East Boston progressed rapidly.

In 1833, the South Cove Associates were organized. They secured title to the land bordering on South Bay in Roxbury, and with the land, the marshy flats and tide land adjoining. The Company moved solid fill on to the flats and tide lands, built a retaining wall to contain the land which they were filling in, and added about seventy-five acres to the city. Some of the new land was pledged to one of the railroads for a station under an agreement made when the Associates were formed, but there remained a considerable area for business or home sites.[1]

By the end of the eighteen forties, it became quite evident that some kind of action had to be taken in respect to the Back Bay. Since the Mill Dam was completed in 1821 a number of things had happened to change the bay which had been enclosed by the dam. Owners of the property bordering on the bay had added fill to the flats at the end of their land, increasing the area of their holdings, but by doing so, cutting down the effectiveness of the water power for which the dam had been built. Two railroad lines, chartered in 1831, had built their rights-of-way across the bay under privileges granted them at their incorporation, and had further reduced the usefulness of the bay for its original purpose. The consequence was that the Back Bay had become "an open cesspool . . . a place of nuisance, offensive and injurious to the large and increasing population residing upon it."[2] Obviously the area had to be filled or some other action taken to change its character. Difficulties and obstructions hindered proposed efforts for some time, so that years passed before anything was done, but everyone remained aware of the situation.

Railroads helped to change Boston. Great interest was aroused in the new form of transportation and the possibilities it opened for many people. Capital funds were invested, and soon Boston was linked to the surrounding country. In addition to the railroads to Lowell, Worcester and Providence, which were put in operation in 1834, the Eastern Road was built two years later, and the Western Road, which joined Boston to Albany was finished in 1842. These railroads were directly related to the growth of industry and manufacturing. In Boston itself, and neighboring communities and towns, factories were built and employment boomed. Cotton, woolen goods, and shoes became important products of the area. And from 1840 on, for some years, a period of prosperity set in, although it was not shared equally by all sections of the community.

By 1840 and increasingly during the following years, the people who had been living in the city began to move out. The wealthy moved first. Earlier they had built second homes for themselves out beyond the city limits, while they retained their homes in the city. As travel between the city and the outlying areas became easier and more rapid they gave up their city houses, lived in the country and came into the city each day for business. Then the middle class followed, building or buying houses that were within their means, and relying on public transportation to take them back and forth to work. There was a land speculation in West Roxbury in the late 1830's when the railroad was built through the district. In the 1850's horse drawn street railways were built; the line running to Roxbury Crossing was started in 1856. Warner says that "in 1850 Boston was a city of pedestrians . . . the area of dense settlement hardly exceeded a two-mile radius from City Hall."[3]

"In the twenty-five years between 1820 and 1845 approximately 3400 foreigners entered New England by way of Portland and Falmouth, 35,000 by way of Passamaquoddy, and 60,000 by way of Boston. . . .[4] These immigrants built the railroads, did the hard work on Boston land, and became the laborers in the mills. They crowded into the city and lived wherever they could find room. In 1846, the great Irish Famine began and its effect continued on for some years. Those who were able to do so got away and came to the States. Groups here raised funds to help the victims, and while much of the money was used to supply food for the starving, some of it was made available to pay the cost of the voyage to America. It is understandable then, how reports could indicate that even though there was widespread prosperity in New England, there was a marked increase in the number of public charges, or those who looked to some private agency to help them solve the problem of living in a strange land. The grants-in-aid made by the Overseers of the Poor annually, increased dramatically after 1840, while the numbers admitted to the almshouse soared. That the new immigrants wanted work is clear from the record of the Boston Employment Society. In 1843, over two thousand individuals applied to that agency for work; scarcely a third of them were placed in jobs; a third were encouraged to go westward in the hope work would be available there; and at the end of the year a third remained unemployed.

Such were some of the facts of the transformation that was taking place. The Board of the Society made a thoughtful appraisal of the situation they faced. From the city assessors they got the population figures, and learned how rapidly the number of people in the city was increasing. That led the Board members to observe that "the enemy [the heathen] cometh in like a flood."[5] They saw Boston as a prosperous city, fifth in size in the country and second in the value of the business transacted. In two years, the assessed value of the increase in property in the city was over twelve million dollars. They saw the railroads being built and the vessels entering and leaving the harbor, and they knew of the hundreds and thousands of people who were involved in those enterprises.

Having looked at the city in that way, they went on to make a study of "the moral conditions of our goodly city." They did this by means of some statistics. Total population, 100,000. Total attendance at public worship in the churches of the Evangelical denominations, 29,000—they arrived at that figure by visiting the churches and counting the numbers in attendance "on pleasant Sabbaths, on both parts of the day, and the average taken, and at a season of the year when the residents of the city were generally at home." Total attendance at places of worship other than the evangelical churches, 25,000—they arrived at that figure in the same way as the previous one. Then they made allowance for errors and for the regular attendants who might have been absent on the days the counting was done and they concluded that a total of 56,000 inhabitants of Boston attended church. Which meant that there were 44,000 people in the city who were "neglecters of public worship." Then they applied the same kind of study to the children and concluded that "at least 7,000 are not even enrolled in any Sabbath School." Finally, they included an additional, but nevertheless impressive bit of data. One eighth of the population of Massachusetts was, at the time, living in Boston; in the state there were over 330 settled orthodox ministers; but in Boston there were only twelve of those ministers. Conclusion: one twenty-eighth of the ministers of the state were trying to serve one-eighth of the population.

The Board of the Society saw that not only was the population of the city increasing, the character of the population was changing. The middle class, who were, as they knew, the loyal and leading members of the churches and the agencies, were moving out of the city into the suburbs, leaving a very few rich and a vast number of poor behind them. "The time is not far distant when the territory comprised within the present limits of the city will be almost entirely occupied by stores, work-shops, boarding houses, and the dwellings of the poorer classes."[6] The Board ascertained that during a single year 25,000 foreigners had come to the city. Since they knew that even though the population was increasing it was not gaining as rapidly as it would if the local inhabitants remained within the city, they had an indication that the growth was really of the poor people, among whom, as they believed, they had a mission. They thought there was a limit to the number of people who could reside in Boston, a limit set by the amount of land available, and the demands of business and industry for large parts of that land—they fixed the limit at 200,-000—and thus they came to see an increasing number of people with whom they were called upon to work.

The significance of these population changes the Board explained in the following way:

> The majority of those who seek their places of residence in the country nearby, while they continue to transact their business in the city, consists of those who in respect to their moral and religious influence in such a community as this, may be considered as 'the light of the world' and 'the salt of the earth.' The removal of residence of so many from the city of this class of individuals, must, in the nature of the case, effect a great change as to the character of the resident population of Boston. An individual's influence is exerted chiefly in the place where he resides. Take away from the city a hundred moral and religious families, and there will be taken away a hundred centers of moral and religious influence, though the constituted heads of those families spend the greatest part of their time in the city, and hold in the metropolis the greatest proportion of their property. Those who remove their residence from the city, remove also their places of attendance on public worship, and the children of those families are removed from our primary and higher schools, public and private. . . . They are not here to visit the poor and degraded, and by their example and conduct to assist in resisting the tide of iniquity that is rolling in on us.

Members of the Board visited the police officials, the City Marshal, and the office of the School Board to learn what those responsible public agents had to report. They learned of "729 houses or tenements of ill-fame," of 1500 places selling intoxicating liquor without any license, of nearly 3500 arrests during the year, about two-thirds of which were of foreigners, or over 3000 individuals sentenced to jail for longer or shorter periods, of the 154 persons, on the day of the inquiry, confined in the jail building which was designed to accommodate 71, and of more than half the children in the primary schools whose parents were foreigners. Surely, they wrote, "it cannot well be denied that iniquity in all its forms of error and crime is rolling in on us like a flood."[7] (The metaphor of "a flood" is repeated frequently in the reports.)

Members of the Board were staunch Protestants and to their way of thinking, however erroneous it may appear to a later generation, the Catholics were clearly idolatrous. They spoke of the Catholic Church as "that great iniquitous system of the papacy" and they believed themselves to be the church of God charged with the task of taking the Word of God to the Catholics "to enlighten their minds and convert them to God." They saw the people who came to Boston from Ireland as deluded and oppressed, at the mercy of their priests, and they were sure that God was leading those people over to Boston in order that they might be saved. God was "bringing foreign missionary and foreign evangelical work for us to do at home."

Lest it be assumed that all this was the work and the opinion of one man, the fact is that, during the years now under review, the annual reports were first prepared and agreed to by a three man committee, then were read to the entire Board who amended them either directly at the meetings or by remanding them to committees for changes; only then were they approved for publication and distribution. The Board may not have realized all that was involved in what was happening to Boston, but at least they came to some understanding of the situation and on the basis of that understanding they went about their work.

Those men were sensible enough, however, not to lose sight of their own position in that setting. They were the Board of a Society representing a few churches, with a membership of, roughly, five thousand. They realized that theirs was but a small part of the Christian task that had to be done. But they were not over-awed, either by their conclusions as to the extent of irreligion in the city or by the relative smallness of the number of church people in whose behalf they were to work. They thought it their duty to put the facts before the church people and ask for sufficient funds to do the job they believed to be theirs. This they did in the Reports they prepared and printed. And they continued, year after year, in every way they could, to drive home to the churches the need they had for more workers and for more financial sup-port.

When the new Board assumed responsibility for the Society they possessed a name and a tradition. Even though the Board was composed almost entirely of men who had not been related directly to the Society before, they could not have been ignorant of its purpose and its past history. There is also every reason to believe that the men on the Board, chosen though they were by their churches, must have shown some interest in the work, or have been enlisted as church representatives because they were ready to become interested. Men then, even more than men now, would not allow themselves, in their absence, to be chosen for some responsibility; this the record makes quite clear as it sets down the names of those who, when elected refused to serve. It would seem then, that the Board members had in their minds principles of operation at the start. They did not begin without pre-conceived ideas, but were already predisposed as to purpose and method.

Moreover, when they began they possessed a staff who were al-ready at work. The two laymen in the employ of several of the churches, in theory at least, came under the direction of the Board, since the Board had become the recognized agency of the churches for missionary work in the city. And the two missionaries had already an established pattern of activity, and certain expecta-tions as to the results that would follow. One of those missionaries —as was noted—chose not to come under the care of the Board but to continue his work with the support of his friends. The new

Board also owned a piece of property, The Mission House, at which there was a Sabbath School holding regular sessions.

Right at the outset, the Board faced two questions which had been raised for them, one by the circumstances surrounding the coming of new life to the Society and the other through the character of the changing population of the city. As the Board began its work those questions were lying in the background unasked, but it was not long before they were brought into the open.

The first involved the issue of just what the Society actually was. Who made up the Society? What was the relationship between the evangelical Congregational churches of the city and the Society? How much responsibility did the Board of Managers actually have? At its beginning in 1816 the Society was composed of all who, because of their interest in the work, contributed to the support of the Society. That was quite clear. When the annual meeting of the Society was held, that is, the meeting of those who had paid to be members, a Board of Managers was elected. Even though the same persons were elected to the Board each year, and the routine grew to be rather traditional, the structure of the Society remained the same, and all who were concerned in it understood the operation. After a time, however, there came the day when members of the Society felt that the organization should, in some explicit way, be related to the evangelical churches. Members of the Society were members of those churches, and the Society was carrying on some of the responsibilities of the churches for the evangelization of the city. Moreover, the problem of financing the Society arose, and the idea was proposed that since the Society was doing the work of the churches, the churches should, in all fairness, support the Society. So the churches were asked to choose members of the Board. That created a tangle of relationships which had slowly grown through the years, which was not unravelled until 1840. And then it was unravelled only in theory.

In the amended by-laws which were adopted at that time, the Society was to be composed of "all past life members of the Society and the members of the Board of Directors." There was the possibility of confusion here in the use of the phrase, "past life members," for that would appear to suggest that in due time all life members would no longer exist. That would leave the Board of Directors as the Society. Then in another item in the amended by-laws there was the provision that the Board of Directors were to be chosen at the annual meeting of the Society. In due time that would result in the Board of Directors, acting as the Society, electing the Board of Directors. As matters worked out, difficulty was encountered at precisely that point. Moreover, the new Board of Directors came into existence when the old Board chose one man from each of the evangelical Congregational churches out of three men who had been nominated by those churches to be on the Board. That device, admirable though it appeared to be, created the problem of just what the Board of Directors were. A group of men acting for the churches in a representative ca- pacity and bound therefore to heed the desires and the counsels of the churches? Or, a Society in their own right, free to act as they chose, regardless of the way they had been selected?

Gradually, those questions of identity and relationships had to be worked out. And they had to be worked out as problems arose. At the outset the new Board started its work with no awareness of the difficulties inherent in their organization, but they discovered those difficulties as time went on.

The second question they faced can be described more briefly, although it was of much more significance than the preceding one. Indeed, it is likely that it is one of the more profound prob- lems of most missionary work. When the Society was formed its purpose was to be wholly in the realm of man's spiritual life. The material needs of the poor were to be cared for by other agencies, public or private, established for that purpose. The Society was not to be "drawn away from preaching the Gospel in order to serve tables!" But as the new Board began its work they were con- fronted with the pressing needs of the people the missionaries dealt with, needs that were so immediate and so overwhelming that action had to be taken in respect to them. "It is not possible to gain access to the hearts of the poor, and attempt to supply their spiritual wants, when they are suffering from almost every comfort and necessity of life." From time to time the Board returned to a discussion of what to do about that dilemma. They were well aware of the ease with which people of kindly hearts could be imposed upon, especially by those who, through long experience with terrible poverty, had learned how to extract generous gifts from the unsophisticated and the unwary. They listened to the arguments of an eminent Scottish divine and felt the force of them, that instead of trying to wipe out poverty after it has come to exist, the Society should be busy "laboring to establish a principle and a habit which will go far to prevent its existence." Poverty, he said, is a virulent and obstinate disease which cannot be cured by handing out relief. Education and the inculcation of religion will do much to ward off the disease before it starts. But even as the Board members were listening to that line of argument they said, "that our prayers and our alms should go together seems, by common consent, to be conceded." They struggled with the problem of how to put the two together all during the years that followed.

One other observation must be made. During the time now under consideration the management and direction of the work of the Society was firmly in the control of the Board. The General Agent and the missionaries made their reports, but the Board determined policy, made decisions about program, and handled the relationships with the churches. The whole enterprise was uniquely a Board affair. There were standing committees of the Board, but they had no independent authority to act. Frequently, special committees were appointed, such was an approved procedure for getting at any matter of concern, but they were never given authority to take action, they could only report back to the Board. The Board kept all authority over the work of the Society in its own hands. This necessitated regular Board meetings. They were scheduled and held every month; sometimes they were more frequent than that.

In 1841, the Board established the practice of working out carefully detailed instruction which the employees were to follow. Today the documents would be called job specifications. They were put in letters addressed to the individuals involved. The letter to the General Agent, after treating of salary, date of beginning employment, and conditions under which the relationship could be terminated, went on to say, "you are wholly to withdraw from other engagements and devote yourself completely to this." Then followed a complete description of the responsibilities the man was to have. Then, "The Board do not expect, of course, that by the acceptance of this appointment you will be called upon to neglect or set aside any duties which devolve upon you as a Christian minister, a citizen, or the Head of a Family, as these things are not necessarily inconsistent with entire devotion to the interests of this Society." The document went on to state that if there should arise an occasion when the activity of the General Agent appeared to be affecting the welfare of the Society, the advice and direction given by the Board "should be the rule of action for their agent."[8] Much briefer letters, although just as explicit, were sent to the lay missionaries.

In 1841, the Reverend Amos A. Phelps became the General Agent, and Messrs. Thomas Thwing and F. D. Stedman the lay missionaries, Thwing being carried over from the previous era. The following year Phelps became the pastor of a church established in East Boston and an arrangement was worked out under which he gave some of his time to the general oversight of the work of the Society. With the money the Board saved through that arrangement, Mr. Andrew Cushing was employed as an additional lay missionary.

That action is worthy of note for Mr. Cushing remained in the service of the Society until he retired fifty years later. Mr. Cushing was a member of the Bowdoin Street Church, and that was significant. In 1825, three men, John Tappan, Samuel Hubbard, and Samuel Walley, two of whom have already been identified as officers of the Society, invited about thirty men from the evangelical churches of the city to meet with them and talk of the need of forming a new church. It was to be a church in which every member pledged himself to active witnessing for Jesus Christ and to unfailing participation in the common life of the covenanted group. "The aim was to form a church which might edify itself in its social meetings [week day prayer and study meetings] without the need of a pastor, and in which all the brethren were to take their part, when called, in all the exercises." It was to be a lay-men's church, a church of men who, while they were bound to have to earn their living, were primarily interested in the evangelization of the city and were pledged to engage in that work. The Reverend Lyman Beecher became the pastor of that church at its founding, happily being in full accord with the purpose for which the church had been brought into existence. That was the company of men to which Andrew Cushing belonged when he entered the employ of the Society, and his whole life was marked by the commitment he had made as a member of that church.

In 1844, the Reverend James Carruthers was employed as a missionary in South Boston, "until further notice." He was "a foreigner," presumably a German, who had been working as a missionary in the State of Maine when he moved to Boston. Beside calling in the homes of the people and conducting Bible study and worship for groups meeting in the homes, he conducted worship services in a hall on Canton Street in South Boston. He gained a ready response from his own people. He remained with the Society for a little over a year, but by that time an informal group had gathered which became the foundation of a later organization.

Beginning in 1847 there was one of those interesting little episodes that often arise when a religious leader comes to be loved by those among whom he works. The record of the case under review is not altogether clear, it was bound not to be since the matter involved personalities, but there is sufficient information to indicate the outlines of the tale. Mr. Thomas Thwing was doing missionary work in the city, supported by a few of the churches, when he was taken into the employ of the Society. Quite naturally he had his own way of doing things and a considerable number of people who depended upon him for advice and help. He was a man absolutely devoted to his work, although he did it as he saw fit. In 1847 the Board asked him, or told him, to do some work on Sundays. From the Board's point of view, that was in line with a change which they were making in the program. But Thwing would not agree to this. He was a layman and while he conducted neighborhood meetings for worship and study on weekday evenings he was convinced that he should not take the direction of congregational worship on Sundays. Moreover, he had never done that, and he knew that one of the reasons why the Board, when they began the revived work, employed lay missionaries was that they did not want to get involved in doing the kind of work that properly belonged to the churches and the ordained clergy. Thwing saw himself as a lay missionary and was opposed to doing anything that would make him appear otherwise. He therefore addressed a communication refusing, plainly and firmly, to do as requested. In reply the Board restated the terms under which the missionaries were employed: that in the case of a disagreement between the Board and an employee, the wishes of the Board were to decide the matter. Thwing was adamant and the Board asked him to leave, giving him the agreed length of time in order to make other arrangements. But Thwing paid no attention and went on with his work. Letters began to pour in to members of the Board asking for the continuance of Thwing's services, and a delegation of poor people waited on the Board at one of their meetings to make the same request. The Board then reviewed the disagreement and concluded they had acted for the best interests of the Society, and gave Thwing six months in which to arrange the termination of his relationship with them. And Thwing left, "the Board expressing to him the assurance of their perfect kindness of feeling, and of their sincere wishes for his future usefulness and happiness."[9] A year later he was back in the employ of the Board. By that time Mr. Cushing had become assistant to the president and the arrangements in the work of the Society were beginning to change under his influence.

During the course of the year 1845 the Board gave careful thought to the wisdom of changing from lay to ministerial missionaries. When the Board was re-established they agreed, as one of their principles, that "while we aim to preach the Gospel to the poor, we are not in favour of supporting permanent preaching in chapels designed for the poor alone" and they had reiterated that principle on occasion since. But they had observed the changes that were taking place in the city and the surrounding areas, and they had come to believe that one of their functions as a missionary agency might be to enter the new areas where the great masses of the poor lived with the deliberate and avowed purpose of establishing churches. They proposed to do this by employing ministers, securing places for meetings, directing the ministers to call in the homes, starting services of worship in the places acquired, gathering children in Sabbath Schools, and when enough people had been drawn together in each place organizing a church. "It is felt," they said, "that at the present moment there is an important call for three or four of these chapels, and that if we neglect to occupy the ground others will occupy it."[10]

The Board realized that this departure from their original policy would be disturbing to the churches. The Board members were sensitive enough to Congregational feelings to know that the slightest appearance of an organization other than the churches presuming to act in the name and on the behalf of the churches without the whole-hearted assent of the churches would arouse both fear and resentment, so they went out of their way to explain to the churches why they were making their proposed change and to try to allay any suspicions that might arise.

> This Society, in reality, is but the embodying of the churches for a harmonious effort to build up the waste places among us. [Further], The Board of Managers of this Society consists of members from each of these churches, so that each church is part of this association; and, of course, nothing will be done intentionally . . . at all prejudicial to the prosperity of any of them.[11]

Then, having indicated in that way, that the churches need not be troubled by the proposed activity of the Society, since the Society was really only the churches at work, (although the argument must have appeared to the churches as a bit of specious theory in view of their experience with the Society during the preceding years) the Board went on to defend its proposal. The case they made out went like this: none of the work the Society was doing would be neglected by the innovations; the change would not be more costly, since "educated and efficient clergymen" would be paid no more than lay missionaries; the clergymen could do more than the lay missionaries could, "many valuable labors which are not appropriate or proper for laymen to do"; the ex-

perience of the Society was that clergymen were preferable to laymen; the missionary societies of other denominations in the city
employed clergymen, which was "a stringent cause why our Society should pursue a similar course"; and "the capitol advantage
is, that the Sabbath is improved." That meant that clergymen
would work on Sundays, which, as they had discovered, laymen
were hesitant to do.

Having worked that all out, the members of the Board made
visits to the pastors of the churches to present the matter personally. But they met with violent opposition, far greater than they
had dreamed. The Board wrote up their side of the argument in
the annual report which was distributed to the members of the
churches. Evidently the pastors had agreed that whereas the Society had been founded as a "Society for the Moral and Religious
Instruction of the Poor," the Board were intending to turn it
into a church extension society, and for this they had no authority. The Board countered by saying that the Society could not be
the former without being the latter, and that inasmuch as it was
the former it was bound to be the latter.

There were meetings between various individuals; a committee
of the Board studied the matter and brought in recommendations; finally there was a meeting of pastors and Board members
at which there was an open confrontation. The Board said the
issue was the continuance of the Society, and they indicated their
intention of disbanding the Society unless they could carry out
the work of the city mission as they believed, in light of all the information they had, it should be done. The Pastors said that since
the Society was an agent of the churches, the Directors of the Society were bound to heed the desires of the churches, and, in any
case, the churches paid the bills. The words do not appear in the
record, but it is easy to imagine the old adage being heard in a
kind of stage whisper: he who pays the piper, calls the tune. But
whether such was said or not, the implication was most certainly
made. At that the members of the Board pointed out that the
churches might talk like that if they chose, but the fact was that
during the current year they had failed by over a thousand dollars to meet the bills. And, the Board added, as a kind of closing

bit of opprobrium, that they had to present the Gospel to fifty thousand people "who are now destitute of the means of grace" with three missionaries and a part-time General Agent at a cost of $3,500, while the ten to twelve thousand members of the evangelical churches, who assumedly were already Christian, had fifteen full time ministers to serve them at a cost of $70,000. The outcome of the matter was that the Board of Managers of the Society was reorganized.

In 1847 an amendment to the Bylaws was adopted providing for a Board of Directors of not less than nine nor more than thirty persons in addition to the officers; and another amendment providing for the election by the Board of an Executive Committee who would be responsible for the conduct of the Society's work and who would report its actions to the Board at certain stated intervals. After those changes were made in the Bylaws the constituent members of the Board changed so that half of them were clergymen and half laymen, and on the Executive Committee were three clergymen and six laymen. These amendments testify to the momentary victory of the ministers. But the laymen were not to be outdone ("the children of this world are wiser," etc.). They began to make use of an article in the Bylaws, which had always been there, providing for the calling of a meeting of the Board at the request of a certain number of members, and by that device they re-established frequent meetings of the Board, at which all the business of the Society came to be handled. The Executive Committee disappeared from the record completely for a time.

While this was going on the Board went on directing the work of the Society. Even while the discussion was taking place, the proposed change was actually made. So that while the argument was a genuine disagreement and a struggle between the power of the clergy and the power of the laymen, the work of the Society went on. In 1847, the Board employed Mr. Patrick O'Brien, a converted Roman Catholic, to work among the Irish Catholics in the city. That seemed to be, from the standpoint of the Board members, a wise appointment, for it brought them the services of a man who, as they thought, understood those people in the population that were seriously in need of saving. The Catholic Bishop felt quite otherwise, and when O'Brien left the Society, which he did after a brief period of service, the Bishop wondered "if honest Irish wrath with this 'turncoat' helped him on his way."[12]

There were a few other personnel changes during the years, but they were of minor significance, simply the replacement of workers who resigned. Otherwise, the employed staff of the Society remained fairly constant, a General Agent and from two to four missionaries. When the Reverend A. A. Phelps resigned his half-time responsibilities in 1846, the Reverend George Oviatt was called to the position.

When the Society was revived and the Board was chosen from among the nominees of the churches, there was a general understanding that the churches would bear the cost of the Society's work by apportioning the financial needs among them. As far as can be learned there was no agreement made about this. The Society authorized its finance committee, when the budget had been drawn up to inform the churches of the proportionate share each church should take. That was done, and the first year the churches paid the amounts asked of them. Nine churches supported the Society in that way. Each succeeding year much the same procedure was followed. Not always did this result in a balanced account; sometimes the expenses went up; sometimes the contributions from the churches went down; sometimes both things occurred in the same year. But at the end of the era under review the Society had a small balance in its account. However, even that was the result of a special collection which had been taken in the churches to wipe out the debt which had accrued at the end of the previous year. The Board continued through the years to insist upon the need for more funds if they were to meet the demands which the circumstances in the city made on them, and occasionally they risked an expenditure before they had the funds to pay for it. On the whole, they managed the business affairs of the Society carefully and conservatively.

As the Society looked at the changing city and saw the religious needs of thousands of people, how did they go about dealing with those needs? First it should be noted that two pieces of work which in 1828 were turned over to other agencies were, in 1841, returned to the Society. The Boston Sabbath School Union, which had assumed responsibility for all the Sabbath Schools in the city, including those developed by the Society, voted itself out of existence. The Union put the schools meeting in churches into the care of the respective churches, and the schools meeting in places other than churches back into the hands of the Society. The Union recommended that all schools retain a relationship with each other under the direction of the Society. A year later, the Boston Seaman's Tract Society, which had been organized within the Seaman's Friend Society, with a relationship both to that Society and to the American Tract Society decided that since the City Missionary Society was about to engage in an extensive Tract program, they would go out of business, and turned its interests over to the Society.

The Board organized a program of Tract distribution so that it would be done regularly and systematically, and would cover the entire city. The plan, in essence, was a very simple one: a distributor, man or woman, would call at a home or a dwelling and offer a tract to an adult person who might be there. If the tract were refused or the door shut against the distributor, that was to be the end of the matter at that particular dwelling; but if the tract were accepted or the distributor were invited into the home that was to be the opening of a relationship which was to be maintained as the distributor returned each month with a new and different tract. The Board divided the city into "Tract Distribution Districts," each district consisting of about thirty families. There were between four and five hundred of those districts. A sufficient number of church people were enlisted to provide one visitor in each district. Then the districts were grouped in Divisions of about twenty-five districts in each, and a missionary was assigned as the Division supervisor. His job was to get the tracts to the distributors, receive the reports of the distributors, counsel with them when they met difficult situations, hold a 'social religious meeting' (a week night gathering in a home for Bible study and prayer) regularly each month in each district, and in any other way that seemed advisable to increase the effectiveness of the program. When the Board started the program with that structure, they included the entire city, the houses of the wealthy as well as the homes of the poor. They believed there were pagans who needed to hear the Gospel, or to be forcibly reminded of it among the well-to-do, just as there were poor people who had the same needs. "It was long before I could summon strength of purpose to enter the dwellings of the fashionable and wealthy on my errand," was the way one distributor expressed himself. After a while, however, the plan was changed, and the calling was directed at the poor only, who, assumedly, would not be reached by the usual ministrations of the churches.

In each annual report of the Board there appeared the following items showing statistically the amount of work done by the tract distributors: "Number of Tract districts 434. Number of Tract distributors 408. Number of Tracts distributed 181,653." In addition to the people working in the city there were 18 distributors working among the seamen. They visited the vessels in the harbor and the seamen's boarding houses, and they made reports, with figures similar to those made by the city distributors.

What were the purposes and the possible results of that work? Tracts were written in order to awaken the conscience, impart some religious truth, recall a religious commitment once made but forgotten, or in some other way to deal with the religious well-being of the people reading them. One of the Board reports put it this way: "Tract distribution serves as one of its grand results, the distribution among the destitute of the Word of God," although it may be, from the context in which those words stand, that the Board really meant that the tract gave the distributor a chance to find out whether the family called on needed a Bible. Yet there was the idea in the minds of those engaged in this work that the tracts, in and of themselves, had the power to work some spiritual good for the readers, or perhaps, that the tracts were agencies through which God might work. The Board noted that "The Great Adversary" used tracts in his work and the "children of the King" should counter with the same weapon. The Great Adversary certainly referred to the Evil One, but there is some doubt as to the guise in which he was to be met. Perhaps the Board thought of tract distribution as a second form of defense against the same activity "extensively carried on by the Catholic Tract Societies of Boston and Hartford."[13] In one report there is an interesting argument presented by one of the workers: tracts are a divinely appointed method of instruction; the first tract was written by God on stone, others were written under God's direction by scribes, prophets, apostles and evangelists; every great reformer has used tracts to do the work God called him to do, and the Society must use the same method.

It is much more certain, however, that in the minds of the Board members the tracts were a most effective device for introducing persons who were strangers to each other. "Tracts serve as letters of introduction." A Christian individual could knock on the door of a stranger and simply introduce himself, trusting that his appearance would start a relationship with the person who answered his knock; if, however, the visitor has a tract to offer and to use as a subject of conversation, a point of contact, the introduction is more easily made. "The stranger, coming on a stranger's errand, becomes a friend, discharging the offices and exerting the influence of a friend. . . . The distribution of tracts affords to those who engage in it, an opportunity for religious conversation with many who otherwise would perhaps never be personally addressed on the subject of an interest in Jesus Christ."

The Board visualized through their program of tract distribution some hundreds of Christian people working all the while throughout the entire city, finding those who had no knowledge of Jesus Christ as they knew Him, or having no contact with the church as they understood the church, and in that way carrying the message of God's salvation. The tract, in itself, simply left at a door, might conceivably do some good, but basically the tract was a sign of the primary interest of the one who brought it.

> Here are 408 pious persons passing through the city from month to month, scattering these pages of truth, these leaves of the good tree, with healing power. These distributors not only leave the tract at the places where they call, but often have profitable conversation with those who are accessible, and thus gain an influence over one here and one there. . . .

The Board prepared a sheet of instructions for tract distributors. The distributor was encouraged to read the tract he was to distribute and then engage in a period of prayer for those he would meet and for his work, before he started out. He was to remain in prayer until he felt himself strengthened for the work and filled with a deep concern for those who needed to hear the Gospel. Then, and only then, was the distributor to set out on his visiting. The essential point of the enterprise came when there was a face to face meeting between a Christian, who cared for the spiritual welfare of his fellows, and an individual who was out of touch with God. If the distributor was refused admittance to a home, or if a family, after learning the reason for his visit, were to refuse to talk further with him, he was to leave quietly and graciously. He was not to return to that place unless he were invited to do so.

The distributor was provided with a report sheet on which he was to record certain information about the people he visited. He was never to let that report sheet be seen and was to get the information sought most discreetly. He was to find out the circumstances of the people, the temporal needs as well as the spiritual, and do all possible to help meet those needs. After a number of visits the distributor was certain to know those who were responsive to his efforts and he was to concentrate his energies on those, for his ultimate purpose was to awaken people "to a sense of their guilt and their danger . . . and to induce them to give themselves to God." When the distributor found a person responding to his religious efforts he was to "use suitable means to have them brought under the care of some pious pastor, and connected, if they should become pious, with some evangelical church." If the distributor came upon a Christian family, as he did occasionally, he was to make sure of their church connection and attendance, and then try to enlist their help in the work he was doing by getting them to arrange for neighborhood meetings.

The distributor was urged to read to the blind and the illiterate, loan books from the Society library to those who were interested, supply Bibles in homes where there were none ("see the missionary if copies are needed"), and make arrangements for meeting temporal needs. Finally:

it cannot be too much recommended to you to 'be patient toward all men.' Should you meet unkind treatment, which in some instances you may, manifest no angry or resentful feelings. Endeavor to exhibit the spirit of your Master, in meekness entreating the truth. The observance of this direction is of special importance when you meet with those who deny the fundamental doctrines of the Gospel, and cavil at the most sacred truths of the Bible. It is of little use, generally, to dispute with such persons. The simple truths of the Gospel, presented in the mild and persuasive accents of love, will be your most hopeful weapon.[14]

The distributors met every month. There was some irregularity of attendance, as was to be expected, but the Board kept urging the importance of the meetings and seem to have had very satisfactory results. At those meetings the distributors were asked to report, and then present any problems they faced. And since the meetings were held in districts the number of distributors present was not so large as to limit effective participation.

The Board were also quite conscious of the impact the program of tract distribution had upon the churches. They knew that through the program numbers of church members were given a means by which they could share their faith with others, and faith shared is faith known and held. "It would be for the welfare of the church could a system of Christian effort be devised which actually secured the labors, in the aggressive movements of the church, of every professor of religion." The Board also understood the importance of the distributors' meeting in giving to those involved a sense of corporate participation in a common task, for they knew how difficult it is for one single individual all by himself to give witness to his faith in the midst of all-encompassing evil. While, on the one hand it was inevitable that the tract distributors reflected in themselves the spirit and character of the churches, on the other hand, the involvement of the distributors in visiting and talking with people about their faith strengthened their lives and that in turn affected the churches.

Month after month the distributors went out. At the beginning they reported on the way they were received. To many of them the task was new and they had no idea of what to expect. "I undertook the distribution with great trembling, but I have been greatly encouraged. I have been very kindly received. . . . I am happy to say that the task has proved very pleasant." That is the type of remark which fills the early reports. As time went on and the distributors learned what to look for on their calls, their reports dealt more in detail with the conditions they found and the results which followed their visits.

Along the road and lanes of the city they went; into houses, garrets, cellars, and tiny rooms on floors in between; a grocery store, a grog shop with men leaning on the bar and the proprietor nearby—a door opening a tiny crack, a face peering out, the door closing—"we want none of you in here"—"my man is so sick, but come in"—Germans, people from the country lost in the city crowd, Irish, backsliders, couples of mixed religious background —"no, I never went to church, no use for religion, don't believe the stuff"—"was regular at church once, but then I married and my man never went"—drunks, smallpox, dead bodies—"no, the kids never went to Sabbath School, they have no clothes"—jobless, hungry, illiterate—"my mother was religious, but she's dead now"—filth, smells, disorder.

Three months later: "The man down the hall wants to talk to you," "but he wouldn't let me in the last time I called," "but he wants you now"—"I'll take the tract, come in and have a visit"— children meeting the distributor on the street, lodging house keeper asking for tracts, the prostitute wanting to chat—"the priest said not to read your stuff, but come in"—"go away, I ain't got no use for you or your religion."

So the visits went month after month. People moved to the city from the country towns hoping to get work, and then were overwhelmed by the situation in which they found themselves. Germans who had clustered together in a tiny area of the city, speaking their own language, holding fast to their own customs, church people without a church since they found none they could understand; Catholics married to Protestants, both having given up their religious duties; members of Boston churches who through their own mistakes or through changes of fortune had lost their places in life and had left their old associations; drinkers and drunks, male and female; the sick with no one to tend them; the

dead unburied; and children everywhere, many who had never
been to school and more who had never been in a church.

The tract distributors did what they could for the physical and
temporal needs they met, but they had only the message of the
Gospel and the most limited of resources to give. Some who knew
well-to-do church members with generous hearts told the stories
of the poverty they found and won helpful interest; others led the
way to city and state agencies which could help. In existence at
the time was the Washington Temperance Society, an early-day
Alcoholics Anonymous, with the same general purpose but not
all the wisdom of the latter, but with amazing effectiveness none-
theless. The distributors introduced many inebriates to that Society and saw a number reclaimed. But always the distributors
looked to affairs of the spirit, always they tried to lead to Christ
and the church. They touched consciences, challenged to reformation, reminded of Christian hope, looked beyond worldly conditions, and since they were Protestants, sought the conversion of
Catholics.

And the results? In their monthly reports the distributors listed
"so many people induced to attend public worship; so many children gathered into Sabbath Schools; so many hopeful conversions."
The last figure was always small, very small; and the reported conversions were only hopeful ones. There came murmurings and
criticisms from the people supporting the Society: why, with all
the effort, all the distributors at work, all the money expended
were there no more conversions? One scans the reports to see
whether, under the force of the complaints, there came an increase of the figures so as to satisfy the complainers, but there is
none.

How, then, can one judge the results? That is an impossibility.
There were children cleaned and clothed and taken to school;
there were back-sliders renewed in faith; there were temperance
pledges signed and kept; there were jobs found for the unemployed. The sick were tended, the dead were buried, the hopeless
were made hopeful. And there can be no doubt that some were
aroused to an awareness of their spiritual needs and responded to
the claims of Christ spoken to them by the persons who came to

them with tracts in their hands and concern in their hearts. But over and above all that there is between the lines of the printed pages and the handwriting of the secretary's reports the story of people interested in the well being of others, and of those others discovering, not in the tracts, but in the look of the eyes, the sound of the voice, the touch of the hand, the patient listening, and the repeated visits, the measure and reality of that interest and responding to it. In the city, where the forces of society, of the economy, of the world, and of religion were setting people apart from each other and destroying true life in the process, the work of those distributors was a tiny bit of healing, bridging the gaps of misunderstanding and animosity and hatred and non-communication that were opening wide.

They did not see their work in that way, for here we use modern language, but it was precisely that job of drawing together individuals torn apart from each other, driven into themselves, and lost in the world, that those distributors did. No doubt in their efforts they added to the brokenness in one way or another, for in man's ignorance the good he seeks to do, and does, always has in it a measure of evil; yet nevertheless, the work that was done in those years by men and women who cared enough to give their time and their dedication to the task of visiting strangers, poverty-ridden strangers, to take them tracts, had results beyond the power of statistics to measure, for wherever and whenever the barriers between men were lowered, even a tiny bit, there life was given.

An enterprise as extensive as this, involving as many people in a city the size of Boston, especially where it touched religious sensibilities, was bound to be noticed. A writer on one of the daily newspapers had this to say, "I am astonished at the effrontery of those persons who are now busily engaged in going from house to house for the purpose of distributing sectarian tracts," and he went on to call the distributors, "disturbers of domestic peace" and "sectarian almoners," and ended by "hoping that the good people of this city and our land, wherever these mistaken efforts have been made, will give evidence of their disapprobation of such measures." Catholic historians have commented:

Already 417 enthusiasts were in the field, distributing religious tracts amongst the people and attempting to persuade them to attend Protestant services. These activities were of such magnitude as to cause the *Catholic Observer* to print a series of articles on how to meet the approaches of these people, and, as a matter of fact, one of the reasons why this paper was started was to instruct Catholics on this very subject. The tract distributors or colporteurs, as they are called, also acted as recruiting agents for the Sabbath Schools and were supposed to try to persuade Catholic children to join them.[15]

But the Board of the Society said that it, and here the reference is to the tract distribution:

is certainly the great instrumentality of the churches in God's hand for reaching the papal population of this city. It is of first importance that we do all in our power not only for our defense against Romanism, but by way of making aggressions on the dominions of the Man of Sin.

The employed missionaries were also at work in various parts of the city. They were on the job every day, whereas the tract distributors visited the homes once a month. This made it possible for the missionaries to deal with a case of human need or an individual "under conviction" until a clear result had been gained. Because they were in specific areas every day they came to know the conditions and the people with considerable intimacy, seeing more clearly than the distributors the poverty, disease, and evil, and learning to distinguish between sincere and sham cases of need. In some ways their work paralleled that of the distributors, so that after a few years their reports and the distributors' reports were merged into one and presented to the churches in that way; they were the agents of the Society ever present among the poor.

In one report they analyzed for the readers the people with whom they came in contact. They divided them into two classes: the pious and worthy poor; the idle and vicious poor. The former were poor through no fault of their own; although they were basically hard working and careful of their resources they became poor. "They were poor, it would seem, according to the all-wise but inscrutable providence of God." They were humble folk, not flaunting their poverty, nor making claims on others because of it, but bearing it patiently and being sincerely grateful for any relief that was granted them. The one thing that troubled them more than the poverty itself was that all too often it kept them away from the fellowship of Christian people and the ministrations of the church. "While the bread, the fuel, and the clothing, were received with the blessing of a soul sincere in its gratitude, the gratitude was vastly deeper for the Christian consolation afforded."[16] The missionaries, in their analysis, called them "the most brilliant exhibitions of the power of the Gospel among the poor, whom the world knows not." Obviously, said the missionaries, the church must seek them out through every means at its command, provide the necessities of life they lack and draw them into the fullness of Christ's human family.

On the other hand, the idle and vicious poor were in their condition through their own sin; they were responsible. The question then arose, in the minds of the missionaries, and it well may be that in this they were stating in their report sentiments that were widely held by church people then, as to why any effort should be made on their behalf. "They have made their beds, let them lie in them." To this the missionaries had two answers. First, that taking the Gospel of Jesus Christ to them is the means appointed by God for their salvation. Since the church and its agencies are those who know that all souls, even those of the vicious poor, are precious in God's sight, and that God does not wish any man to die in his sin, they are the ones who must see to it that the Gospel is made known to them, idle and vicious though they be. The preaching to them is God's command. Second, the Gospel must be taken to those people because it is the only sure means for wiping out pauperism. Feed, clothe, and support the idle and vicious poor and they remain idle and vicious, or even become worse than before. The reason for this is that affording them relief from their poverty does not touch the cause of their condition. Man must come to know and acknowledge his sin, then, perchance he will turn and be changed. "The Bible shows his sin to the vicious poor man, and the judgments from God which impend over him." When the poor of this type are given religious instruction, it may be "that, by the blessing of God, their souls may be saved."

With that understanding of what they were doing, the missionaries went about their work. As previously noted, they supervised the tract distributors. That took some of their time, and through it they learned of places and people needing their ministrations. Then, they called in homes, not necessarily following the tract distributors, but going often where those had been repulsed. They visited "the poor, sick, afflicted, serious, vicious and neglected." They sought out the objects of their ministry, going from house to house and door to door. They knew full well that "taking the Gospel to the poor" meant far more than preaching to them. But they also knew that the task included preaching, which to them meant the telling in as simple a way as possible the story of God's action in man's behalf. They arranged and conducted "social religious meetings." Poor people who were Christians welcomed the missionaries to their homes and invited their neighbors to come in for Bible study and prayer. Slowly there were established throughout the city a number of such meetings. In the year 1846, for example, there were over three hundred such meetings, which means, roughly, about twenty-five a month. Sometimes a meeting would be led by the person in whose home it was being held, the missionary being simply among those present. And sometimes a meeting went on without the missionary in attendance.

Through those gatherings, companies of Christian people were formed, into which the pagan and evil ones could be led. At the meetings hymns were sung, the Bible was read and studied, and prayers were offered. "The good news was heard."

The missionaries were called upon for other services of what would now be called a pastoral nature. They sat with the dying and at times were the ones to offer an encouraging word and to hear the final response before death. They conducted funerals for people who passed away with no one to care for them and no one interested enough to arrange the disposition of their remains. They dispensed relief. At first they did this out of their own money, but they quickly realized that would never be enough. They convinced the Board to include the taking of a collection for the poor at the Quarterly meeting of the Society, and they raised money on their own. During the year 1847 they received $611.96 for relief. "Of this sum, $220 were given by two individuals without solicitation, $160 by an anonymous friend, and $60 by a tract distributor." Which means that about $150 came from the collections at the Quarterly meetings. The amount of money given for relief increased each year. The missionaries distributed the money carefully, ending each year, almost without exception, with a balance. The money was used only for emergencies; there was no attempt to give systematic and continued support of a family. This is clear both from the amount of money involved and the reports of the way the money was used. In the year 1849, for example, $260.40 was received for relief; 180 families were assisted, and $271.63 was spent. The money went for: a bottle of medicine here, coal for a fire there, bread and meat for a meal, shoes for a child, a secondhand coat for a man with a new job; such small needs were met when no other resources were available.

The missionaries were required to report regularly to the Board on the conditions they met, the work they had done and any results of which they knew. Doubtless they used cases, in their reporting, which they knew would make the greatest impression, but from the picture which they drew over the years it can well be believed they described the city with accuracy. "I attended the funeral of an only child, at which I tried in vain to arouse the mother from her drunken sleep." "Children are often found in dens of infamy . . . one of the duties of the missionary is to secure them homes where they will be surrounded by better influences." "The man died a few days after his arrival in this country, leaving his widow and six small children. After the funeral I learned that she had but twenty cents left." "In a garret room there is a widow with three children. The only furniture are two chairs and a chest. The family came from the country. The father took to evil ways, sold their possessions to get money for gambling and drink, and died in a fit of intoxication." "Found a family on a very cold day, upstairs, with five children, miserably cold. I loaned them a stove to make them comfortable for the winter." Thus the stories went.

In the 1848 report the missionaries described their work thus:

This is the only organized instrumentality [tract distributors and missionaries] that aims to reach the entire community within the field of its operations. In its aggressive character, it literally obeys the command of our Saviour, "Preach the Gospel to every creature". There are no depths of degradation into which men have fallen, from which it does not try to elevate them. There are no trials of life, from which it does not aim to relieve them. None have wandered so far in the paths of the destroyer, that it does not follow them, saying, "Turn ye, for ye will die." It enters every garret and cellar and there proffers the Gospel of Jesus Christ as the only panacea for human ills.

For all the while, in everything they did the missionaries held one great purpose and that was the bringing to those who, in their judgment, were lost, the message of the Christian faith, fully trusting that if they did their work faithfully God would use them for His saving purpose. They persuaded people to attend church, they took children to Sabbath School, and they were convinced that some with whom they dealt were "hopefully converted." Those were the results for which they labored.

The missionaries also shared with the tract distributors the work among seamen. The responsibility they took for those men was in seeing to it that tracts, Bibles, and Testaments were made available. When a seaman gave up his job and settled in the city, the missionary found him; when a seaman had a family living in the city the missionary often kept in touch with them. However, since seamen came and went with the movement of the vessels, the missionaries had casual contacts with many men over brief periods of time.

Aware of how insignificant the Society was in the face of the size of the city and the rapidly growing number of the poor, the program the Board created and carried on, had audacity and faith. Few though they were, they dared to see the whole city as their God-given sphere of responsibility, and they set in motion a program designed to carry God's Word and the personal touch of a Christian into every home. And they had faith enough to believe that though their efforts were relatively insignificant, and frowned upon by the "cultured despisers," God would use all they were doing for His ends. Perhaps one of the secrets to the work of those years is that the people involved did not theologize about what they were doing. In obedience and trust they did it.

When the Board began the renewed effort in 1849, there was no chapel program under their direction. The Society owned the Mission House on Buttolph Street, but services of worship had been discontinued. A Sabbath School held its sessions in the building. Early in 1840, some of the members of The Free Church, Marlborough Chapel, of which the Reverend Amos A. Phelps became the pastor when he resigned from being the General Agent of the Society, decided to form another evangelical congregation. The group was given their release from that church in order to do so. They asked the Society for permission to use the Mission House property. The Society granted their request and spent some money repairing the building so as to make it more usable. A regular lease was written under which the proposed new church was given the right to use the Mission House provided they would maintain the building in good repair. The congregation became the Garden Street Church in 1841, and called the Reverend W. R. Chapman to be the pastor.

As time went on the missionaries came to feel that their work would be more effective if there were chapels at which Christian congregations might be gathered. They were aware of the earlier decision of the Society not to establish churches for the poor alone, and they felt the force of the reason why that should not be done. But they came to believe even more strongly in the fact that the poor had no churches to which they could go. The poor could not afford the expense of attending one of the established churches, because the pew rents were beyond their resources, and even when special pews were provided for them they felt out of place. And the special pews for the poor were often located in the balcony, which resulted in a type of segregation even more invidious than chapels would be. Furthermore, the missionaries watched the rapid growth of the Garden Street Church and discovered that they were able to relate the people on whom they called quickly and effectively to that congregation. So they began to urge the Board to undertake more chapel work, because it seemed to them the one thing lacking in their enterprise. And they suggested that the South End of the city was an area where a chapel was needed at once.

The Board secured the use of a hall on Suffolk Street, and services of worship were started. Mr. Carruthers conducted the services at the outset, then the pastors of the city churches took turns. No reason is given in any of the reports for that change of leadership, but knowing the suspicions which the pastors had of the Society, and the agreement under which the life of the Society had been restored, there was probably a desire on the part of the pastors to have control of the new enterprise. The response to that chapel work was immediate from the people in the neighborhood. The limited accommodations of the hall were quickly outgrown, and a larger hall was found. Then some of the people who were attending the services approached the Society with a request that a church be organized. The Society responded by making a survey. They sought to learn what "the prospects of the proposed effort in that section of the city would be." The survey showed that the proposed church would be three-quarters of a mile from any other orthodox evangelical church; that the number of people to whom the proposed church would be the nearest evangelical church was between 1,500 and 2,000; that the number of those people who then attended an evangelical church was from fifty to sixty families, of which from thirty to forty families desired the proposed church; that the population of the area was increasing rapidly; and that an unusually large number of homes were then being built in the district. The conclusion to be drawn seemed clear.

At that time the lease on the Mission House property expired and the Garden Street Church notified the Board that they did not wish to renew it since they intended to unite with the Green Street Church and establish the merged congregation elsewhere. The idea then occurred to a Board member that the property on Buttolph Street might be sold and the proceeds used to buy land and erect a building in the South End. The Society considered the matter, authorized the proper officers to proceed and soon were "in possession, on very advantageous terms, of one of the most eligible lots in the vicinity named."[17]

But the churches in the city were troubled. A meeting of laymen and pastors was called at the Pine Street Church, at which the action of the Society was discussed. The leaders of the Society started out by acknowledging the 1840 agreement that "they were not in favor of supporting permanent preaching in chapels designed for the poor alone," and then went on to insist that in the new enterprise they were not in any way transgressing that agreement; they were planting the "means of grace" where none was available, doing only that work which was preliminary to the organization of a church. After arguing the matter on principle they illustrated from the history of the churches in the city how each one which had been organized since 1815 had come into existence through the agency of existing churches. In light of that, they insisted, the Society, as the agency of the churches, was simply acting as the churches had acted in the past. From the record it would appear that the representatives of the churches were convinced, for a resolution was adopted approving "fully" the plan of the Society to build a chapel in the South End. From subsequent developments it may be judged, either that the churches were temporarily overwhelmed by the lucidity of the Society's spokesmen, or that they graciously bowed to a *fait accompli.* In any case, the Society having won the battle, if not the war, built a chapel, which was dedicated in July of 1845. Four months later there was an organized congregation at the place over which a pastor was installed. The building was designed to seat 350 people, yet not long after the organization of the church it became too small for the numbers who came. Plans were made for putting up an addition. All indications were that the Suffolk Street Union Church was a vital organization.

That move was such an obvious success and such a confirmation of the recommendations of the missionaries and the growing convictions of the Board that it was not long before proposals were made for the opening of other chapels.

It is thought that the chapel effort may be prosecuted with success.

> The centre of the city is filled up, and is well supplied with churches. The population is spreading out on all sides where there is yet ground to be occupied. There are among them more or less professors of religion, some of them from churches in the country, who have not yet removed their relation from those churches. But many of these are poor people, or at least few of them have any property at their command.

And the Board urged upon the churches the wisdom of locating chapels at strategic points as soon as possible.

In 1845, the Board proposed opening work at South Cove, and work at a place near the Boston and Lowell Railroad depot. They reported that they had surveyed both fields and that both of them warranted going ahead at once. By 1846 use of the Ward Room on East Street, in the South Cove neighborhood had been secured and the Reverend Mr. Dyer, a newly-appointed missionary, had begun to hold services there. The following year, the congregation having far outgrown the Ward Room, the services were moved to a hall over the Old Colony Railroad station; and, Mr. Dyer having left the Board, the two ministers of Central Church alternated in conducting the worship. A Sabbath School had been started which almost from the opening day enrolled more pupils than could conveniently be cared for. During that same year a hall was found, at the corner of Lowell and Causeway Streets, and public worship and a Sabbath School were started there. Soon afterwards, that place, seating more than three hundred was filled for each service.

Then the churches of the city made it clear, in the most final way that could be, that they did not approve of the extension of the chapel program. Funds were withheld from the Society. The Society was forced to tell the people using the Old Colony Hall that they would have to pay the rent if they continued to meet, and also to pay the rent for the previous period since that had not been paid. The Society notified the group at Lowell and Causeway Streets that they could not expect any further subsidy payments. The board reported:

> Some of the churches are adverse to the policy of chapel enterprises. In withdrawing support from the chapel efforts just named, the

Board, influenced by the state of the treasury, and in part, the wishes of the churches, do not take a stand against the policy of chapel enterprises, because they entered upon the policy at the instance of the majority of the churches [evidently a reference to the meeting referred to earlier] . . . The responsibility in reference to the mode of operations adapted to accomplish the ends of the Society, rests with the churches, whose organ the Society is. . . . The Board of Directors has no disposition to pursue a policy which does not receive the approbation of their constituents.

Having responded to the wing-clipping operations of the churches, the Board went on to point out that from 1840 to 1845 the population of South Boston had increased more than 62%, "more in proportion by poor foreigners and their children," and that members of the Board were being asked to do much more for them than simply to distribute tracts; and then the Board noted that from 1840 to 1845 the population of East Boston had increased almost 245% and that such an increase obviously called for a tremendous effort by the evangelical forces of the city. But at that apparent impasse the chapel effort rested during the years now under review.

It has been noted earlier that the Sabbath School Union disbanded and made suggestions as to the future of the schools. It is of interest to record the reason the Union gave for its action. The officers said that "more would be done to promote the cause of Sabbath Schools in each denomination, and with as much or more real Christian Union, if each denomination were left to manage its Sabbath Schools in its own way." The Union effort had failed on the rock of denominational loyalties. When the Union was disbanded there were eighteen Sabbath Schools connected with Congregational churches. Some of them were local schools and the others parish schools. Under the arrangement which was worked out at the time the parish schools went to the control and support of the churches, each church becoming responsible for its own school; and the local schools were turned over to the Society. Three of these schools immediately worked out relationships with churches for themselves, leaving four schools for which the Society was responsible. In addition, the Society was to undertake the promotion and the conduct of the Quarterly Rally of all the Congregational schools, or the Quarterly Concert of Prayer, as it was called.

Within a year two of the local schools closed; the number of pupils in attendance decreased and the difficulty of securing teachers increased, and the Board felt justified in stopping the two activities. At the same time one other school was transferred to the Baptists, since practically all the children enrolled were Baptists. That was evidence of the growth of denominational consciousness which had brought about the dissolution of the Sabbath School Union. One new school was opened under the leadership of Deacon Daniel Safford. The school met at the Masonic Temple on Tremont Street and was the precursor to the formal organization of the Mt. Vernon Church.

The Board met with increasing difficulty in its work with the Sabbath Schools. Church members who were interested in Sabbath School work almost invariably served in their own churches, so that the Board could not find teachers for the local schools. In any case the interest and the attention of the Board had shifted to other activities. In 1844 the Board asked the churches to send representatives to a meeting to consider what action should be taken. The purpose of the meeting was "that something should be done to increase the number of Sabbath Schools—or in some way to bring under a Sabbath School influence the large number of children in the city who are now destitute of such instruction."[18] At the meeting the Board representatives stated their understanding of the responsibilities they had for Sabbath Schools: to secure reports from all the schools, collate the information and make it available to the churches; maintain local schools and establish others if they were able to do so; and to indicate to the churches, whenever the situation seemed to warrant it, actions which might justifiably be taken in respect to the schools. The Board leaders said they had done the first duty and the annual reports had been placed in the hands of the church officials. In respect to the second duty, while the Board clearly understood that the hope was that through local schools many children who would not go to the schools in the churches might be brought under Christian instruction, the Board had been quite unable to maintain such schools or increase their number, and that the meeting then in progress was in fulfillment of the third duty.

The Board then went on to report the needs of the city. The census of the city showed, they said, that there were nearly 23,000 children between the ages of four and sixteen living there. Members of the Board had visited the Sabbath Schools in the city, of which there were eighty-seven, including the schools of all denominations, and by inquiry and observation had learned that there were 16,452 children enrolled in the schools with an average attendance of 11,796. Of the number enrolled about 2000 were over eighteen years of age [sic] which left "14,390 in all schools, of every name, between the ages of four and sixteen in the schools." The need for more schools, or the enrollment of more children in existing schools was clear.

The meeting adopted three resolutions and sent them to the churches by the representatives who were present: one, that the churches make special efforts to increase the number of scholars in their own schools; two, that the churches should undertake to establish branch schools wherever they can; and third, surprisingly, "that it be recommended to the churches, to cooperate with the City Missionary Society, by contribution of their means, and members if necessary, in establishing a chapel and church in the south part of the city, and other chapels afterwards, as they may be required."

In 1845, a new Sabbath School was added to the number from which reports were received, a school at the Suffolk Union Church. In 1846, the Board called a meeting of superintendents and teachers of all the schools "for the purpose of mutual encouragement and familiar inquiry." The outcome of that meeting was the formation of "The Union of Orthodox Congregational Sabbath Schools." In the report of the Board for that year there is added, after the story of the above meeting, "As a tabular view of the schools for 1846 is given in the annual report of this Sabbath School Union, it is not necessary that it be presented in this report." There were sixteen schools, enrolling some 3600 children which composed the new Union. In 1847, two of the missionaries employed by the Board opened a Sabbath School at the Mill Dam;

that school joined the Sabbath School Union. After that, there is no further reference to the Sabbath Schools except through the work of tract distributors and missionaries children were "gathered into the Sabbath Schools."

By the year 1849, the fortunes of the Society were once again at a rather low ebb, not as low as they had been earlier, but certainly not as bright and encouraging as formerly. The program of tract distribution continued throughout the year, although the number of people involved in it was somewhat reduced. The missionary force consisted of two men, Mr. Cushing, who during that year had been in such bad health that the Board had released him for two months in order to recuperate, and Mr. O'Brien, whose work was only among the Catholic people. The chapel effort had been stopped. The Sabbath School responsibilities had been turned over to a newly-formed organization, and the Society was $2,000 in debt.

Then, at a meeting of the Board in October 1849:

> The president presented from the executive committee the proposition to extend the organization so as to embrace all the Evangelical denominations. After a full expression of sentiments of the members present, Dr. Adams [the Rev. Nehemiah Adams, pastor of the Union, or Essex Street church] moved the following Preamble and Resolution, which were adopted: Preamble, The Executive Committee having submitted to the Board a proposition to change the Society's present form of operation so as to unite other Evangelical denominations in the City Missionary effort; Resolved, as the sense of this meeting is that it is expedient to change the plan of this Society's operations as to combine the several evangelical denominations of this city in one organization in the work of extending the Gospel to the destitute of this population; Resolved, that the president, [Deacon Daniel Safford] Dr. Adams, and the Rev. Mr. Kirk [pastor of the Mt. Vernon Church] be a committee to make arrangements to carry the above resolution into effect and report their doings at an adjourned meeting of this Board."[19]

Eight days later the Board met again. Dr. Adams, of the special committee appointed at the last meeting, made a verbal statement, when the following resolution was passed—"that if a new organization for city missions, as contemplated by the preamble and resolutions adopted at the last meeting, should be formed, it should be done independently of the Boston City Missionary Society."[20]

That is not quite the way the episode appears in the published record of the Society's doings. According to that account, the Board, having agreed that it would be desirable and expedient to unite all evangelical denominations in a single missionary organization for work in the city, thought, first of all, to call a meeting of the pastors and some laymen from the churches to present the proposal to them, but then, deeming that unwise and a bit presumptuous, invited a few people from the other churches for an informal conversation. Out of that there came an inter-church committee, which called a meeting of pastors and laymen. That gathering appointed a committee to prepare a plan for the organization of such a missionary agency as had been proposed and to report as soon as possible. "In the end, the conclusion was reached, that it was impracticable to effect, at present, such a united association of all evangelical denominations in the city, to give the Gospel to the poor."[21]

The minutes of the Board meeting and the report of the Society to the general public do not agree as to what really happened, but the result, as far as missionary work was concerned was the same. There may have been a well prepared plan for the joint conduct of missions in Boston, similar to the plan under which the Sabbath Schools had been carried on, or there may have been nothing more than an idea which arose in the mind of some Board member and shared with others who had grown discouraged by the continuing difficulties which beset the labors of the Society. Yet all is guess work, for the truth of the matter is hidden behind the enigmatical language of the secretary's report.

The idea of a united Protestant City Mission disappeared at that point, but the Society, in the hands of church laymen as the Board of Directors and a church layman as the chief missionary, continued on.

CHAPTER VII

The Cushing Era 1850–1892

FROM 1850 TO 1892, the life and work of the Society essentially revolved around one man. It would not be correct to think that he was solely responsible for the direction of the Society or the development it underwent, for he was only an employee under the supervision of ministers and laymen, and an associate with other members of the employed staff. Yet he was the one who through the years was looked to for leadership in the enterprise. While inevitably the people with whom he worked influenced not only the work of the Society but also the man himself, the years were, most assuredly, Cushing's years.

There is something fascinating about this, for it is symbolic of the inner essence of the Christian faith. The world of humanity changes all the while, and the changes in Boston during the Cushing era were many and violent, but the Christian Gospel, the living reality of God's action in man's behalf, never changes. The seventy-fifth annual report of the Society made this point in another way: "The generations come and go, but institutions based on the unchanging needs of the people abide, and grow stronger and more useful with the passing years."[1] Cushing, while part of the changing scene, in himself pointed to and labored for the unchanging God.

Andrew Cushing was a layman, and it is well to hold fast to that fact. He was a member of the Bowdoin Street Church. He entered the employ of the Society on March 1, 1842. "Voted, that Mr. Andrew Cushing be appointed a lay missionary of this Society with a salary of $800 per annum, payable quarterly, it being understood, should he accept, that the connection may, at any time, be dissolved by either party on giving three months' notice."[2]

Although the Board met a number of times during the months that followed, there is no record that Mr. Cushing accepted the appointment or that his appointment was confirmed. With such meager notice began the career of a man who was destined to remain with the Society for half a century. Evidently, however, Cushing remembered the stipulation that three months' notice must be given by either party before the relationship could be dissolved, for the letter he addressed to the Society in 1891 met that provision of the original stipulation. That letter is dated December 14, 1891.

> If my life is spared to the first of March next, I shall have completed fifty years service in connection with the City Missionary Society, and a sense of duty to the Society and to myself requires me to tender my resignation to take effect on that date. . . .[3]

Not long after his resignation Mr. Cushing died. And if the Board was offhand and unconcerned when he began his work, it was almost equally so at his resignation and death. A brief, three-paragraph note of appreciation in the Minutes of the Society at his resignation, and a clause, within a long paragraph listing the members of the Board who had died during the year, "and Andrew Cushing, of the Mount Vernon church, elected [called from their earthly labors]—in 1891," at his death. One looks in vain for an obituary fitted to a person who had served as long and effectively as Cushing, but there is none. Perhaps the Board was content to let his memory linger in the hearts of those who knew him, and let "his works follow after him."

Andrew Cushing was born in South Scituate, Massachusetts, on September 24, 1814. He was the seventh in the line of a famous family known as the "Cushing judges." In 1686 Matthew Cushing came to New England and settled in Hingham, becoming a deacon in the church and a leader in public affairs. His grandson, Joseph, born in 1677, was a deacon of Second Church in Boston. The generations that followed were equally devout men and equally given to assuming responsibilities in the common life. One of Andrew's ancestral relations was a trusted advisor to George Washington and appointed a Federal judge by him. A great uncle was a Supreme Court judge in Massachusetts and judge of the Admiralty during the Revolution.

Andrew Cushing attended the district school near his home. Then he was apprenticed to his maternal uncle, James Loring, who was a printer and bookseller. Andrew Cushing intended to go into the publishing business, but in 1842 he began to suffer from eye trouble. While casting about for some solution to the problem this posed for him, he was approached by Julius Palmer, then president of the Society, and asked to enter their employ, an invitation he accepted. That was not the only important decision he made that year. About the middle of 1842 he was one of nearly fifty men and women who, having received honorable letters of dismissal from the churches to which they belonged, covenanted together in the formation of the Mount Vernon Church. The Reverend Edward N. Kirk, a well-known evangelist and lecturer on missions, temperance and the anti-slavery movement, had visited Boston and preached at the Park Street Church. A number of men were so deeply moved under his preaching that they determined to form a new church if Dr. Kirk would agree to be the pastor. Kirk consented, and the church was organized, with Andrew Cushing one of the charter members. Later on in 1842 Cushing was married to a daughter of Ezra Lincoln, who was printer and sometimes editor of *The Recorder*. In 1847 Cushing was elected a deacon of the Mount Vernon Church, a position he held to his death. At Cushing's death there was a meaningful coincidence. On Sunday morning, November 6, 1892, the last service of worship was held in the old Mount Vernon Church building on Ashburton Place and that afternoon Cushing died. On November 9th the new Mount Vernon Church building was dedicated and the next day Cushing's funeral service was conducted in the new building.

The pastor of the Mt. Vernon Church, the Reverend Samuel Herrick, preached a sermon in memory of Andrew Cushing on December 4, 1892, praising him for:

> . . . a fine and ever true and loyal sentiment of justice, combined with a calm and equable temper. He would pronounce his judgement impartially in view of all the facts, whether it favored friend or foe . . .

his opinion was waited with interest, and when it had been given with its reasons, it was so clear, so fair, so palpably reasonable and just, that it was nearly always the final word. This faculty of calm and careful judgement was doubtless an heirloom, a fine strain in the very current of his blood.

He was true to his birthright, also, in maintaining through life all that was noblest and best in the Puritan character. He brought down into the heat and haste of modern life, the old-time ideals of religion, of reverence, of worship, of thoughtfulness, or moral earnestness. Life to him . . . was a place and a time for serious endeavor to do and to be what a son of God, accountable to Him, ought to do and to be.

But Puritan as he was, holding fast to all that was fundamental, he was no indiscriminate worshipper of whatever is antiquated. He was intelligent in his appreciation of the past, but equally shrewd in his interpretation of the present, and keen in reading the signs of the future. His was one of those well-balanced minds, which, as though hung on double acting hinges, open readily backward into the old and forward into the new without losing their hold on either.

He possessed no ordinary fund of knowledge in many directions, and, what is better, knew how to use it. He was a wise man, which cannot be said of many men who know more. It [his deaconship] brought him into contact with the widows, the fatherless and the poor. The poor confided to him their needs and sorrows, and the rich trusted him to be the executor of their charities, and neither confidence was ever abused.[4]

When Cushing began his work for the Society, Boston was for all practical purposes a city within the confines of its original peninsula with a population of slightly more than 100,000. When he retired, Boston was a vastly expanded city: the Back Bay had been filled in and built up; other land on the opposite side of the city had been reclaimed; the Church St. improvement, the Suffolk St. improvement, and the development of Atlantic Avenue had been completed; Fort Hill had been reduced; Roxbury (1867), Dorchester (1869), Charlestown, Brighton, West Roxbury (1874) had been annexed; and the population was nearly 450,000. When he began, places such as Watertown, Jamaica Plain, and Brookline were rural areas, where the wealthy of the city had their country homes; when he retired they were included in the metropolitan district by transportation and a number of public services, even if they retained their political independence. When he began, the way to get about in the city was on foot, and the transportation to Dorchester was by horse-drawn omnibus; when he retired, six horse-drawn street railways had been built, carrying people well out into West Roxbury and most of Dorchester, and the West End Street Railway Company had begun to operate an electric car on one of its lines. At the same time the connections between Boston and other parts of the country, which were limited when he began his work had been vastly expanded, no less than eight different railroad lines having been built and put into operation, some of them consolidated and made more efficient, establishing rapid communication with cities and towns in all directions.

There were changes in the way people lived too. When he began there were less than one hundred fifty primary schools in the city, enrolling about 10,000 children with a poor average attendance; when he retired there were over four hundred such schools, with over twice the number of pupils, most of whom attended regularly. When he began, some arrangements had been made through the Overseers of the Poor, the House of Industry and the House of Correction to deal with the poor and the idle of the city; when he retired the number of public agencies and funds had been substantially increased to thirty, a Department of Institutions had been established (1857), nearly two hundred voluntary organizations had been formed for the same purpose, and many of the latter had united for more effective performance of their work in the Associated Charities (1879). When he began there were thirteen Congregational churches in the city; when he retired there were thirty-one. To paraphrase a sentence from the report in 1891, the Boston that existed when Andrew Cushing began his work with the Society had almost disappeared by the time he retired.

Besides these changes, there were other events of national and international scope which had an impact upon Boston, and therefore upon the work of the Society during this half century. There were two major economic depressions. The panic of 1857, brought on by overexpansion and speculation, aggravated by the weakness of the banking system of the country, caused the failure of over two hundred fifty business houses in Boston alone. A period of hardship for the poor followed, through the rise in prices and the reduction in employment. The second depression came in 1873, and continued for a number of years. Business was demoralized, unemployment rose, panic swept through the populace, and some of the savings banks in which the poor had deposited what little money they had accumulated, failed. Many of the banks which closed their doors, later reopened under new legal provisions which enabled them to recover money loaned on mortgages, but by that time the damage to people had been done and the suffering was acute.

The Civil War occupied all minds from 1861 to 1865. At the start, the men of Boston volunteered in sufficient numbers to meet the quotas assigned, but by the year 1863 a draft had to be imposed to fill the ranks, and there was opposition and threatened rioting in the city. Young men from families in all levels of society were called into service. That brought particular hardships to the poor, when the earners were taken away, leaving the incapacitated and the unemployable relations behind to get along as best they could, which in all too many cases was not adequate to ward off starvation and suffering. The war also disrupted the staff of the Society and lessened the number of workers available to cope with increased responsibilities.

The great Boston fire of November, 1872, was another disaster for the poor. While many warehouses, shops, and factories were burned, only a few dwelling houses were destroyed. However, the fire threw many out of work, creating an amount of hardship which not even a very substantial relief fund, raised immediately following the event, was able to allay. And, as at the time of other disasters, the staff of the Society not only had to deal with the increased need caused by the fire, but were also called upon to aid in the work of the Relief Committee.

But those events, upsetting though they were and temporarily disruptive of the ordered conduct of the Society's affairs, pale into insignificance before the most important and continuing happening of the Cushing era: the Irish immigration. Beginning in the mid-1840's and continuing on for a period of years, crop failures in Ireland caused untold suffering and a great number of deaths by starvation. Those who were able to do so, literally ran for their lives, using the last resources upon which they could lay their hands in order to effect their escape. Not only were substantial sums of money raised in Boston and New England and sent to Ireland to help those in distress, but one committee, The New England Relief Committee, provided passage money to the States for many who were unable to pay the cost themselves. But whether they came by paying their own way or were helped to come by others, Irish people landed in Boston, and having no funds to move farther took up their residence in the city. Thus, many were without any money when they arrived, and some of them, due to the crowded, unsanitary, almost inhuman conditions of the voyage, were ill. They then had to make their way in a city ill-prepared to receive them.

The result was "the fateful decade of the 1850's," as Henry Commager called it, after quoting from Jefferson's first inaugural address, "that religious intolerance under which mankind so long bled and suffered."[5]

It is difficult to learn exactly how many people from Ireland came to Boston during the years of the great immigration; figures differ as individuals attempted to reach a total from the available statistics. "In 1847, so we are told, there were landed in the city of Boston twenty-five thousand foreigners."[6] "In 1845, the number of foreigners and their children in the city was ascertained to be about 37,000—at the present time [1848] it must be something more than 45,000."[7] "In 1865, there were 183,777 individuals in Massachusetts who were born in Ireland."[8] "By 1875 sixty thousand foreign born Irish were living in Boston. During the balance of the century immigration from that poverty stricken island continued so rapidly that despite the growth of the city the Irish newcomers and their children made up from 30 to 40 per cent of Boston's total population."[9] "Boston by 1850 contained a foreign born population about equalling its native-born; five years later the natives were outnumbered by some 10,000."[10] Whatever the actual number of people coming to Boston from Ireland during the years of Cushing's leadership, it was substantial.

So many people came that Boston was quite unable to absorb them into the existing society. Not only were the public institutions unable to cope with the sick, the poor and those needing and expecting to find employment, there was no housing for them and no adequate provision for any of their simplest requirements. This has to be seen from both sides, the side of those living in Boston and the side of the newcomers. Take, as an analogy, a group of people enjoying themselves in a swimming pool. They would be quite able to make adjustments were newcomers to arrive in small numbers, some getting out of the water to rest, others willingly leaving to go to some other activity, and so on. But let a group, as large or larger than the one already in the pool, arrive and jump in, and immediate and almost unconscious reactions are bound to follow.

The newcomers were crowded into the poorer sections of the city; South Cove, and the West End north of Cambridge St.:

> In their localities there were numerous narrow alleys, courts and streets . . . that had never been properly constructed and were equipped with a makeshift sewerage system or none at all. Many of the homes . . . had been built to accommodate one or two families but the immigrants were literally packed into them. One house in North Square had a family of nine living in one room, in another, fifteen people slept in three attic rooms. . . . On Broad Street and Fort Hill were buildings from three to six stories high that sheltered from forty to one hundred inhabitants each. Fort Hill was an especially bad district, the houses were without common comforts and 'mostly without common necessities.' It was quite usual to have only one sink in a building, the drain of which opened into a small poorly built sewer or into the street. Some buildings had no conveniences or sanitary facilities.[11]

That description was made from reports of city commissions. Oscar Handlin, in his book, has the same kind of picture.[12]

Owners of property leased it to middle men who crowded the immigrants into every conceivable bit of space and charged what were for the time and the accommodation extortionist rates. Inevitably, disease was rampant, outbreaks of cholera and smallpox were common, and the death rate terribly high. Efforts were made by government agencies and private organizations to deal with the situation, but years passed before any substantial measure of order was brought about, and then it came as much through the industry and patient bearing of hardship by the immigrants themselves as through any other force.

Most of these immigrants were Roman Catholics. Their coming created for the Catholic church as great a problem as that which they presented to the city. During the twenty years that followed the accession of Bishop Fitzpatrick to the head of the Boston Diocese, that Diocese was divided into three, and in the area which remained as the Diocese of Boston, there were built four times the number of churches as were in the original organization. When Bishop Williams succeeded to the head of the Diocese in 1866, there were 109 churches and 116 priests; at that time the Diocese included a much larger area than present metropolitan Boston. The Diocese of Springfield was created in 1870; and the Diocese of Providence in 1872. Those separations removed from the Diocese of Boston, Bristol and Barnstable counties, Nantucket and three towns in Plymouth county. Even then, in the Diocese of Boston, as it was after those losses of area, there were in 1875, 120 churches and 189 priests. And before the Cushing era came to an end, Boston became an Archdiocese. The reports of the Catholic church do not show clearly the growth within the city itself. According to the reports of the Society, in 1844 there were four Catholic churches in the city, in 1866 there were thirteen, and in 1890 there were thirty-four. In Winsor's history there is this summary, "The probable Catholic population of the city in the year 1880 was about 150,000 souls. These worship in 30 churches, attended by 90 priests, under the guidance of their archbishop."[13]

From this it is clear that the leaders of the church struggled with an almost overwhelming problem as they undertook the task of providing for the religious needs of the numbers of immigrants who entered the city. For a period of thirty years, people with a Catholic heritage came in increasing numbers. Only towards the last two decades of the century did the size of the numbers grow less, relieving the pressure, somewhat, for the provision of new facilities. In addition to the numbers of the people involved, was their poverty, which added two complications to the terribly difficult situation. On the one hand, the needs of the immigrants made claims upon the financial resources of the entire community including the Catholics already living there, and, on the other hand, the poverty of the newcomers made it impossible for them to contribute to the substantial sums required to provide churches for them. If the actions of the Catholic leaders at the start of the "immigrant flood" were quite slow and accelerated only gradually as the years went by, it is understandable. The resources of the Catholic community were not available to make more rapid expansion of the church facilities possible.

All through the period, but especially during the earlier years, the Catholic church suffered under the opposition, antagonism, and outright persecution by combinations of Protestants and the non-religious. This had begun earlier. As the tide of immigration increased, so did the hostility toward the Church and her people. The attacks grew less during the years of the Civil War, when the entire population was drawn together by a single enterprise, but when the war was over, the anti-Catholic spirit manifested itself again.

It took two forms. One was the open, ruthless actions that stirred the masses of the people into highly emotional states and which led many to see in every Catholic, and in the Catholic church, agents specifically engaged in the work of destroying the freedom of the nation. Societies were formed, newspapers were founded and published, spell-binding speakers toured the land, books were written, and various characters claiming to be ex-priests and ex-nuns were put on platforms to tell what purported to be the inside stories of their experiences in the church. While all the various forces that were working in those ways did not unite, there was enough unity in the attacks they made, to turn the whole business into a vicious anti-Catholic campaign. The public hysteria was further increased by the meeting of the Vatican Council 1869-1870, at which the dogma of the Pope's infallibility was enacted.[14]

That dogma seemed to confirm the charges being made

against the church and served to substantiate prejudice and add to the fanaticism of all who had entered the lists against the church. During these years a strong spirit of fear and opposition to the church took hold of men and became one of the motivating forces in life. When men are moved by such a spirit all tests of logic and reasonableness and common sense by which men ordinarily control their behavior are over-ridden and they act out of sheer perversity.

The other form of anti-Catholicism was more subtle, and much more difficult to deal with. In face of the overt hostility, the Catholic people could either fight openly or put up with the condition in patience, countering the falsity and calumny sufficiently to reassure themselves of the truth. The wonder is that the Catholic people did not react more violently than they did. In addition to that, however, through the years, as the Catholic people sought to establish themselves in Boston and become an accepted part of the body politic they were blocked at every move. When they wanted to secure property for a church building, they found opposition arising and rules invoked against their attempted purchase which had not been applied when non-Catholic groups were involved. When their pastors sought entrance into public institutions in order to visit their people and to conduct the last rites for their dying, they were refused admission. And after they secured permits allowing them to go on public property, they found those permits ignored on the whim of the officials.

Other serious issues arose. There was the matter of obtaining grants from public funds for their various charitable institutions. It had long been the practice for money to be allotted to certain agencies which took responsibility for people who otherwise would be in care of the state. Protestant agencies had benefitted from this practice. But when a Catholic institution made application for such aid, the request at first was refused, and then the institution was subjected to a series of most annoying investigations. Finally a modest grant was allowed.

There was the matter of the religious activities required of the inmates of public institutions. Services of worship were held in prisons, reformatories and homes for the indigent, and all the inmates were required to attend. The services were conducted by Protestant clergymen. It made no difference that some of those involved were Catholics, attendance at services was required. Catholic leaders began to effect a change in those arrangements, but some years passed and a number of rebuffs were met before the Catholic Mass was conducted at the institutions, and still more years before Catholic chaplains were appointed to the institutions on the same basis as Protestant chaplains.

Then there was the matter of religion in the schools. It was customary for the school day to be opened with Bible reading, the singing of hymns and prayer. All that was in the Protestant tradition. And the practice was upsetting to Catholic parents when they sent their children to school. Moreover, the textbooks in use had been written by non-Catholics and contained false and unkind references to that faith. The teachers in the schools were non-Catholics who were not at all averse to giving their understanding of the Catholic church and its practices to their pupils, even when there were Catholic children in the classes. When the Catholic leaders proposed establishing a school system of their own in which their children might receive an education consonant with their religious beliefs, there was a great outcry. Attempts were made to thwart the effort and to interfere with its effective operation after it was started.

The story is not a pleasing one, and yet it is understandable. On one side, a vast number of Irish Catholics, escaping from terrible suffering and almost certain death in their homeland, came to Protestant and Puritan Boston. They were forced into dark corners, places where no one else wanted to live, and when they laid claim to public services in order to meet their most elementary needs, were made to accept services given in an ungracious and niggardly manner. They struggled for their very livelihood and many died in the process. They were subjected to the worst kind of exploitation and open public abuse. And then, when they trustingly followed the guidance of their own religious leaders, who moved forward in faith, to gain the rights that belonged to them in a city whose citizens insisted upon the freedom of all men, they were hindered at every point.

On the other side of the situation, however, were the people of Boston, descendants of those who had made the city what it was, sure of their accustomed ways, free churchmen when they were churchmen, counting the entire citizenry as individuals who should be regular church attendants, and discussing whether or not there were enough seats in the churches to accommodate everybody and giving generously through a number of effective agencies to win all men, the world over, to their understanding of Christianity. They faced a flood of strangers, whose religious faith was a form of Christianity which they repudiated, and which they thought of as no Christianity at all. They knew why the immigrants came, and were at the outset deeply sympathetic, but as they kept coming they inevitably sought to protect their own ways and make the newcomers conform.

The whole of the Cushing era was a time of intense, deep-seated struggle that arose from the souls of men; that was why it was so serious, its forms so manifold and expressive of the fight for life on both sides, and its outcome so determinative of the future. At the end, the Catholic people gained control of the city, which was the most overt sign that the Boston of young Andrew Cushing had been radically changed by the time he died.

In 1883, the man who was elected mayor of Boston had been born in Ireland and had landed in Boston when he was five years old. And in 1887, men of the Catholic faith won the leadership of civic affairs—the mayor, the chairman of the Board of Aldermen, the president of the Common Council, the city clerk, and the chairman of the School Committee.

People of other races and nations besides the Irish came to Boston during this period. Some of them had little effect upon the work of the Society. But the Germans, the Jews, and the Chinese did become the subjects of concern for the Society. They began coming in numbers, making their homes in Boston. During the last ten years of the era the Italians came in substantial numbers. Their arrival created some problems for the Catholic church. But it is interesting to observe how infrequently they appear in the records of the Society, and how little interest appears to have been taken in them.

When Cushing began his service with the Society there were thirteen Congregational churches in the city with a membership of 3750; when he ended his service there were thirty-one churches with a membership of just over ten thousand. Much of that increase was due, of course, to the churches which came to be included within the city boundaries when the towns in which they were located were annexed. But other events accounted for part of the increase. During the years a number of revivals were conducted in the city, arranged, in the main by a Congregational church or a few of the churches. The series of visits by Edward N. Kirk in 1841 were part of a fairly lengthy evangelistic program carried on during the years 1841 and 1842. It is reported that more than four thousand people joined the churches of the city during that revival.

In 1877 Moody and Sankey came to Boston at the invitation of the city churches. A tabernacle was built on the new land being made in the Back Bay and at every service the place was crowded. Not all the Congregational churches were interested in the campaign, some of them shunning the effort officially. In the report of the Society for that year is this comment:

> It was to have been expected a year ago, that the Tabernacle work then being inaugurated under the leadership of Messrs. Moody and Sankey, would be felt as a powerful auxiliary to the labor of our Society. It has indeed been so, but not so immediately, perhaps, as some may have anticipated. Its effects were felt in the general quickening of religious feeling in the community at large, making individuals and families more accessible, and increasing the attendance upon our chapel meetings. The record of hopeful conversions during the year stands 162—as against 90, in 1876; these were not in many instances from the Inquiry-Room of the Tabernacle, but the results of our own missionary labor, under the generally awakened interest of the community.[15]

Cushing began his service with the Society as a lay missionary. He was assigned to work in the western part of the city. As was required of the employed missionaries he made his reports regularly. They indicate the understanding Cushing had of his work. In 1843, he wrote, "As your missionary, it is mine to alarm the careless, direct the anxious, confirm the feeble, comfort the afflicted, and point the dying to Him who died for them. These are my duties." He was unshakeably firm in his conviction that the only way a person could gain salvation was through faith in Jesus Christ, and the experience of being accepted and redeemed by Him; and he was fearless in the presentation of the claims of Christ to all whom he met. On one occasion he was ordered out of the house by a man whose wife was a Christian but who was unable to attend church because of her husband's opposition. As Cushing talked with the wife, the husband paced the floor smoking a cigar. As soon as he could, he broke into the conversation and told Cushing never to come to his house again. "I then set before him God's claims upon him . . . he repeated his request that I cease to visit him; after taking him by the hand, and urging him to prepare to meet me at the judgment, I parted with him."[16]

Cushing observed in one report that "he had little confidence in death-bed repentance," but it is clear that he willingly put aside everything else to answer a call from one who was dying. He came to believe that repeated visits to specific families were a much more useful way of spending his time than making single visits indiscriminately over his whole area, and he said that to the Board of the Society, "My visits have mostly been confined to families with which I was previously acquainted; believing that the prospect of usefulness was greater in frequently visiting the same families, and following up any impressions that may be made, than in extending my calls to a greater number." Right at the beginning of his work he became conscious of the dilemma confronting a missionary to the poor, of how to deal with the spiritual needs unless something is done to alleviate physical suffering. In making his report for the year 1848, Cushing used an argument which he repeated a number of times in reports during the years that followed:

A missionary once applied to a gentleman for funds to relieve the destitute. He was told that the missionary's office was to do good to the souls of men, and when asked to supply the wants of the poor to answer, with Peter, "silver and gold have I none, but such as I have give I thee." This gentleman forgot that the missionary had no power to say with the apostle to the disabled poor, "in the name of Jesus Christ of Nazareth, rise up and walk." Where it can be done, it is far better to furnish employment than alms to the poor.[17]

But to do this, said Cushing, takes up the time of the missionary.

At the meeting of the Board, February 18, 1850, a committee which had been appointed to propose plans for the future work of the Society reported:

> . . . that a man of devoted piety, sound judgment, industrious and systematic habits, experiences in the work of a city missionary and well acquainted with the conditions and wants of the different parts of the city be appointed as a missionary whose duty it shall be to aid the president in superintending the labors of the assistant missionaries, subject always to the directors of the Board. . . .[18]

Cushing was chosen to fill the proposed post. Under that arrangement, Daniel Safford, who had become president of the Society at the beginning of the year, actually had the authority over the program and the affairs of the Society. He received no salary, but actively watched over the operations of the Society, and wrote the introductions to the annual reports. Cushing was his assistant, working with him and under him. There is no way of knowing how the two men got along together and how they managed their working relationships, but since they were among the founders of Mount Vernon Church and both were deacons of that Church it can be assumed that there was a large measure of harmony between them.

The Board voted at the time that the president's assistant should attend their meetings when he was requested to do so, and only then, but there are no indications in any of the records for a few years that Cushing was ever asked to appear. Apparently he was the working partner on the team, the president being the executive partner. The first Sunday in February 1856, Daniel Safford died. In that same year, although no reference to any action by Board or Executive committee appears in any of the records, Andrew Cushing became the Superintendent of the work of the Society and continued as such until his resignation.

During the Cushing era, ten men served as presidents of the Society; it is practically impossible to tell how many different men served on the Board of Directors. When Cushing began his work the four officers and nine others constituted the Board. In 1857 a change was made. The Bylaws were amended to read, "not less than nine nor more than fifty others," and up to the end of the Cushing era the Board was elected under that provision. More importantly, however, the Executive Committee was resurrected under the earlier provision that the Board was to choose from among their own number nine persons, "who shall have such power as the Board shall give them each year." Each year after those arrangements were put into effect the record of the Board of Managers contains these words, "Voted, that the Board hereby delegates to the Executive Committee power to adopt whatever measures they may consider expedient or necessary to promote the general interests of the Society, which shall be reported to the Board, and subject to their approval."[19] Each year, at the annual meeting of the Board an "abstract of the work of the Executive Committee" was given, which was always approved. So that in effect the Society was managed by an Executive Committee of nine persons.

One of the nine all through the years was the president, without exception; another of the nine was the secretary of the Board, who was always a clergyman. During the Cushing era forty-eight different individuals served on the Executive Committee, of whom seventeen were clergymen. But that does not give a true indication of the number of people who really assumed responsibility for the work of the Society, for some of them were on the Committee for only one or two years, scarcely time enough for them to become acquainted with the activities. Three ministers and five laymen were on the Committee from five to ten years, three ministers and four laymen from ten to fifteen years, and two ministers and five laymen from fifteen to twenty years; no individual served for more than twenty years. Thus, it might be said, that twenty-two different individuals directed the affairs of the Society.*

* Dr. Blagden of the Old South Church was on the committee for seventeen years (1852-1885); Reverend B. F. Hamilton of the Eliot Church, Roxbury, for eleven years (1876-1886); Reverend Albert Plumb of the Walnut Ave. Church, Roxbury, for fourteen years (1872-1885); Reverend Edmund K. Alden of the church in South Boston, for ten years (1862-1871); Reverend A. L. Stowe, pastor of Park St. Church, for seven years (1852-1859); Reverend James Means, pastor of Second Church, Dorchester, for six years (1870-1875); and Reverend Samuel Herrick, pastor of the Mt. Vernon Church, for five years (1876-1880). One minister, the Reverend Baron Stowe, who served from 1857-1862, cannot be identi-

Of the seven ministers with the lengthy terms of service, six of them were graduates of Andover Seminary. That theological background of the men who had the most continuous influence on the affairs of the Society, may mean very little, but it does indicate the particular Christian perspective which was dominant through the years.

The same kind of analysis cannot be made with respect to the laymen who served the Society long and faithfully: Henry Hoyt, who was treasurer for twenty years; Samuel F. Wilkins, treasurer for thirteen during the Cushing era, remaining on into the next era; Executive Committee members Charles Demond (18 years), John Denison (16 years), Richard H. Stearns (20 years during the Cushing era, and on to his death in 1908), Arthur Tufts (20 years), George Coburn (who died after he had served 17 years), and Luther Wright (13 years). It is of interest that during the last four years of the Cushing era the Executive Committee was made up entirely of laymen.

One of the tasks of the Board of Directors and the Executive Committee was the supervision of the finances. It is not known how much time the various individuals spent raising the annual budget, although since substantial amounts of each year's needs came from the churches it can be assumed that they at least spoke with some conviction in the councils of the churches when the request for the annual contribution was received, and certainly they scrutinized expenditures with care. When Cushing began his work, the Society raised $3,596 from nine churches, took in some rent, which another agency paid for the use of the Society's office during the evening hours, and borrowed $293 from a legacy in order to pay bills amounting to $3,890. The year Cushing retired, the Society raised and spent $44,450. Of that sum, $19,659 went for missionary work, $5,375 for the relief of the poor, $13,412 for the Fresh Air Fund and Rosemary Cottage, and $6,007 for Thanksgiving and Christmas programs. The expenditure for missionary work had multiplied six times during the era and other activities had been added to the work. At the beginning of the era

fied in the records as associated with any church; he may have been one of the professors of Andover Theological Seminary.

one page in the printed annual report sufficed for the financial record; at the end of the era the treasurer's record took up five more pages in the report than the account of the work which had been done. During the Cushing period the Society raised and spent nearly a million dollars.

There were two anxious financial times during the era, and they coincided roughly with the two periods of business depression. During the first period the salaries of the missionaries, which were $700 for the men and $300 for the women, were reduced 25% and a number of workers were dismissed. But that was not enough to save the Society from another deficit the following year, and the Board, fearful of the situation, voted, "that the usual notice of three months be given to all the missionaries in the employ of the Board, that in consequence of the falling off of the subscriptions their services will not be required after the first day of January next.[20] That vote of the Board was never carried out. Some months later, "The president made a statement of the financial affairs of the Society, showing a probable deficit at the end of the year .... After a free exchange of opinion, upon motion of the Rev. Dr. Blagden, it was voted, that it is inexpedient at the present time to dismiss any of the missionaries."[21] What was the reason behind this change of mind? It is there in the record. The treasurer, evidently without the knowledge of the Board, or the membership, had in his possession $4,000 which had been realized by the sale of the Mission House property some years earlier. That item had never been included in the financial reports and had apparently been quite forgotten.

When the next depression came along, the Board was completely sure of itself. The treasurer's report showed an indebtedness of over $2,000 the first year, and the secretary observed, "this has probably been caused by conditions which are temporary and we hope for an advance in the future." A loan was made, all bills were paid, including the interest on the loan, and three years later there was a balance in the bank with which to start the next year.

Two general observations should be made about the financial operations of the Society. First, when Cushing began his work, finances were handled in the simplest manner, with no attempt to follow any systematic accounting procedures. When he ended his work, the reports indicate the most meticulous kind of bookkeeping and careful attention to every separate account. In the early years, legacies and reserved funds and willed estates were simply put into current income and were used if and when they were needed; at the end, there is an endowment account, separate from other accounts, to which legacies are added, the interest on which is allocated to the purposes for which the gifts were made, and all other accounts are carefully itemized. That development over the years doubtless reflects nothing more than the evolution of approved business practices and the growth of the Society's operations.

The other observation concerns the extension of the support for the Society over the years, which not only shows a considerable amount of effort expended raising money, but also a slow transformation in the relationships of the Society. In the beginning of the era, the Society was the agent of the churches of Boston for a specific work, and the churches paid the bills; at the close of the era the Society spoke of itself in much the same terms as it had earlier, but in its efforts to pay its bills it received money, not only from the churches in Boston, and their Sunday Schools and young people's societies, but also from churches and church members throughout New England, and across the country, from places in New York, Kansas, Missouri, Virginia and Illinois. That development had a number of implications. On the one hand it meant, that the relationship between the Evangelical Congregational churches of Boston and the Society was beginning to be a bit more tenuous. The churches of course continued to support the Society. Out of the more than nineteen thousand dollars contributed for missionary service in the city, over fifteen thousand came from the city churches, and the members of the Board were from those churches and therefore reflected, in some measure, the thinking and the interests of those churches. But as the resources of the Society supplied by churches and people beyond the city increased, the Board became more free to conduct its program as the members saw fit. The Society became somewhat independent of the churches.

On the other hand, that extension of the supporting base for the Society's work affected the program. A large proportion of the money coming from outside the city was in behalf of new lines of activity which the Society had undertaken. To the extent that the Society came to be free of obligations to the city churches and took upon itself obligations to represent others beyond the city, the Society was led to engage in those enterprises to which the supporters made their contributions. This shift went on without those involved in it being consciously aware of what was taking place, for it happened gradually, and the Board had their attention fixed upon the necessity of financing the work. Furthermore, since each move the Society made in adding to its program elicited much favorable comment in the public press and loud expressions of gratitude from all who benefitted, the Society was encouraged to continue. The Society became, in effect, through its financing, the agent for a far wider circle of churches and people than it had originally been.

Who did all this new and expanded work? When, in 1850, the Board re-organized the work there were two men working as missionaries, Mr. Patrick O'Brien, who was charged with the work among Catholics, and Andrew Cushing. Six months later O'Brien departed and, "as he left no report, we can give no account of his labors."[22] Then the Board agreed to a substantial extension of their operations, because the needs of the poor in the city "required constant and varied action," and that agreement was implemented by votes to employ two missionaries and three female assistant missionaries who were to give full time to the work. The Board instructed the president, Mr. Safford, to see that the number of neighborhood meetings were greatly increased, "and that members of the churches be requested to sustain these with occasional assistance from the missionaries." At the same time, the Board delegated certain members to make special appeals to the churches for money to pay the indebtedness and underwrite the proposed program. The Board members performed admirably for more money than had been anticipated came into the treasurer's hands. Indeed, the contributions were so substantial that "when past bills were paid, and current salaries paid, there remained

Deacon Samuel C. Wilkins
Missionary, 1862–1899

Miss Harriette Carter
Missionary, 1871–1915. Worked with the Chinese population

some two thousand dollars yet unexpended." On the strength of that response by the churches, the Board employed as missionaries four men, and as assistants ten women. From then on through the rest of the Cushing era the Board continued to employ men and women as full time workers. Each individual was voted upon by the Board at the time of employment, and when each one resigned or sought some change of relationship, the Board handled the matter. Cushing was the superintendent, but his authority did not extend to hiring and firing personnel.

Through the years the number of missionaries serving the Society varied. There were never fewer than twelve and never more than twenty-five employed during any one year, although, because of overlapping of terms, there were on occasion numbers lower and higher than these. The average number was roughly seventeen or eighteen. There were one hundred-eight different individuals employed as missionaries during the era, twenty-four men, of whom six were ordained ministers and eighty-three women. Some of those individuals served only short periods of time, but there were seven men and twenty-four women who remained with the Society ten years or more; two men and six women with more than twenty years; and one man and two women with more than thirty years. When the Cushing era came to an end, Mr. Samuel C. Wilkins (30 years), Mrs. Lorena Field (21 years), and Miss Harriet Carter (20 years) were still in the employ of the Society. There was, then, a considerable measure of continuity in the employed personnel. Whether this was for the best interests of the Society or not is a question that cannot be answered. Such a continuity may result in a conservatism of action, a disregard of changes in the situation and the suggestions of newcomers on the staff, especially if the newcomers remain on the job for relatively short periods of time. Alternately, however, the degree of continuity in the personnel may have been enough to provide stability in the work of the Society while new ideas and new proposals for action were adopted, and while the changes in the community were taking place.

When Andrew Cushing became assistant to the president in 1850, with responsibility for overseeing the work, the activities of the Society consisted primarily of two things: the Tract Distribution Program carried on by the members of the churches, and the work of the employed missionaries. The only difference employment of a larger number of missionaries made in the tract distribution was that the distributors had a much closer tie to people who were permanently employed by the Society and thus were able to gain a readier response to their reports of families found needing closer attention than they were able to give. For the missionaries themselves, the city was divided into districts. The three main divisions, which had been worked out earlier, north, south, and west remained, and an eastern section was added, each of which had a population of about thirty thousand people. Each district was in the charge of a missionary (male). Then each district was sub-divided into sections. To each section an assistant missionary (female) was assigned. For example, Mr. David Pike (a member of the Old South Church who became a teacher in the Sea Street Sabbath School in 1825, and entered the employ of the Society in 1850) was the missionary in the eastern district, including South Boston. He had three assistant missionaries working with him, one in the "city proper" and two in South Boston.

The general plan of these arrangements continued for a number of years, with changes in the boundaries of the districts as additional missionaries were employed, or as the population of the city moved, or as the surrounding towns were annexed and made part of the city, and as women were given the status of missionaries and assigned areas of their own. There was one important change made in the year 1861. At that time, the missionaries were assigned, not to districts marked out on the map in terms of the distribution of population, but to the churches, and they were to work in areas delineated as particularly the responsibility of each of the churches. The Board made that change because they believed that "each church of Christ should, in its own neighborhood, be actively and directly engaged in efforts to relieve the wants of the poor, to console the afflicted, to lead within the walls of the sanctuary such as neglect public worship." Missionaries were appointed with "regard to an equable representation of the churches contributing to the treasury," and the districts in which the missionaries were to work were "marked out with reference, as far as may be, to the position of the several churches." The Board asked that each church appoint a committee to consult with the missionary assigned to it and indicate to the missionary any special interest the church might have."[23] District No. 1, for example, was assigned to Maverick Church, East Boston, and Miss Armeda Gibbs and Miss Anne M. Smith were appointed as missionaries related to that church. District No. 14 was assigned to Highland Church (all the territory south of Camden Street, and west of Tremont and Pynchon Streets.) with Miss Ellen E. Metcalf, missionary. Subsequently, while that arrangement of relating missionaries to churches was maintained, a few shifts in areas and churches were made as changes occurred in the city.

This, then, is the picture of the Society and its agents during the Cushing era. A Board reviewing the work done; an Executive Committee directing the affairs of the Society, raising money, hiring personnel, approving or disapproving proposed changes in the program, and overseeing the promotion of the Society's interests in the churches and among the general public; and out in the city an employed staff and hundreds of volunteers—men and women, visiting, distributing tracts, arranging meetings, and participating in other parts of the program. The report for the year 1868 shows that more than 450 individuals were associated in the work of the Society.

What then were these people about? How did they understand their efforts? And did changes occur in that understanding through the years of the Cushing era? In other words, was there an underlying rationale for the work? The Society knew the conditions of life in the city in two ways: through consultation with public officials and through their own personal experiences. They tried to keep a vision of the total city before themselves so as not to misjudge the situation out of the limited contacts they had. They paid occasional visits to the city police, and published reports so the church constituency might know the facts. They did not depend upon guesswork nor on personal impressions. They knew that in 1862 there were 16,088 arrests for drunkenness; they knew that in 1866 there were 1,800 juveniles committed to jail during the year; they knew that in 1875 there were 62,740 idle beggars lodged over night in the station houses of the city; they knew that the number of Chinese who were living in Boston in 1883 was a certain figure; and they knew the other agencies organized from time to time in the city to deal with the poor and the needy and the criminal. The one thing they did not know exactly, nor did anyone else, was the number of Irish people who came to live in the city during any one year. But they were sure that the number was large and that it was growing larger all the while.

They also knew conditions in the city through personal experience. They knew where people lived,

> . . . the room was cold and damp. A dim light was burning on the table. In one corner, on a bed, without sheet or pillow case lay a boy eight years old, with an old woolen shirt on, suffering from scarlet fever of the worst malignant type. The father sat over the stove. Upstairs, in their other room, I found five children. On a bed, as comfortless as the one below, were two children, two and four years of age. The mother held the baby in her arms with an old garment pinned about its body and its legs exposed to the cold weather.
>
> Visited in a miserable garret which was filthy in every respect. The husband had been sick several weeks and they had no means of procuring food except by begging.
>
> I called at a house occupied by seven families. In the first room was a girl sick with the measles. There was no fire in the room. On the floor lay a lad of sixteen, intoxicated. The mother could scarcely stand up. I passed from room to room, witnessing scenes of filthiness and disorder scarcely conceivable.

They knew all about drunkenness, for they met it every day in their work, often in its worst form:

> . . . called to visit a dying woman. When her husband came in he was intoxicated. He ranted and shouted and abused his wife. Then he went out saying he would go for a doctor, but he went to the saloon. The wife died before he returned.
>
> Requested to visit a dying woman but before I got there she had died. When I entered, the body was on an old chest, with a dirty shawl wrapped around her. The room was filled with women, all intoxicated. The woman who died had been drunk.
>
> I was visiting a young girl dying of consumption in one of the

worst localities of the city, when I heard of a family who had moved
to an adjoining cellar. Upon calling I found a man and his wife and
two children, one of whom was almost helpless from lack of proper
food, sunlight and pure air. The family had no money, food or fuel.
The waste pipe of the house ran through the room, and was badly
broken, making the air so foul that when I entered, I felt that with
every breath rank poison was taken into my system.

And they met other conditions of which the officials spoke: ignorance, degradation, disease, debauchery, crime, and death; all
of these conditions became very familiar to them. There is no way
of being able to say with certainty whether conditions improved
during the years of the Cushing era. There are indications in the
reports that a slight bettering of circumstances took place. But
such indications are few, for it was the job of the Society's workers
to search out the poor and the ignorant. And as families, through
work and patient industry reached a better standard of living they
were bound to move away from the run-down sections of the city.
Thus, in the later reports, amid stories that are much the same as
those in the earlier years, there are glimpses of people who are
establishing relationships with others, working at remunerative
jobs, and seeing to it that they and their children enter the public institutions open to them. Then, finally, the missionaries,
every day, wherever they went, met the Irish. For it was the Irish
who had to crowd the tenements and hovels, who suffered severe
privation before they could find a place for themselves, and who
were caught up in the evil that was indigenous to the areas to
which they were forced to go. The reports refer again and again
to "the immense Catholic population of our city."

The City Missionary Society was the Boston Society for the Religious and Moral Instruction of the Poor, with a new name, but
the same task. The Society proposed to evangelize the poor of the
city, to confront them with the message of Jesus Christ and to call
them to faith in Him.

We must make room for them by our altars and extend to them the
precious truth of Jesus . . . we must go among them in the earnestness of Christ-like compassion, watch and follow guiding provi-
dences, be patient with every prejudice, gain our ground inch by

inch, and expend all the endurance and activity of our utmost Christian heroism to win them to the true faith of the Cross.[24]

That was at the beginning of the Cushing era. In 1855, the Society said,

> . . . we do not wish to become a public eleemosynary institution, though we have facilities for this work which no other society enjoys; we do wish to keep our distinctive character as a proper missionary society, whose most precious trust, whose richest treasure, is the Gospel.[25]

In 1865,

> . . . let us go forth on our visitation, trying at all times to exert a directly religious influence, endeavouring to bring the soul to genuine repentance, to prayer, and to faith in Christ, seeking to awaken the careless, guide the inquiring, and comfort the desponding.[26]

And at the Semi-Centennial Anniversary in 1866, as the president of the Society summarized the lessons that had been learned, he laid stress on the fact that "the aim of the City Missionary Society must be the religious instruction of those visited . . . and the temporal wants can be incidentally cared for."[27]

While the workers of the Society understood that their particular work was to convey the Gospel of Jesus Christ to the poor, they believed firmly that all men, rich or poor, learned or ignorant, are in precisely the same condition in the sight of God, all "belong to the sinful race of humanity." And on occasion the reports of the Society spelled this out explicitly. "Are there not in our Sabbath audiences"—and then followed a description of the decent, law-abiding, well-to-do, church attending citizen—"as they take their seats [in church] with the respectful proprieties [some who] never come with contrite spirits, to be guided personally to the Saviour?" The poor were described with the same kind of observant detail. The conclusion was that both, the substantial church-goer, and the degraded poor, were in the same position before God. In fact the poor were better off, actually, for they could hear the promises—of a Father's house, of a great supper, of an inheritance of true riches,—and they could obey the command 'sell all thou hast' far more readily than could those who had good homes, plenty to eat, money in the bank.[28] All men needed to hear the Gospel; no man could be saved without responding to the Gospel.

The workers of the Society had a fairly clear idea of what was involved in the hearing and responding. The first step was the awakening on the part of the individual to the question of his eternal destiny. Man was certain to have many temporal needs, but the missionaries were sure that concern over those, pressing though it was, was not the primary concern which man should have. Man was a child of God, with an immortal soul, and he should seek the well-being of that soul. And man had to know this, admit it, see what he was like, before he granted it. The way the workers of the Society understood the process of salvation can best be shown by using a case one of them reported. It is not at all unique, for its parallel can be found in practically every annual report. The year was 1869. One of the workers had been able to get a girl from one family to attend Sunday School. After some weeks the girl spoke to the missionary about her father who, she said, was irreligious. The missionary invited the father to attend the neighborhood meeting, but "he met the invitation with ridicule." The girl finally persuaded her father to go with her, and he came "light and trifling." Later on, however, "his heart was touched by the seriousness of the presentation of the truth. He was led by the Spirit to see his lost condition as a sinner before God; he was driven almost to despair. All the awful threatenings of God against the unrenewed sinner, he applied to himself." That was the personal experience the missionary hoped for and expected. That was the awakening of a person to the issue of his eternal destiny.

The next step was the acceptance by the one whose concern was thus aroused of the reality of Jesus Christ and His power to save. That acceptance, the missionary believed, was brought about by the Holy Spirit. The missionary's job was to tell the story of Christ, and that was all he could do. Returning to the sample case: "not a promise of God would he accept [the missionary assuredly, had let him hear all he knew] until, one evening, light broke in upon his soul." Similarly in every report there is the account of individuals, "troubled by the Spirit" over their lost state who are suddenly or gradually brought to the experience of inner peace.

Then, finally, the missionaries knew that this experience was not enough. One further step was needed. The experience of Christ had to be given practical expression. There had to be a commitment to some form of action. If the convert were a woman who let her family live in filth and disorder, and her children go ragged and dirty, she was called to reform her ways. If the convert were a drinker, he signed the pledge. If the convert were a wife beater and brutal to his children, he promised to change his ways. And always, came the agreement to attend the neighborhood meeting or a church regularly. The missionaries followed up each individual as closely as they could.

> The Spirit of Christ, introduced into any heart and home, effects this very result. It brings with it peace, joy, purity and the hope of a Christian heart—that will restrain intemperance and crime, that will banish the curses of a vicious pauperism by drying up its sources, and will hallow and illumine whatever toil, discomfort and poverty may be appointed by God. . . .[29]

Sometimes the individual failed to keep his commitment; the worker expected to find that individual "seven times worse than at first" but tried the redemptive process again. Sometimes it happened that the missionary failed completely, and that happened often enough to make him discouraged. Then he had to give up the individual involved completely.

This redemptive process, as the missionaries understood it and used it in their work among the poor, had one great danger in it. It depended upon conversation, or talk, through which the worker addressed some other person. The risk was that the conversation would become "aimless or vapid," or that it would consist only of the worker's ideas or seek to propound the worker's moralisms. When the talk did that, it was worse than useless, for it was false, spoken in the name of Christ but not carrying His words. "The Word of God, accompanied by the power of the Spirit, must be our chief reliance in the efforts for the evangelization of the world."

But there was that ancient question of why there were

poor people and the Society's workers had to raise it anew for
themselves and work out an answer. If all men were God's children, and all were equal in His sight, why were some rich and
some poor, some favored and some burdened almost beyond the
strength of man? The workers never tried to settle the matter by
saying that people were poor because of their sins, that their condition was a punishment for the evil they had done. They knew
that some were poor because they were "idle, lazy vagabonds, mis-
erable sticks of men, driftwood on the current of humanity, coun-
terfeit manhood." But they also knew that others were poor
through no fault of their own: men were victims of fraud; a manufacturer shut down his plant; a work of public improvement was
stopped in mid-course; a blight killed the crop; a bread winner
died; long sickness created a heavy debt. Yet the workers were
sure that God was the ruler of the universe and that all things were
in his hand, operating "by a divine arrangement and under divine
control."

As the missionaries sought an answer for all that, they held fast
to Jesus' saying, "the poor you have always with you" and they
took those words to be, not a remark applicable only to the setting
in which they were uttered, but "a prophecy of perpetual force."
They saw that rich and poor, under the mysterious working of
the divine, are together in the world because that is God's plan.

> It seems to be the arrangement of Divine Providence, that some
> should be wealthy . . . that some should have a competency . . . that
> some by hard work should be just able to provide for themselves and
> their families . . . and that some should be poverty striken. . . .[30]

That arrangement, however, had as its purpose the spiritual welfare of all men. God intended men to learn respect for all persons, regardless of their condition, to become mutual helpers of
one another, the rich and the poor each contributing to the other's needs.

> What is wanted is a simple recognition of the divine appointment,
> by virtue of which each holds his place. When every man shall look
> upon his brother, no matter what his condition and say within him-
> self, 'that man is my brother; he was not meant to stand alone: I
> have need of him and he has need of me; each of us is a thread in

the social fabric, and he is as important in his place as I am in mine: he must hold me up, I must hold him up. . . .'[31]

Such an understanding of society had a continuing effect upon the way the Society's workers went at their task. They were much more interested in the spiritual welfare of the poor than they were in their material condition. They were prepared to give emergency help to families in dire need, but that was not what they were about. They expected the poor to be poor, but they believed the poor should be the "saved poor." They sought to express and imitate "the Saviour's care for the poor." "Christ put honor upon this condition of life by being born in it himself; He knows the poor, He is one with them; He seeks their salvation." That was the ground on which the workers proceeded. As time went on, and the terrible plight of the people with whom they had to do worked upon their sensitivities, the generally held understanding of the meaning of the Christian faith changed, and their thinking and their actions changed.

The situation the workers found was an overwhelming one. There was no end to the immigrants and seemingly no limit to the hovels and garrets where they found living space. Thousands upon thousands of poor and a few hundred workers of the Society, less than two dozen of them, at the most, giving full time to the work. How could anyone think an enterprise so clearly infinitesimal was worth the effort? People asked that question; and they asked it out loud. Once in a while the officers of the Society begged the churches for more funds in order to employ more workers, but they realized their begging was largely in vain. There was, however, the parable of the leaven, and they used that:

> Silent, inconspicuous, seemingly disproportionate and inadequate to the accomplishment of the work proposed, the leaven, nevertheless, attacks the mass . . . Such the principle and such the practice, emphatically, of our missionary work. It brings the Christian heart into vital and living contact with unleavened life . . . and you cannot score the silent infusion of thought with truth, and of heart and feeling with pure and holy spiritual influence . . . all our calculation must be of faith and not of figures. . . .[32]

The Society was content to go about its work and let God use their efforts for His purpose.

Occasionally, voices in the churches wanted to know why there were not more obvious results and the officers of the Society tried to explain. Sometimes the officers were troubled themselves when seemingly so little happened in spite of all the efforts put forth. And it may be that underlying the changes that took place in the Society's program as the years went by, there was the desire to have some tangible evidence, in some measure at least, of the usefulness of their enterprise.

At the beginning of the era the core of the program was the house visitation, carried on by the missionaries and the tract distributors. The latter reported to the former when they found families needing or deserving more attention than they were able to give, so that the two groups worked together as they entered homes, talked to the people, and sought their spiritual welfare. During this period there are no figures in the reports giving the number of visits made by the tract distributors. The reports show that the number of visits made by the missionaries remained relatively constant, over 40,000 in the year 1852, and over 49,000 in 1891. The lowest number made was in 1862 with 26,000 visits, and the highest in 1885 with 57,400 visits. The curious statistician may want to work out the number of calls per working day for each missionary: allowing twenty working days a month, the figures mean that the missionaries averaged nine calls a day.

A day in a missionary's work was described thus: third story of a lodging house to a dying woman; poverty ridden home with clothes for the children; to catch an intemperate man while he is sober, perchance he will listen; to get a man a job; heard of strangers recently arrived, went to find out how they were faring —lonely, disappointed, confused; answered a message from a prostitute, went and got her away; a family of Romanists to tell them the Gospel; then to a mothers' meeting.[33] They went through lanes, alleys, and the streets of the city, into tenement houses, and they dealt with people. They found hunger, destitution, nakedness, drunkards, criminals, sickness, loneliness, old age, orphans, and death. And they tried as best they knew how to show that they cared, and to bring the word of the Christian Gospel to bear on the lives of those who were caught in these conditions. They had little else to give, for the money put in their hands for relief was a mere pittance—in 1852 there was $2,117 to be divided among the 18 missionaries, not $120 for each one, $10 a month—but they had themselves, their faith and their knowledge of other agencies in the city, public and private, able to help the needy.

As they visited, the missionaries found an occasional person who was an evangelical Christian. To the missionaries a person was a Christian when he had known the experience of salvation and demonstrated by his life the results of that experience; all others, Universalists, Unitarians, Catholics, and the irreligious were lumped together as lost and were the objects of their evangelical labors. They were especially concerned over the Catholics, for to them the members of that church were the victims of an idolatrous system which was of the devil's doing. Since there were so many Catholics living in the places they visited, they were bound to deal with them. There is no indication that the missionaries were directly involved in the anti-Catholic movements described earlier, but there is no doubt that they believed as did those expressing their antagonism openly, that the Catholics were no better than sheer pagans and therefore proper subject for their efforts.

They visited Catholics, took the children to Sabbath School if they got the parents' permission to do so, gave them Bibles and tracts, told them of salvation through faith, invited them to attend the neighborhood meetings and surrounded them with every Protestant influence available. When they came across a Catholic who was adamant, or as they said "bigoted," they let him alone; although the reason they ceased to visit him was not that they had respect for his faith, but that they gave him up for lost. When a Catholic responded to their visits, and in their loneliness and need many of them did, they saw the Holy Spirit at work and did their best to be of assistance. Yet regardless of the conditions they found or the state of the people they visited, they tried to talk with them of the faith they had and of the Saviour they knew. They tried to get the children into the day schools and the Sabbath Schools; if a child had no fit clothes to wear they found some for him; and if a child feared to go alone for the first time, they went with him. When they found a sick person, they visited regularly, found a doctor, or went to the drugstore for some simple remedy. All the while they looked for a chance to speak of Him who was able to give healing of soul to the sick in body. They went to the dying and when they found one afraid to face the end, talked quietly of God's promise of eternal life to those who believe. When they dealt with a drunkard they made use of the temperance pledge, doing so, not indiscriminately, for they refrained from mentioning the device when the person with whom they were dealing was not concerned about himself, but making good use of it when the individual appeared ready for it.

They entered many places where the family, having lost all hope, had stopped struggling against the awful conditions and had drifted into irresponsibility and filth and degradation, and they tried to arouse a sense of personal responsibility by pointing to Him who is Lord regardless of conditions. They sought out the prostitute and found a new home for her. They picked up abandoned or orphaned children and either took them to a public or private institution or arranged places for them with families they knew. Regularly they made their reports, putting into tabulated form what they had done: number of sick visited; number of funerals attended; number of tracts and Bibles given out. The results were given as they believed they knew them: number of children taken to Sabbath School; number of temperance pledges; number of persons furnished employment; number of persons hopefully converted. The former set of figures relating what they had done were, through the years, uniformally large, showing the faithfulness with which they did their work. The latter set of figures were always comparatively small. To illustrate: in the year 1872 there were twenty missionaries at work; they made 41,660 calls, visited the sick 7,082 times, gave out over 97,000 pieces of literature. But, they took 338 children to Sabbath School, there were 166 temperance pledges signed, 368 persons found employment and 46 hopefully converted.

Through the years of the Cushing era a number of changes took place in the program of home visitation. First, that part of the work not appearing in the statistical reports, which had been done by volunteers from the churches, the Tract Distribution Program, gradually changed hands. The number of distributors grew less. In 1853—"The interest in, and the results of this branch of our operations, it is feared, have somewhat diminished." However, the report for that year shows that about four hundred volunteers were at work, and the statement was made that "we place so high an estimate upon the influence and labors of these our volunteer helpers, that any depreciation of their value touches us dearly." By 1855, "It has been found difficult to sustain the systematic distribution of tracts, while the number of districts in which it is hardly proper or safe for females to visit has increased, the number of male distributors has diminished." And the report went on to lament this trend, since the work of distributing tracts, believed to be of the utmost significance, would have to be done by the missionaries. In 1864,

> Some distrust this method of doing good and suppose that the tracts are destroyed without being read. Admit this to be true in many cases; it is also true that some are not destroyed; they are not only read, but read with prayer, and with the accompaniment of the Spirit of God enforcing the truth.

Then in the following year, 1865,

> An effort has been made to change somewhat the character of tract distribution, and to engage in it only those Christians who are able to accompany the distribution with other missionary labors. The missionaries have been much more largely supplied; and have distributed personally more religious reading than in past years. The difficulties in the way of and the objections to universal and indiscriminate distribution of tracts have greatly increased. It is hoped that a more judicious, though less extensive distribution, will be more productive of good.

By the early 1870's reference in the reports to Tract Distribution has disappeared as a separate item, and the giving away of literature has become part of the job of the missionaries.

Second, there was a clear and decided change in the attitude of the missionaries of the Society toward the Catholics. During the early years, Catholics were people who most desperately needed to hear the Gospel of Jesus Christ and be led in the way of salvation. During the closing years, Catholics were, in the main, left with their own faith, unless there were situations in which the individual had already turned away from the church. For example, in 1884, one of the missionaries did a complete survey of four streets in her district. "Many of the calls were not of sufficient importance to be counted in the list of the families visited; but, so far as Roman Catholic families generally were concerned, were merely to ascertain the denomination and place of worship." In 1885, "As I was visiting in a neighborhood, calling on many families, all of whom were Roman Catholics, I found one woman who was nominally a Protestant, but who had not been to church for years." The Protestant woman was finally drawn back to the church, but the report says nothing more about the Catholics. In 1886, there is the account of a missionary visiting a woman dying of consumption. She was a Catholic married to a Protestant. The woman's sister was there, keeping house. The missionary gave the husband a Bible, since he did not have one. Later on, the missionary called again, and the sister asked if she might have a Bible, which the missionary gave her. The sick woman and her husband both died; the sister married a man from Sweden, a Protestant. The missionary reported finding the woman reading the Bible on a subsequent visit, but there is no indication that she became a Protestant or that the missionary made any attempt to talk with her to that end. In 1887, there is the account of a missionary calling on a widow with four children living in a crowded tenement. The Catholic children of the neighborhood were accustomed to play in the street during "most of the hours of the Holy Sabbath." The Protestant widow had refused to allow her children to join the group, although they had been asked; "she discharged her duty as a Christian mother." But apparently the missionary did not think of getting the Catholic children into the near-by Sabbath School. In 1888, a missionary entered a home to find a very unhappy woman. She was a Catholic, married to a Protestant. The first two children had been baptized in the Catholic church, but when the third child was born the father refused to have it baptized by the priest, and a serious quarrel had broken out. In answer to the missionary's question the woman said that her husband was a good man, "there never was a better." "Then," said the missionary, "do not be troubled; you and he worship the same God, and pray to the same Saviour. I think God would be better pleased if you had peace in the family." Those are nearly all the accounts having references to Catholics in them during the years indicated. The contrast with the earlier years is marked.

Third, there is a noticeable change in the purpose, or perhaps, in the way the missionaries understood the working out of the purpose of the Society between the earlier and the later years. In the earlier years there is a picture of a dismal setting into which the missionary goes armed with the Gospel of Jesus Christ to win souls from evil and despair and hopelessness to a trust in the Saviour, the missionary sure that right in the midst of that terrible setting the light of new life in Christ "will shine." In the reports of those years the emphasis was on conversion, on reformation, on the finding of inner peace, the coming of hope. During the later years, while there are accounts of need and destitution the scene is not as dark and dismal. And the missionary goes with resources to meet the needs, to provide new experiences, and to lift burdens. The emphasis is placed on service rendered and invitations to chapel services nearby. The difference as it was stated, is between "bringing people to a knowledge of the Saviour" and "bringing people within the influence of the religious institutions of our society." In 1859, the Society, through its workers, "pointed people to Christ as their only hope for pardon and salvation"; in 1890, the Society, "while primarily religious, does a constantly increasing work that is philanthropic and charitable." There were three major reasons for that change. One, the arrangements under which the missionaries worked were changed so that they were related to the churches and the areas of the city in and about the neighborhoods of those churches, which put them within specific settings. Two, the increasing concentration of the interest of the missionaries on Protestant and non-committed families, which again sent them into certain homes, rather than into whole areas. And three, the change in the general understanding of the meaning of the Christian faith which had taken place during the era. The day of the Social Gospel was dawning and the thinking that was expressed in that took form in the Society.

Home visitation was supplemented by group meetings. One was linked to the other as two parts of a single campaign designed to reach the poor of the city with the Gospel. A writer in one of the reports using Biblical imagery likened the home visitation to the attack upon the enemy, and the group meeting to the gathering of the prisoners. The analogy breaks down at a number of points, as the writer acknowledged, but it served to put into pictorial form the pattern of the Society's program. The group meetings did more than gather those who had been awakened to a concern for their eternal welfare by the visits of the missionaries, for the meetings were occasions where the experience of Christ's saving power might and did occur. These neighborhood "social religious meetings" were continued from the earlier years and were increased in number as missionaries were added to the staff. During the year 1849 there had been 129 such meetings, while twenty years later there were 2,176. The plan of the meetings remained simple: the singing of hymns, the reading and study of the scriptures, the giving of testimonies or the sharing of concerns, and prayer. The records indicate that frequently those in attendance felt free to speak of their anxieties, their sorrows, and their needs, finding in the group sympathy, advice, and often direct relief, which is surprising in light of the poverty of the participants.

It was not long before the missionaries noted two things about the people with whom they dealt: Neither the women nor the girls knew how to sew. Consequently they could not make the clothes so badly needed by their families and were unable to earn the money that was paid to seamstresses by the dress and suit manufacturers of the city. At the same time the missionaries saw babies die not long after birth in shocking numbers, and while they realized that some were lost through starvation and disease, they noted that many deaths resulted from mistreatment or lack of proper care. To deal with those circumstances the missionaries began to conduct sewing classes and meetings for mothers. In both series of meetings, the sessions were opened and closed with devotions, but they were held primarily for their intended purposes, the one, to teach women and girls plain sewing, and the other, to teach mothers how to handle their babies and bring up their children. For years those two types of meetings, held in homes, and led by missionaries or church women whose aid the missionaries enlisted, were well attended. The sewing classes ceased somewhere in the middle 70's, we may judge because there were other agencies doing the job, but the mothers' meetings continued through the whole era. Both meetings accomplished more than their stated purposes for they brought individuals together to share their troubles and to give support to each other.

Then there were the Sabbath Schools—they were not called Sunday Schools until 1884. The Society had turned over to the churches the schools they had established, believing that this work with children properly belonged to the churches. Only if there were a direct and immediate connection between Sabbath School and church could the individuals who had been trained during their growing years in the ways of the Christian faith readily become members of the Christian fellowship. And the missionaries of the Society continued to make it an important part of their work to get the children they met while visiting into the Schools.

> The missionaries cooperate with the members of the churches, in bringing into the parish schools such children as are not connected with other Sabbath Schools, and in visiting them, furnishing them with clothing when necessary, and promoting their constant attendance. Where there is the necessity for the establishment of a mission Sabbath School, their advice will always be given. It is thought that such Schools had better be under the care of some church, which shall be responsible for their support.

Even in the case of the mission schools, that is, those schools not directly part of church programs, the Society felt the need for some church connection. Of course, there were financial and personnel sides to that: if the churches were responsible for the mission schools they would pay the bills and provide superintendents and teachers, thus relieving the Society of both responsibilities. But there was a principle involved, which the Society had been led to see: the place of the church in the life of the Christian faith. An evangelism which ended with the conversion of the individual was inadequate and truncated. The converted individuals had to be brought within the company of those who were the saved of the present generation, and that was the church. The two great agencies for promoting, strengthening and extending the Christian faith, the Society said, were the church and the home. "The Christian family and the Christian Church are the two institutions which stand forth prominently as the divinely appointed instruments of Christian power among men; the family, properly trained being 'a church in the house'; the church being a congregation of Christian families. From these as sources, every Christian enterprise must derive its life."[34] Hence the conviction that Sabbath Schools should be conducted by and in relation to churches.

The poor had certain convictions of their own. The missionaries discovered that the children were enrolling in several schools of various denominations and then attending wherever there happened to be something worth while going on, or wherever they could benefit most. If there was a picnic planned at one school, the children went there for a Sunday or so previous to the announced date. If a youngster needed some new shoes, he went to one school after another until, as an enrollee of some school he got the shoes. When one school offered its pupils prizes to bring in new students, the attendance at the other schools dropped; and the school that arranged the largest Christmas tree with the most presents on it, had the largest attendance at that season of the year.[35] When these tricks were learned and "the baleful influences upon children and parents" were seen, the superintendents and teachers of the schools in the city met to work out ways of dealing with the situation. "An excellent catholic [cooperative] spirit has prevailed, and it is hoped will be productive of good."

At the beginning of the era there were three Mission Sabbath Schools in operation. These were the Old Colony School, which beginning in 1825 as the Sea Street Sabbath School had been adopted by the Central Church in 1845 when it met in the hall over the Old Colony Railroad Depot; the Revere Street School, which had been started in 1829 in the West End, and for which Park Street church had assumed responsibility when the Society changed its policy; and the Mariners School which, because its work was primarily with seamen and their families, was in a dif-

ferent class than the others in respect to the possibility of sending
other children to it. Then there were the parish schools and the
two church-run mission schools. These were the schools to which
the missionaries could direct the children they found in their calling. They experienced difficulty getting their children into parish
schools: "there are social barriers to be overcome; the difference
in clothing, manners and habits of the children of well-trained
Christian families and those which have been deprived of such influences" is too great.

Other schools were started, but the development was not a simple one, for the growing sense of the importance of the church,
and the belief that church and school should be connected, and
the dilemma of the poor children and the parish schools were
mixed together in thought and action; not as three distinguish-
able strands, but as one united whole which resulted in what came
to be called, "Chapel and Sabbath School Work." As the years
went by it was not possible to tell which was which. Chapels developed out of Sabbath Schools; Sabbath Schools conducted services of worship and group meetings of various kinds similar to
chapels, yet remained as schools; and the Society assumed responsibility for some of the enterprises and left others completely to
the churches.

The report of the Society for 1859 begins, "It has not been the
policy of our Society to organize churches, but in humbler ways
to carry the blessings of the Gospel to the destitute," which was
simply a reiteration of the policy that had been agreed upon in
1848 between the churches of the city and the Society. But the
repetition was not for the sake of reminding readers of the report
of something that had previously taken place, it was an introduction to the announcement of the formation of a church. This
church was not the result of a deliberate effort on the part of the
Society, but "evidently a child of Providence."

In the fall of 1851, the year the Society was reorganized with a
working president and an assistant, Cushing went over to East
Boston and found the Fourth Section, so called, in a deplorable
state. The inhabitants were a long distance from a church or from
contact with other orderly society and "their degradation was

proverbial; the place sustained a most unenviable reputation."
Cushing asked Miss Armeda Gibbs, who for years had been one
of the volunteer tract distributors, if she would become a full-time
missionary and go over to the Fourth Section to see what could be
done. Miss Gibbs agreed and set out for her new field. One day
as she was going about her visiting she stopped in the home of a
Christian family. They were overjoyed at the thought that religious activities might be started in their area and they volunteered to find a place where a Sabbath School could meet. They
knew another Christian family who had a fairly large parlor in
their house, so the school was started there. After some weeks the
city authorities allowed the use of a room in the local schoolhouse.[36]

There was an immediate response from adults and children
alike. The project appeared to be well launched. When spring
came the missionary and her helpers were ordered to vacate the
school room. There was nowhere else in the neighborhood to go.
Cushing started out with a subscription paper in his hands. He
went through the Fourth Section, other parts of East Boston, and
to some of his friends in the city. In a short time he had collected
money enough to build a chapel, "thirty-five feet by fifty, seating
nearly four hundred persons." Meanwhile he had gone to the
East Boston Company and had leased a piece of land from them,
as he put it, "free of expense." That was the Bennington Street
Chapel. But, he said, in reporting his activities to the Board, "it is
not intended to organize a church in connection with the enterprise." Cushing was a poor prophet or else a good diplomat. By
1854, the work of the chapel, carried on in part by some members
of the Maverick Church, had developed in surprising fashion, and
the Society, reviewing the situation and the possibilities, employed the Reverend Lumen Boyden to "preach on Sundays and
do the usual missionary work on week days." In 1859, matters having progressed further and there being a demand for action by
some of the regular attendants, the Evangelical Union Church
was organized around carefully worked out "Articles of Faith."
Trustees were elected, representing the religious backgrounds of
some of the people in the congregation—Baptists, Methodists, and

Congregationalists. Two years later, two businessmen who owned contiguous parcels of land in the district gave a sizeable area to the new church and the chapel building was moved.

A Sabbath School had been started in the North End by one of the missionaries sometime in the middle 50's (the reports do not always give names and times), but after getting a large response from the people at the beginning, had run into difficulty through "the inconvenience of the place and the opposition of the Catholic priests." The School was then moved to a hall on Hanover Street which was rented for the purpose, and the attendance increased to over one hundred children who had "grown up in ignorance and sin." The work was then taken in hand by the Park Street Church. The Sabbath School was maintained and services of worship for adults were started on Sunday evenings. Thirty years later there were more than two hundred fifty in the Sunday School, and the chapel program included week-night meetings in addition to the Sunday service.

A poor, elderly widow lived in a single room in a tenement on Harrison Avenue. One of the missionaries of the Society, Mrs. Sarah Paul, found her and used to drop in occasionally for a visit and to make sure that her basic needs were supplied. One day the old lady talked to Mrs. Paul about her concern for the children who, all day long on Sundays, tore up and down the street shouting and fighting and causing no end of trouble, and she said she wished she could do something to help the youngsters. She told Mrs. Paul that if she would take the matter in hand she might use her one room for a meeting place. Mrs. Paul corralled the youngsters and "The Kitchen Sabbath School" was born. The number of children attending soon became too large for the small room, and a carpenter who had a shop further along the Avenue offered his space for use on Sundays. That was in 1859. In 1865 the Shawmut Church became interested in the work through a few of the members who had been enlisted to help in the school. The church raised some money and built a chapel on Harrison Avenue near Malden Street. This became the Shawmut Chapel, where there were services of worship, group meetings during the week, as well as the Sunday School.

In 1863, Miss Soviah Burgess, one of the missionaries, was assigned to an area in and around Carney Place. She was appalled by the conditions she found; she described it as the most wretched place she knew and as "one of the most unpromising mission fields." In the course of her visiting she came upon a Protestant family, living in a room on the ground floor of one of the houses. She and the couple finally decided they would try to hold neighborhood meetings in the couple's room. Word of the plan was passed around among the people living nearby. On the appointed day, the number who came nearly filled the limited space, and the meeting seemed to have been appreciated. A time was fixed for the next gathering. But then a noisy crowd of ruffians appeared with the announced determination to stop such meetings. A policeman was sent for, the crowd was dispersed, and the service proceeded without interruption, the policeman standing guard at the door. A day or so later, Miss Burgess was told by men who were the ringleaders of the mob that no more such meetings would be allowed in the area. Miss Burgess, not wanting to put the family in whose home those events had transpired into further danger, found a vacant flat on the first floor of a nearby tenement, rented it from the owner who was apprised of the circumstances, and who gave Miss Burgess permission to have some of the partitions between rooms knocked out so as to make a sizeable meeting place. The "Myrtle Mission Room" thus came to be. The police were needed whenever the Room was opened during the following week, but gradually the opposition subsided and the enterprise became known as Berkeley Street Mission No. 1. The meeting hall was at the corner of Washington Street and Carney Place. The mission got its name because members of the Berkeley Street Church became involved in the work, and the church took over responsibility for it.

With a Berkeley Street Mission No. 1, one would expect a mission No. 2, and so there was. In an old tavern in the South End known as Washington House, sometime in 1863, a Protestant woman who lived nearby started a Sabbath School with the permission of the tavern keeper. As the numbers increased, some members of the Berkeley Street Church were asked to help, and under their leadership a building was erected on a piece of land they leased on Lenox Street. The report said, "it is not only occupied by the Sabbath School, but preaching is sustained there every Sabbath afternoon, and prayer meetings on Sabbath and other evenings." Berkeley Street Mission No. 2 then became the Lenox Street Chapel.

While all that was going on, the Old Colony Sabbath School had been forced out of the hall in which it had been meeting and was being conducted temporarily in some leased space. The Central Church, which had responsibility for this school, set to work, raised some money, bought land, and erected a building on Tyler Street near Harvard Street—total cost $17,700 and the Old Colony School became the Tyler Street Chapel.

Other schools were started as the years went by, some becoming chapels, and at least one becoming an organized church before the era came to an end. 1867—a school in Washington Village, Dorchester; 1891—a school in Mattapan, started by a newly-appointed missionary; the Eliot Chapel in 1874, which merged with the Old Colony Chapel; the Bay View Mission in South Boston, 1875; the Winthrop Hall Mission in Charlestown in 1878, under the auspices of the Winthrop Church; the Salem Street Sabbath School started by the members of Park Street Church in the building of the Seaman's Friend Society in 1881; the Melrose Street Sabbath School opened by the Old South Church, 1883, which became the Hope Chapel; and a Sabbath School opened in a hall at Field's Corner by members of the Second Church, Dorchester, 1885, which became the Bethany Church in 1878 with the Reverend C. C. Kellogg as the pastor.

In 1872, the Board of Managers of the Society expressed themselves as being desirous of enlarging the work the Society was doing and if possible of trying out some new methods. The decision was taken to employ an ordained minister as "a clerical missionary" in order that he "might give new interest to the social religious services, devise new methods of usefulness, and by addressing the churches at their prayer meetings and on the Sabbath, promote a better acquaintance with the spiritual wants of the city, and the efforts made to relieve them." That appears to have meant a job of promotion among the churches by an ordained man whom the churches would respect more than they would a layman. On the Board at the time was the Reverend Daniel Waldron, pastor of the Maverick Church in East Boston, who had been a member of the Board for a little more than a year. When the action was taken to secure a clerical missionary, the Board turned to Mr. Waldron and invited him. By 1874, the Chapel work of the Society had been put under his supervision and he was preaching regularly in the chapels. He was deeply interested in that part of the Society's program, and under his leadership the number of chapels and schools was increased and the programs in all of them made more extensive and more orderly.

Home visiting led to social religious meetings in homes, to sewing classes and mothers' meetings, to Sabbath Schools and chapels, and ultimately to churches. That was the basic pattern which the Society had developed over the years as they pursued the purpose of taking religious and moral instruction to the poor. Such a cold, factual summary tends to obscure the hundreds of church people, visiting and teaching and directing, who, with the missionaries, carried on the work. There were meetings held for this sizeable company of people—area meetings and teachers' meetings—which gave a sense of unity and provided inspiration and sustaining power. But more than that, there was to begin with a basic social and religious oneness. The middle class of society from which those workers came had begun to disintegrate. People belonging to the city churches were moving out into the suburbs and other forces were at work breaking down the social cohesion which held people together in oneness of belief and interest, purpose and spirit, but enough cohesion remained to reproduce the army of people who really were the active Society.

Mrs. Lucretia Boyd was a missionary of the Society who worked in the West End from 1855 to 1861. She became deeply concerned over the fate of the single young women coming to Boston to find work, for she found them living in the poorest of quarters and getting involved in the evil enterprises of the city. In November

1858 she went to Mrs. Edwin Lawson and laid this situation before her. Out of that visit came the Boston Y.W.C.A.[37]

During the Cushing era the Society made special efforts to reach and work with three particular groups. This should be understood in the way the Society understood it. The workers of the Society were dealing with people of various racial ancestries all the while: the Irish, for example. But the workers were not assigned specifically to seek out the Irish; the one attempt that had been made to do that had not proved to be very successful. The missionaries were to present the Gospel to all people with whom they came in contact. On one occasion the Society made a public statement to the effect that, "it has not been customary for the City Missionary Society to appoint missionaries for distinct classes of people or nationalities," but there were three exceptions to this.

In 1858 the Society employed Miss Elisa Kersten to work among the German population. "Being of their number and speaking their own language, she has been able to labour more effectively for their good, than one who could speak the English language only." In the background somewhere, although there is no reference to it in the records of the Society, is a German congregation which, beginning in 1839, was aided by the Massachusetts Missionary Society.[38] The aid was continued for some years, but was withdrawn when the congregation divided after a serious disagreement. Eventually one side of the division was absorbed by the church on Suffolk Street established by the Society, with the Reverend George Oviatt as the pastor. When this took place the Massachusetts Missionary Society resumed its financial support of the enterprise until the church, able to meet its own expenses, gave up the gift.

From 1858 to 1869, when Miss Kersten's name disappeared from the list of missionaries, there is no direct reference to her work. And when her name disappears from the roll of missionaries there is no word of her going. However with careful scrutiny of the reports of the missionaries, which are never signed, here and there a brief reference to a German family on whom a missionary called can be picked out, but that is all. In 1863, the Society employed the Reverend A. H. Bechtold to "work among the Germans and the Hollanders." He reported in the following year that a group of fifty-five adult Hollanders, and their children numbering seventy-three, had been meeting in a hall for worship and Sabbath School, that the adults had united with the Springfield Street Church of which they considered themselves a branch, and that conversations had begun about the possibility of erecting a chapel for their use. But in 1865 Bechtold departed, having received a call to a Dutch church in New Jersey. Then, in 1867 his name appears unannounced and unexplained in the list of missionaries of the Society, and it is repeated in 1868 and in 1869, after which it·disappears. But for those years there is no mention of any work he did.

The only other reference to work with the Germans is in the 1869 report which speaks of "one of the female missionaries, herself a German, though thoroughly Americanized." She had gathered a group of Germans and had begun to teach them English. She had based her teaching upon the New Testament, using the edition with the two languages printed in parallel columns. She also started a sewing class for the women and girls.

In 1881, a woman supporter of the Society offered to pay the salary of a missionary to work among the Jews. In 1883 one of the missionaries then in the employ of the Society agreed to undertake the work. Mrs. Julia White was a native of Germany and spoke the language which "qualifies her the better to work among the Jews." At the time there were ten synagogues in the city. Mrs. White started two Sabbath Schools and two mothers' meetings. The Sabbath Schools enrolled about two hundred, adults and children. In 1885, Mrs. White was taken seriously ill and had to relinquish her work, and Miss Anne Watson took her place. She concentrated upon visiting in the homes, but at the same time continued the organized activities which her predecessor had started. The Sabbath School became a part of the Old Colony School, where classes for the Jewish adults and children were separated from the other classes. That arrangement continued until the end of the Cushing era. By that time Miss Charlotte Sisson had taken Miss Watson's place. From the statements made in the reports, the purpose of the Society in undertaking that work was to present Jesus as the Messiah to the Jewish people, in the hope they would believe and be converted. There are no records of such conversions.

Miss Harriet Carter was a member (in the 1860's) of the Chambers Street Church, which was supported at the time by the Old South Church. In 1871 she entered the employ of the Society and was assigned to work in the area of the church where she had her membership. Sometime later, in the course of her visiting, she came upon two Chinese men. They aroused her interest, and discovering that they were anxious to learn English, she invited them to come to her rooms for some instruction. That continued during the summer of 1876. In the fall of that year she started a language school on Monday evenings at the Chambers Street Church. A sizeable number enrolled, but the percentage of regular attendants was relatively small. Few of the Chinese remained long in any one place and even those who stayed in Boston for a time were not sufficiently interested in the program of the school to be present at every session. As the school continued, Chinese appeared who already knew some English and they were able to assist in the instruction of their countrymen. There was always a group of them who appeared at every class session and made consistent efforts to master the language and the other subjects taught in the school. The Bible and other religious literature were primary resources of instruction.

In 1879, two events added to the effectiveness of the school. An ecclestiastical committee had been asked to consider the future of the Chambers Street church. They recommended that the church be disbanded and the members transferred to other churches because of the changes which had taken place in the district where the building was located. The recommendation was followed and the church was closed. Miss Carter joined the Mt. Vernon Church, then located on Ashburton Place, and transferred the Chinese School to the chapel of that church. It was immediately apparent that this was much more satisfactory for the Chinese, as they had been subjected to ridicule and annoyance when going back and forth to Chambers Street. The second event of consequence was a visit of three months by the Reverend David Jones. Mr. Jones was an evangelist among the Chinese in and around San Francisco. He visited in the growing Chinese community of Boston and developed an effective organization for the work Miss Carter had started. By the time he left, the school had increased in numbers. Teachers, members of Mt. Vernon Church and from among the Chinese themselves, had been recruited, and a start had been made toward helping the non-Chinese understand Chinese ways. That year, for example, relationships between the two groups had progressed to the point where the Chinese invited the teachers to join in celebrating their New Year.

All that time Miss Carter had carried on this work as part of her total responsibility. She was also making home visitations and conducting social religious meetings in her assigned area. In 1881, the Board of the Society, having become aware of what she was doing, made her "missionary to the Chinese," relieving her of other tasks for, they said, "it finds that among the poor of late there are hundreds of yellow-visaged heathen who have come to dwell at our doors."[39] The purpose for which the Board made that assignment was that the Chinese might hear the Gospel of Jesus Christ and be converted. The work was expanded; a Sabbath School was started; the evening school increased its sessions from one night a week to three; and an afternoon school meeting five days a week was begun. A few Chinese Christians came to Boston, and they added impetus to the work. Correspondence with the Reverend Mr. Jones, who by that time was in China, set up an arrangement under which gifts from the Boston school were sent to China to help with the Christian program there; and a regular program of visiting among the Chinese was started.

At the end of ten years of work among the Chinese, Miss Carter made a summary of what had been done. Nearly a thousand different individuals had been enrolled in the activities. Since the number of Chinese in Boston had remained fairly constant during the time, between four and five hundred, the number of enrollees indicates the extent of the movement among those people. Some who had been in the program went back to China, others moved to cities and towns of New England, still others went to other parts of the country. As they moved away, Miss Carter said, they took with them the knowledge they had gained in the schools or the church, especially the knowledge of people who had "done something to show them the true spirit of our Saviour, Christ the Lord." Miss Carter said that she hardly ever had been asked to help a Chinese who was sick, for they looked after their own. Occasionally she had shown them how to get into a hospital, and how to use the courts of law when they had been assaulted by a non-Chinese. There had been some avowed converts to Christianity. The number was not completely known, for news had come of men who had joined churches on profession of faith after they had left Boston. Eight had joined Mt. Vernon Church.

A Sunday School was begun at the Charlestown Y.M.C.A.; another school was started at the Temple Methodist church that same year. Two years later, Clarendon Street Baptist church, the Warren Avenue Baptist Church, and Berkeley Temple opened schools. Visitors from other places who were involved in work with Chinese people, the Superintendent of the Chinese Mission in San Francisco, Mr. F. W. Damon of Honolulu, and others added impetus to the work. When the Cushing era ended, Miss Carter was busy with the program she had developed.

The records would indicate that early in the Cushing era the missionaries of the Society were not visiting the institutions of the city. Occasionally, when a person known to a missionary was taken to one of the institutions the missionary would call, and once in a while a missionary would make it his or her business to go to the institutions. "Nowhere am I more gladly welcomed than at the City Hospital which I visit from week to week," but there was no plan worked out by the Society for that activity. When Mr. Waldron joined the staff he launched such a program. He noted that there was no chaplain at City Hospital and that the Roman Catholic priests went there regularly, seeing their own people and being "not wholly unmindful of others." Three of the missionaries were asked to include that hospital in their visiting. Calling was also started at the "Charitable Eye and Ear Infirmary, the Penitent Females Refuge, and the Home operated by the Children's Friend Society." Services of worship were conducted at the

Refuge and the Home. In 1884 the list of institutions at which visits were made and services conducted had been more than doubled. An account was published in *The Congregationalist,* shortly after Easter that year in which Mr. Waldron's activity on that day was described, "he made a tour of twenty-three hospitals or homes, providing for religious services at eleven of them." In the report for 1882, the Directors of Public Institutions made reference to the resumption of Protestant worship services and the organization of a Sunday School at the Marcella Street Home by Mr. Waldron and acknowledged the "elevating and moral influence" of the activities. This extensive program continued through the end of the Cushing era.

The report for 1850, in defending the workers of the Society against the criticism that they were spending far too much of their time caring for the temporal wants of the poor, said:

> The object of the Saviour's mission on earth was to seek and save the lost; but while here He was often touched with compassion for the physical sufferings of those about Him. By His miracles He supplied their wants, and thus proved not only the divinity of His mission but the kindness of His heart. He was the friend of the poor. Thus must it ever be.[10]

As the years went by, this line of argument was worked out more specifically. In 1854, the report again noted objections to relief work, but insisted that the missionaries acted on the example of the Saviour "whose miracles, while principally designed for moral effect, were also miracles of relief from physical wants and maladies." The following year the defense had taken a much more practical turn: it portrayed a missionary going into a household for the first time; as a perfect stranger he gets in the door and he looks at people in a state of sheer wretchedness and destitution. Now, the report asks, what shall he do? Does he offer them a tract, inquire if they go to church, or what they do to assure their eternal well-being, or tell them that they are in God's care? And the report answers that if the missionary acts like that he can add 'one' to the number of visits made on his report, "but the kingdom of God has not come nigh that household." Then the report proposes an alternate way: relief of need given with a loving heart first, then other hearts will "be unlocked to hear of Him who loves us all." Ten years later the entire matter has been turned completely around. The work of the missionaries "will not be regarded as Christian, unless it is humane." Church members are urged to make their gifts for the needy through the missionaries because they are well acquainted with that class of people and can discriminate between the worthy poor and the imposters. In 1874: "But we need not argue the case. A pure and living church never has existed, and never can, where the relief of the poor is neglected."

In 1879, the Associated Charities of Boston was formed. The purpose was to unite all agencies doing charitable work in the city in an organization that would be a clearing house for cases, thus eliminating duplication of effort as far as possible and as a means through which the various societies might learn from each other. The City Missionary Society was asked to join. There were those on the Board and in the churches who thought the Society ought to join since it carried on an extensive relief work. But in the end the Society voted not to become a member, "we are not a society for the temporal wants of the poor. That is not our mission." The Society further said that the missionaries knew their cases so intimately that the danger of their being imposed upon was slight; that they dealt with some families who would rather starve than have their names "entered on the lists of promiscuous charity"; and that if the missionaries came upon a doubtful case they would check with the Associated Charities.

Each year the Society maintained a relief fund. This was kept separate by the treasurer from the missionary funds; churches and individuals gave separately to the two funds. The Society insisted that the money for relief should not be taken from the regular income. In 1850, the amount available for relief was $850, and in 1890, $5,564. The fund had risen to $9,952 in 1880, but after that it slowly declined. During the whole era $200,111 was contributed for relief. Thus, when the number of missionaries employed, the number of visits the missionaries made, and the number of destitute, needy people they met, is all taken into account, the amount put in their hands for relief was indeed small. And when the total

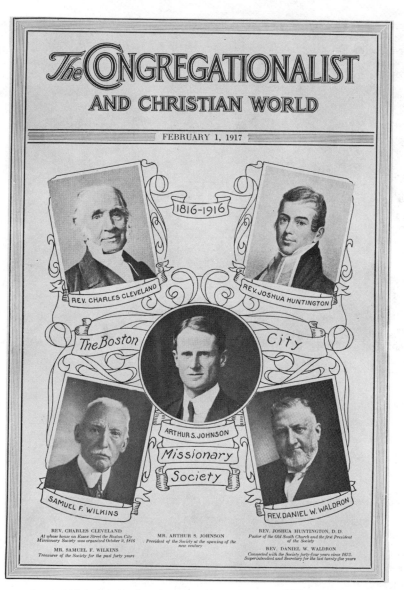

The CONGREGATIONALIST
AND CHRISTIAN WORLD

FEBRUARY 1, 1917

1816–1916

REV. CHARLES CLEVELAND

REV. JOSHUA HUNTINGTON

The Boston   City

ARTHUR S. JOHNSON

Missionary

Society

SAMUEL F. WILKINS

REV. DANIEL W. WALDRON

REV. CHARLES CLEVELAND
*At whose house on Essex Street the Boston City
Missionary Society was organized October 9, 1816*

MR. ARTHUR S. JOHNSON
*President of the Society at the opening of the
new century*

REV. JOSHUA HUNTINGTON, D. D.
*Pastor of the Old South Church and the first President
of the Society*

MR. SAMUEL F. WILKINS
Treasurer of the Society for the past forty years

REV. DANIEL W. WALDRON
*Connected with the Society forty-four years since 1872.
Superintendent and Secretary for the last twenty-five years*

100th Anniversary Issue of *The Congregationalist*

International group of children celebrating the
100th anniversary of the Society, February 5, 1917

is broken down in terms of work, it appears even smaller. Making $9,952 available to 20 missionaries in one year means about $500 for each; the twenty missionaries were in touch with 11,832 families, meaning that each missionary had visited nearly 600 families one or more times. The twenty missionaries had rendered "pecuniary aid" to 2,659 families. Surely, that does not suggest a lavish showering of wealth upon the needy. But relief work had become an accepted part of the Society's program.

Another field of endeavor for the Society developed in an unexpected way. The year was 1865: "The children of our mission Sabbath School had been promised a picnic by the superintendant." Early in September two hundred parents and children went to Hingham by boat, rode three miles in carriages to the beach, had a feast in the public house and returned to their homes by the same means as they came. The year was 1868: "one missionary has been very kindly supplied, by a benevolent gentleman, with a large number of steamboat tickets, enabling invalids and other poor women, who have no country-seat or watering place to which they can resort in the long hot days of summer, to take a pleasant and healthful excursion in the harbor." The year was 1871: "through the kindness of one it was my privilege to confer the pleasure of a trip to Hingham, or Nantasket, upon about sixty persons connected with the families in my district." In 1897, the Young Men's Christian Union gave money to some of the missionaries so they could take a number of infirm people out for a ride; a well-to-do gentleman paid for seventy-five parents and children to go by boat to Nantasket, and for tickets on the horse-cars so that a number could have a ride into the country; and a lady hired a large sleigh "with plenty of warm robes," took twenty girls on a ride, and then gave them a feast at her house.

In 1880, those spontaneous and unrelated episodes were the inspiration of an article in *The Congregationalist* which suggested among other things that people with some extra money might donate it to the Society so that the poor and sick might have a day in the country. The response was immediate. One man, Mr. R. L. Day, a State Street broker and a loyal church member, sent a sum of money to the Society with the instruction that it be used to establish "The Fresh Air Fund." Another man reading the article offered the use of a house in South Framingham for the summer. And sufficient money was sent in to pay for more than a thousand street car rides. Annual contributions mounted rapidly; after eight years the total passed $10,000. The street car lines— Highland Street Railway, Metropolitan Railway, Consolidated Horse Railway Co., the West End Street Railway, and the Boston, Revere Beach and Lynn—gave hundreds of dollars worth of tickets year after year. The steamboat lines—Boston and Hingham Steamboat Co. and the Hingham, Hull and Downes Landing Steamboat Co.—did likewise. Mr. William Tufts donated hundreds of dollars worth of ice cream. Thousands of individuals, adults and children, were given a day out of the city during the summer months, and many thousands more were given an excursion of briefer duration, either to a park, or on a boat cruise around the harbor. The Fresh Air Fund became an established part of the Society's program.

In 1878, D. L. Moody, while having a holiday in Northfield, had an idea. He found the farmers in the area with more apples than they were able to sell, so he suggested giving them to the Society for distribution among the poor. The young people of Northfield picked the apples, two firms donated bags, a trucking company carried the bags to the railroad station without charge, and the railroad transported the bags to Boston free. Two years later, the idea of making such donations having spread beyond Northfield, "over four thousand bushels of apples, besides pears, peaches, and vegetables were received from upwards of two hundred contributors, and were distributed among more than one thousand five hundred families, selected by our missionaries," while some were given to various charitable institutions. There is no further reference to that activity after the year 1881.

Funds to provide Thanksgiving dinners for the poor were raised for the first time in 1878. That year enough money was given to the Society to provide for more than four hundred families. By 1886, more than 1200 families were being given Thanksgiving dinners. That same year, 1878, members of the Board of the So- home for poor children reported progress." Boston, May 14, 1888

Miss Steel Elliott, who had been troubled when she learned that there were people in hospitals at Christmas time who were not remembered by anyone. She wrote letters of Christmas greeting, and late on Christmas Eve took them to the hospital near her home and put them under the pillows of the patients. Miss Elliott's work grew into the Hospital Pillow Mission. The Society borrowed the idea, renamed it the Christmas Letter Mission, and purposed to greet the inmates of homes and hospitals with letters and cards at Christmas time. In 1883, over eighteen thousand separate greetings were sent to people in nineteen institutions, and to shut-ins whom the missionaries knew. The cost of that program was met by special gifts; the greetings were sent by mail. The program was continuing at the close of the Cushing era. Another idea, picked up from England at about the same time was known as the Easter Card Mission. Cards were addressed to the inmates of the city institutions, appropriate for the Easter season. On Easter Sunday, beginning fairly early in the morning, these were taken personally by workers of the Society under the leadership of Mr. Waldron, and handed to the individuals for whom they were intended. In 1885, over 23,000 Easter cards were distributed in thirty institutions and in the homes of the aged and the sick whom the missionaries knew. Those two missions, the Christmas and the Easter, were carried on as a means by which the message of the Christian Gospel might be heard by those who, on those high, holy days, might not otherwise hear it.

Toward the end of the Cushing era an event occurred which further added to the program of the Society; however, all the details are shrouded in mystery. Boston, March 19, 1888 ". . . A proposition having come from the family of H. T. Farmer to make over to the City Missionary Society a building recently erected for a summer home for poor children in Eliot, Maine, it was voted to refer the whole matter to Messrs. Tufts, Waldron and Stanwood, with full power."[41] Boston, April 9, 1888 ". . . The president [Mr. Tufts] in behalf of the committee to whom was referred the proposition of Mr. Farmer of Eliot, Maine, to make over to the City Missionary Society a building to be used as a summer home for poor children reported progress." Boston, May 14, 1888

". . . interesting facts were also given in regard to Rosemary Cottage at Eliot, Maine, and the statement made that over $2000 in money and goods had been secured or pledged for that object."[42] And that is the record. Shortly thereafter Mr. Waldron was taken ill and was given six months leave of absence. In the annual report of the Society for the year 1888, distributed early in the year 1889, there is a picture, and a detailed description of Rosemary Cottage, and a statement about it which begins: "It is known to most friends of the city missions that Rosemary Cottage has been given . . . for a summer home, where tired mothers, feeble children, and overworked shop girls can find a temporary respite from the burdens of poverty and toil." In 1890, 263 persons spent an average of two weeks each at the cottage, "at an expense of $6.88 for each person."

Other developments involved decisions with larger implications. In 1863, the Board sent Cushing to New York to investigate a plan of work among the poor which had been adopted there. The plan had its origin in Great Britain and was the result of consultations between the Bible Society and the City Missionary Society in London. Under the plan, poor women of limited education, but of good character and sincere Christian commitment were employed to visit among the poor, to read the Bible to them and get them to participate in a savings plan under which a poor family would make a deposit with a Bible woman regularly, the fund so accumulated to be used for the purchase of needed supplies—fuel, clothing, etc., and a Bible. The Bible women were under the direction of a superintendent, who supervised the work, gave the women instructions and served as banker for the money put into the workers' hands. There were a number of ideas behind the plan: a poor woman, being one of the poor, was in a much better position to understand those she sought to help than was a woman in comfortable circumstances. The poor needed to learn how to save, for one of their greatest weaknesses was their complete inability to plan; and when a person paid for a Bible he was more apt to take it seriously than if it had been given him. The superintendent, in addition to supervising the Bible women, also conducted the mothers' meetings. The plan had been adopted practically as it was conducted in England by the New York City Society.

Cushing returned from his tour of investigation and made a detailed report to the Board. He made a number of observations: that the success of the plan actually depended on the superintendent; that poor people, hard pressed for funds, are not apt to buy Bibles; and that the reason why poor people did not save was because they had nothing to save, not because they were improvident. The Board discussed the plan and Cushing's report at some length, and voted against adopting it, either as a whole or in some modified form. They agreed that the plan of the Society "of employing more intelligent, experienced and better educated women, in works of benevolence and piety, is far preferable."

The Society had been established after a survey had been made to discover the needs of the city; thus, objective analysis and idealistic purpose were linked at the very outset. Now again in 1883, the Society made use of the same device. Through the years, the workers of the Society visited in the districts assigned to them and made their own decisions as to which families they would continue to visit and which families they would drop. There thus developed, actually without any recognition of the fact, a group of clients, cases, beneficiaries, visitees, call them by any useful term, among whom the work of the Society was being done. When a missionary made himself responsible for a family, so that he called on that family repeatedly, and had gathered to himself a good number of such families, he did not go searching for more. With that as a background, the Board set aside one month when the workers were to call on new families in so far as possible, and to keep accurate records of what they found. Primarily, they were instructed to seek for Protestant children not in Sunday School. Nearly two thousand families not visited before were called on that month. The Board were surprised to learn "that fewer children of school age are out of Sunday School than is generally supposed; and that, in the case of many, there are obstacles in the way of gathering them in."[43]

Two years later the Board tried another survey with a somewhat different plan. A house to house census was taken in a particular area of the city (bounded by Dover, Northampton, Washington Streets and the water). Professional canvassers were employed, nearly three weeks was taken for the job and the results were carefully tabulated. The Protestant families not attending church were called on by the missionaries and some church members enlisted for the task, and invited to the Shawmut Chapel. The Jewish families were called on with the same invitation. The sixty-eight children in Protestant families who were not in Sunday School (the smallness of the number was surprising) were personally approached to secure their attendance. There is no mention, in the report, of any action to be taken in respect to the Catholic families which constituted about 50% of those visited.

Before the Cushing era ended the Board of the Society had become conscious that the religious "sentiment," as they called it, had changed. They had come to recognize the Catholic people in the population as having a faith of their own, even though the Board members thought it far from Christian. But, they had come to sense that there had been a "change in the tone of general religious feeling." In order to describe what they were talking about, they contrasted Socialism, which proposed that men could solve their own problems, peacefully if possible, but by revolution if that were needed, and Religion, which knew that men were sinners and were saved only through faith in God. Men and women were growing to be more and more sure of themselves and their own abilities to manage themselves. As this happened they turned away from God and denied religion any place in their lives. "It is not difficult to see . . . the decay of religious faith, and the spread of various philosophies which remove from man all sense of responsibility to a personal God." The Board realized, dimly perhaps, that the movement of the population from the country into cities had something to do with this, "men, roused and anxious for more stirring life, or drawn by the hope of larger returns for labor or trade, are seeking the great centers."[44] And they were much clearer about the increasing unwillingness of men to listen to the Christian message and respond to its claims. Yet almost at the end of the era, the Board made public a statement reiterating their trust in the way they had been carrying on the Society's work:

> There are vast multitudes living among us in neglect of God. They must be brought in to the Gospel feast or perish in their sins. Their day of grace is swiftly passing. [The] Lord's imperative command to every follower of Christ is 'compel them to come in.'

Andrew Cushing retired from the service of the City Missionary Society, March 1, 1892; he died a few months later. A great era in the life of the Society passed with him. But the work of the Society stretched out on all sides. Other hands took up his task.

CHAPTER VIII

The Waldron Era 1892–1918

THERE IS A TRADITION in lands ruled by a monarch that when a king dies the seneschal announces the sad event by the words, "The king is dead; long live the king." That phrase suggests both the change of leadership that took place in 1891 and the unbroken continuity that remained in the Society. But that is all it can do. In the life of the Society it is not at all clear who the reigning factotum was in the years just previous to 1891, whether Cushing or Waldron. The fact remains that upon Andrew Cushing's resignation in March 1892, Daniel Waldron succeeded him. But the succession was not a simple one, the putting of Cushing's mantle upon Waldron; instead it was as though there had been a change in dynasties. The transition was much like going from a democracy, in which the executive office is the servant of the people, to a monarchy, in which the ruler may and does accept advice from his counsellors, but in which he rules.

Cushing was a layman; he was the superintendent of the work of the Society; the Board and the Executive Committee had their officers and managed the affairs of the Society by their decisions. Waldron was an ordained clergyman with a true sense of the dignity and power of that position; he was the secretary of the Board and the Executive Committee, and at the same time the superintendent of operations. The contrast was all important. Cushing had his eyes fixed on the needy and the unconverted poor. He directed the work of the Society to the end that the Gospel of Jesus Christ would be proclaimed. Waldron had one eye, if not one and a half fixed on the Society, that it might be an efficient and an effective operation. Cushing directed a loosely organized evangelistic program; Waldron was an executive of high competence. Such was the change that came in the work of the Society. Daniel Waldron was born in Augusta, Maine, in 1840. He graduated from Bowdoin College in 1862, attended Bangor Theological Seminary for a brief time, then transferred to the Andover Theological Seminary, graduating from that institution in 1866. He supplied the church at East Braintree for the better part of a year, and then was called to East Weymouth, where he was ordained. In 1871 he moved to Maverick Church in East Boston. From that position he was called to the Society as clerical missionary in 1872. He had been made a member of the Board of Managers the year previously, but the reason behind that is shrouded in mystery; the Society did not usually turn to newcomers to the city for Board members. Maverick Church had been contributing to the Society for some years before that time, so his appointment to the Board could not have had financial implications. The members of the Executive Committee must have had some idea in mind when, after he had been at the Maverick Church so short a time, they asked him to join the Society's staff. Knowing Cushing's unshakable faith in individual evangelism and his almost exclusive emphasis upon that part of the Society's program, both in his direction of the activities and the reports he wrote for dissemination among the church people of the city, perhaps some of the businessmen on the Executive Committee had come to feel that a somewhat different approach was needed.

There is one tiny clue. 1872 was the year of the great Boston fire, in which many businesses were wiped out. That must have had an effect on the thinking of the laymen on the Board. When the Executive Committee had agreed to invite Waldron, three men were deputed to approach him on the matter: the Reverend James H. Means, pastor of the Second Church, Dorchester, and a graduate of Andover Theological Seminary. Mr. Arthur W. Tufts, and Mr. Richard H. Stearns, both leading businessmen of the city, the former a member of the Walnut Avenue Church, and the latter of the Old South Church, both subsequently to be presidents of the Society. The three men laid their case before Waldron, telling him that as clerical missionary one of his jobs would be to cultivate the interest of the churches, which was a polite way, even though an indirect way, of saying to Waldron that he would have to raise his own salary. Waldron could appreciate the meaning of the remark the men made, for as a Board member he had scrutinized the annual reports and he knew that for some years the Society had barely remained solvent. If he were to accept the invitation extended to him, either one of the missionaries then employed would have to go and the salary given to Waldron, or the Society would have to run a deficit with no assets to cover it, or Waldron would have to produce new income for the Society sufficient to pay for himself.

The alternatives were clear. In the same conversation the three men told Waldron that the Society wished to expand its work, which meant the expenditure of even more money. As the four sat talking Waldron could see in his mind's eye the ruin of the burned out city; perhaps he even looked out the window at the destruction; and he demurred. Why leave a growing church to which he had so recently gone for a gamble like that? It is not known whether the businessmen talked out loud, or whether Stearns took Waldron aside and talked with him personally, but one or both of those businessmen assured Waldron that if he did not succeed in increasing the gifts to the Society during the first year he was on the job, they would pay his salary. On that assurance Waldron became the clerical missionary.

During the years that followed, while Cushing remained the superintendent, there are references to Waldron's work: ". . . our clerical missionary has preached very frequently in the Chapel in Harrison Avenue." "Our clerical missionary has presented our cause in churches outside of, as well as within, the city limits, and the response made to his appeals deserves our grateful acknowledgement." "The Chapel work has been under the care of the Reverend D. W. Waldron." "Under the guidance of our clerical missionary, the Chapel preaching services have gained increased interest and success." "Reverend D. W. Waldron preaches at Shawmut and Phillips Chapels, and is responsible for services at Austin Farm, Marcella Street Home, City Hospital, and the Young Women's Christian Association." "A novel picnic for the benefit of the poor took place yesterday . . . the plan and management were in the Reverend D. W. Waldron's care." "Reverend D. W. Waldron, . . . has both experience and skill in the management of the Fresh Air Fund." "Reverend D. W. Waldron, in company with an earnest Sunday School superintendent, carried over five thousand Easter cards to various charitable institutions."

Beginning in the year 1878, the section of the annual report dealing with the chapel programs was given extended space, and a statement about the activities at each chapel was made. And that emphasis continued to be made during the remainder of the Cushing era. It is also quite clear that the Fresh Air, Recreation, and the Christmas and Easter activities were in Waldron's hands. And when the Board appointed a committee to work out the details of the gift of the cottage in Eliot, Maine, Waldron was made the staff member of the committee, not Cushing. It may be concluded that during the years Waldron served as clerical missionary he directed the Society into additional lines of work which were of particular interest to him. These did not clash with the program already going on, instead, in a most effective way they strengthened that program. There are no indications, and no reasons to assume, that Cushing and Waldron clashed; every evidence points to the most harmonious relationships between the two men.

Two years after he took office as secretary and superintendent Waldron had the affairs of the Society in the kind of order he wanted them, and he kept them that way during the years of his regime. He was an expert executive. It is easy to think of him as "a clean desk man," as an administrator who "ran a tight ship." The affairs of the Society were completely under his control. He was a money raiser of the first rank. He won and kept the respect of the businessmen of the city. Arthur Johnson, a member of the executive committee of the Society from 1908, and president from 1915 to 1920, said of him:

> I must say, as one who works with the executive committee, that there is no committee in which I have the greater pleasure to serve. When we arrive for our meeting we find everything in order and readiness; everything is prepared, so that in a limited time we are able to transact whatever business comes to us.[1]

During Waldron's era there were three presidents of the Society, R. H. Stearns, Jacob Bates, and Arthur Johnson, all well-to-do, successful business men, and only one treasurer, Samuel F. Wilkins, a leading banker of the city. Some of the men who were on the executive committee were highly respected in city and state.*

All were churchmen, all active in civic affairs, all having responsibilities in other philanthropic organizations. They would not have given so much time and effort to the Society if they had not been impressed by the integrity and competence of the executive officer. Dr. Gordon, pastor of the Old South Church, said:

> Mr. Waldron has graced this Society . . . by this central fact, that he has won the confidence of men of wealth throughout our whole city . . . winning to its Board of Directors wise men, to the office of president wise and influential men, and winning the confidence of the coming men and women in all our churches.[2]

He was good at promotion. The printed annual reports during his era are interesting and readable. He rarely used, as it was handed to him, a missionary's report, or even an excerpt from a report. All too often these were dry and uninteresting, sometimes bordering on the sheer sentimental. Waldron took the reports, and by using a case from one, he made the account of the work of all the missionaries vivid and alive. A reader was literally made to go with the missionaries into the situations they faced every day. Turning the pages of the reports of his era, it would be easy to think that he devoted altogether too much space to finances. Often the number of pages filled with money matters ran to fifteen or more, sometimes occupying the bulk of a report. But he knew the people of his day, and he well understood that when Mr. A. gave $5, Mr. A. wanted to be noticed for his gift. Waldron saw to

* Samuel Shapleigh (Board of Managers 1880 to 1915) a tea and coffee merchant; Jacob Bates (president 1910 to 1916; member of the executive committee, 1904 to 1916, and of the Board, 1898 to 1916) president of Cobb, Bates and Verra, a manufacturing concern, and a banker; Frank Wood (executive committee 1891 to 1914) a business man; Frank A. Day (executive committee 1900 to 1913) banking and brokerage; Arthur Stanwood (executive committee 1886 to 1907, vice-president 1904 to 1907) a leading business man; and R. H. Stearns (executive committee 1871 to 1907, president 1892 to 1907) department store executive.

it that he was noticed. Hence the long lists of names in the reports.

To see the other side of this matter, we must also note that in 1900, he cut the space taken up with finances by recording only the total of the gifts for the Fresh Air Fund, and the Thanksgiving and Christmas programs, rather than list all the givers, thus saving a number of pages. He spoke at many of the churches in behalf of the Society. From the financial results and the glimpses of that work, he was most effective. The minister of the Eliot Church, Newton, said on one occasion, that to the long standing rule of that church "that no organization should be permitted to present its appeal from the pulpit" there was one exception, Daniel Waldron, and that he never once spoke a minute longer than the time allotted to him. Eliot Church, Newton, gave generously to the Society during the Waldron era. He knew how to dramatize the work of the Society: he would invite a giver to a picnic at Franklin Park; he took a childrens' chorus to sing in a church; he got another generous individual to go with him to Rosemary for a day; and put pictures, well-chosen pictures, in the annual reports. He had a retentive memory, and had read carefully the reports of the Society previous to his day, so that he could quote from the earlier pages almost at will when a suitable occasion arose. He was skillful with finances. His budgets were clear and concise; and when the year for which they were planned ended, there was a balance. His proficiency in that part of the Society's life was proverbial. Even the banker who was the treasurer had, on occasion, to turn to him for an answer to a financial question.

When, in the report for the year 1912, he announced that the Society had suffered a deficit, "the first time in thirty-seven years that such a condition has existed," a careful appraisal of the financial reports for that year does not show what Waldron was talking about. The figures say that the income for 1912 was greater than the income for the previous year, although some of the churches which were substantial supporters of the Society had lowered their gifts slightly—Old South by $120; Immanuel Walnut Church by $250; Second Church, Dorchester, by $150. Those three churches were the largest givers in the city—but the losses had more than been made up by new gifts. And the expenses for the year were approximately the same as for the preceding year. What, then, was behind Waldron's remark?

In 1909, the Congregational churches had launched the Apportionment Plan, under which a church was assigned its share of the general and missionary work of the denomination, the church paying the designated sum to a central office which then distributed the money to the various agencies of the denomination. Waldron was nervous about this; he could not be sure of the effect it would have on the Society's income. He saw that if a church were to include the Society in the apportionment gift it "might work to the disadvantage of the City Missionary Society." He also saw that his work would be altered, if instead of being one person among a number of other persons, each appearing before a church to ask support, in which competitive situation he came off rather well, he was a lone voice speaking to a congregation who knew, before he spoke, of a large financial obligation which they were morally bound to meet. There was some discussion of the matter in the Executive Committee, and a disposition on the part of some members of the Committee to make the Society one of the church agencies included in the Apportionment Plan. That idea, however, was not adopted. And Waldron, wise businessman that he was, acknowledged that, "it [the Apportionment Plan] is certainly the right method; all the City Missionary Society asks or expects is that it shall have a fair percentage of the contributions under the new system." When he announced the deficit in 1912, which turned out to be no deficit at all, he went on to say, "This is due to several causes which we need not name. . . . May we reasonably hope that the churches which have adopted the Apportionment Plan will keep up their contributions to City Missions, never more important or useful than at the present time?"

Or, there may have been another reason for the deficit. Waldron was a bit proud of the financial record of the Society. Every year he announced, in a tone of satisfaction, the number of years in which there had been a balance. "We are glad to be able to report that the present is the thirty-sixth consecutive year closed

without debt, and the twenty-ninth year in succession that this result has been brought about without asking for special contributions." He also talked a great deal about "pay-as-you-go," and he
used to recount stories of men who sent checks because the Society conducted its affairs on that basis. "Another gentleman, not
a Congregationalist, sent $200, suggesting it be credited to pay-as-
you-go." But as the years went by, Waldron grew a bit fearful that
he was over-doing the business, that the annual balance, and the
emphasis on always meeting all bills when due, might come to
have a reverse effect. He read a letter in Board meeting one day,
"I am glad to continue my subscription to your work. If only you
had a debt I might make it double. But since that is a fashionable
luxury you are not able to afford, I reward your thrift by keeping
to the smaller amount." And having read the letter, he delivered
the Board members a gracious but firm lecture on the dangers of
the year-end balance.

The financial facts of the Waldron era testify to his ability. The
annual income and expenditure remained relatively the same
throughout the whole time—in 1892, the budget balanced at nearly $47,000; in 1912, it was just over $45,000; and in 1916, $52,000.
In addition, there were the substantial bequests that were made
to the Society during those years which were handled carefully.
Doubtless Mr. F. Wilkins, the treasurer, should get some of the
credit for putting the endowment funds in order, but Mr. Wilkins
became treasurer in 1877, and the special funds do not appear to
have been systematically and separately handled until three or
four years after Waldron took control. After all, even a banker is
impotent unless aided by the Board of a Society and the executive
officer. The number of bequests that came to the Society, especially from men who knew Waldron and worked with him, testify to the trust others placed in him, a trust that was clearly justified.

Waldron directed the staff of missionaries firmly. Some had
high respect for him and gave him their utmost loyalty; others
could not accept the kind of discipline he imposed. The former
remained on the staff for years. The latter appear in the reports:
"Miss X., who entered our employ last year found herself unfitted

for the work and resigned"; "Miss Y. began her work with us and then was called home by a sick mother." There were quite a number of sick mothers during the era. Every Monday morning, promptly at nine o'clock, Waldron met with the missionaries— and that meant nine o'clock, not five minutes past. Even on the one hundredth anniversary day, which was a Monday, he was in the office ready for the regular meeting, and "wondered why only one person had appeared at the appointed time." Before each meeting he had read the reports of the missionaries and he was ready with comments, suggestions, and directions for the following week. As one of the missionaries said, "ordinarily we come there not to speak but to be spoken to and to receive orders from our commander-in-chief."

Often he heard reports from the churches of the work done by the missionaries assigned to them, and when those reports were critical, he made it very clear to the missionaries that such should not happen again. Evidently, such criticism came with some frequency for at one meeting he observed, "I have heard nothing unfavourable from the churches recently." At the same time he continually praised the missionaries to the Board for the work they did. He was fond of using some words once used by the Reverend Edward Alden, pastor of the Phillips Church, and a member of the Board of Directors of the Society from 1862 to 1876:

> A more faithful and self-denying company of Christian laborers than the missionaries of this Society during the past fifty years we do not believe has anywhere been engaged in the service of Christ. It is an honor and a privilege for the members of our churches to be associated with such a fellowship.

Waldron must have heard Dr. Alden say that, or something like it, for he repeated it again and again.

When reporting on the work that had been done, Waldron always used the first person plural, "we", never "I" or "they". When a missionary who had served for a long while retired or died he made it a point to include a statement about her in the annual report. He may have been an exacting superintendent, but he had respect for the missionaries and he accorded them the utmost consideration as persons in their own right. At the close of his career, in speaking of his relationship to the staff, he said, "though at times there were experiences which were trying and difficult to adjust, I think all [the missionaries] have felt that I desired to do what was just and fair."[3]

He maintained a close relationship to the churches, and saw to it that the missionaries did their work in association with the church to which they were appointed. This was not so much based upon theory with him, that the Society was the missionary agency of the churches, as it was based upon sheer practicalities. There were two sides to this. On the one hand, Waldron was very much aware that the churches paid the bills, and that therefore, they had the right to expect some service from the Society, indirectly, if not directly. On the other hand, there was in Waldron's thinking a sense of the corporateness of the Christian faith, so that, to him, an individual who made a Christian confession must of necessity become a partner in the Christian fellowship. Waldron's deep interest in the chapel program testifies to his insight here, and he gave further evidence of this by his directions to the missionaries. Doubtless he never worked all this out consciously, yet he knew it, and therefore sought to keep the missionaries working in close relationship to the churches.

Waldron worked through, and with, the laymen of the churches. He knew laymen, understood their approach to life and their way of handling business and people; and what is more, laymen understood Waldron. He was not too much at ease with ministers. He was not certain that ministers were helpful to the Society when they knew too much about its affairs. He wanted them on the Board of Directors because there they could be told of the Society's work and the need for funds. He wanted to be sure they were happy with the missionaries assigned to their churches. But he did not want them on the Executive Committee, where the real decisions were made. Only two ministers got on that committee during the whole of the Waldron era, and then only as vice-presidents of the Society: The Reverend Samuel Herrick, pastor of Mt. Vernon Church, with whom Waldron felt especially close because of the Chinese work carried on at Mt. Vernon, in which Waldron had the deepest of interest; and the Reverend

William Campbell, pastor of the Highland Church, Roxbury, who succeeded Herrick when the latter died. When Campbell was made vice-president it was decided to have two vice-presidents of the Committee, the other a layman. Waldron did not want a number of ministers, with their propensity for raising questions and disagreeing with each other and talking endlessly about minor points, on the Executive body of the Society; he wanted them where and as they were needed. And he succeeded in maintaining such relationships with laymen and ministers throughout his era.

Waldron was conservative, thoroughly conservative. There were no new ventures undertaken during his era, no launching into the unknown, no innovations, no asking strange and upsetting questions, but a careful, orderly, refined carryout of a well-tested program. The parts of the program for which he had been responsible before he became superintendent were either expansions of activities carried on before, such as the chapel program, or the formalizing and generalizing of incidental events that were appealing and helpful, such as the outings, or the outgrowth of suggestions for work that other city mission agencies had started, such as the Christmas and Easter activities. One or two of the activities, started before he became superintendent, which were departures from the more traditional, were dropped. He wanted a well-understood, effective operation which went on undeviatingly. He preached at the Shawmut Chapel for twenty-five years, 1873 to 1898 and was chaplain of the Massachusetts House of Representatives for forty years, 1878 to 1918.

The turn of the century was a time of outstanding individual leadership in the religious and philanthropic agencies of the western world. The leaders were men who embodied the spirit of Christian business, a kind of combination of concern for the needy and the pagan, and a mastery of the executive practices that made for a successful and effective organization. Such leaders as John R. Mott, Sherwood Eddy, and Jane Addams, came to the fore. They were laymen, dedicated to Jesus Christ as they knew Him. They saw great visions and won the respect and support of the wealthy business community and thus were able to give form to their dreams. They were the ones who brought order to the institutions they served and made those institutions leading agencies of the time. Waldron belongs in that company of men. His field of labor was much more limited than were the fields of those individuals named, but even as they, Waldron incarnated the religious interests of church laymen of Boston in that age when laymen turned over to competent professionals responsibility for carrying out the religious concerns and the religious obligations which they made their own. Waldron was known, in public, as Mr. City Missionary Society. The term described the man.

He loved, as does every person from Maine, to tell stories. He did not have too many, but those he knew he repeated again and again. One of his tales concerned Deacon Samuel C. Wilkins, who was a missionary of the Society from 1862 to 1899. A member of the Shawmut Church from its very beginning, the organizational meeting having been held at his house, he was a deacon of that church from 1855 to 1899. "When Deacon Wilkins was no longer able to teach his large Sunday School class," went Waldron's yarn, "the request was sent to his home that, if possible, he would be present and occupy a seat beside the teacher. And," concluded Waldron, "his presence was felt to be a benediction." The same story is told of the Reverend William Jenks, the first employed worker of the Society,[4] and perhaps with Waldron's retentive memory, he may well have read it there and confused it with Wilkins.

In Waldron's period it was quite clear that the old Boston was gone. Before the Waldron era ended, the only Congregational church remaining in the same location as when the Society began was Park Street Church. In various ways the city had been made over: Fort Hill was removed and the Back Bay was covered with fine homes. "Where were once the homes of the well-to-do have become the haunts of poverty. Where the salt grass waved above the marshes a great and wealthy city has grown up." The population of the city had changed and was continuing to change. The Roman Catholic part of the population was in the majority and the Protestants had come to see that their faith was strong and viable. People of other races had come to the city, some of them from Protestant countries. At one of their meetings, the Board of Directors were handed a statistical table showing the foreign-born

population of Boston; a pertinent comment and a question were
added: "There has been a large influx of Jews and Southern Italians during recent years,—how far do Protestant influences reach
this host of [the foreign born]?" Moreover, the population was
continually shifting, the more affluent moving out into the suburbs, "most of our wealthy citizens have preferred to reside at the
Back Bay, Brookline or Newton, rather than at South Cove and
similar locations,"⁵ and the poor who remained in the city
changed from place to place with great frequency. The missionaries noted that the Irish remained in the same residences longer
than any other race. The movement was obvious:

> A steadily increasing outflow of residents from the central dis-
> tricts of Boston is one of the signs of the times. . . . The churches
> within the city are losing men of large affairs by removal to the sub-
> urbs, the fields of the inside churches are becoming more and more
> difficult and the financial strength of the churches is growing less.

In a summary statement, the city as the Society saw it, was like
this:

> Children who are not connected with some church and Sunday School
> are hard to find; we have the use of free hospitals for every kind of
> human malady; the city has a wonderful system of compulsory educa-
> tion; there are homes for the aged, for the orphaned and the in-
> curable; a great chain of settlement houses in different parts of the
> city is combating ignorance and superstition among the alien races
> who come to us in such numbers; highly organized societies for the
> protection of men, women, and children from vice and cruelty have
> come into existence; child welfare work, which has stimulated public
> interest in the better care of children, has brought about childrens'
> gardens and playgrounds, the Boy Scout and the Camp Fire Move-
> ments, and has made possible the maintainence from year to year of
> the summer recreation work, by which thousands of mothers and
> children are benefitted.⁶

All of which raises the question whether the Society had given
thought to relating its work to the city that had so markedly
changed.

It is worth noting the events, local, national and world-wide,
which, affecting Boston as they did, caught the attention of the
Society or failed to do so. The removal of the Dowager Empress

from the throne in China, the Boxer Rebellion, and the Revolution are all referred to in the reports. They were of great interest to the Chinese with whom the Society was at work, and affected that work. The death of Queen Victoria is duly recorded in the pages of the Society, although what that had to do with the work is not clear. But the panic of 1893, in which Boston along with the rest of the nation suffered, is not mentioned, indeed, the Society had a substantial financial balance at the end of that year. In 1898 came the Spanish-American War, and regiments from New England were involved, yet there is no mention of it in the records. In 1902 there was the great coal strike, which had terrible repercussions among the poor of the Northeast. The event is not mentioned directly, although to all who lived in Boston at the time, this reference in the report, "the cold December storm brought the shortage of fuel strikingly to the notice of our missionaries . . . coal by the pail and bag at famine prices is the last resort of the poor," would be clear enough. And in connection with the same event so would this sentence from the report of the following year, "the vacation granted our missionaries was never more needed, on account of the severe tax on their sympathies through the previous winter visiting families in need of fuel."[7] There was a financial panic in 1903; but for the Society there was a balance in the bank at the end of the year of $4,000. In 1912 came the textile strike which shut down the mills and threw the employees out of work. The only reference is that an unusually large number of people "were found employment by missionaries" that year and the next. This would indicate that the Society was coming to see itself from within its own perspective rather than from a dynamic relationship to an ever-changing city subjected to frequent deeply-moving events in the midst of which it was placed.

How, then, did the Society think of its work or its purpose, not alone theoretically, but practically? In earlier years the Society saw itself as an evangelical agency, and it carried on its activities as such: practice was the expression of principle. During the Waldron era the Society insisted that it was not a church extension agency. In the past, the Society had established chapels, or chapels had come into existence because of the work done by missionaries, and there was no doubt as to the appropriateness and the wisdom of that activity at the time, but the day for such activity was gone. Circumstances had changed. At the beginning of the era, the Society continued work at two chapels, Shawmut and Old Colony. At Shawmut, the services were conducted by Waldron himself. In the report for 1896 there was reference to a new Sunday School started in the Savin Hill area by the missionary there, and the comment is made that the enterprise should most surely be supported by the Society, since the area appears to be a most promising one. In the same year there is mention of the start of another Sunday School, but there is no indication of where it was nor of the church to which it was related, if any. And then the reports repeat the determination of the Society not to engage in such efforts again.

As though to emphasize their belief that circumstances had so changed that a chapel program was no longer wise, the Society argued that there existed in Boston sufficient church equipment spread equally across the city to accommodate all of the population who were not Catholic or Jewish. During the year 1897, a statistical study of the situation was made in order to show this to be true. This was more than a bit of office reckoning based on figures borrowed from other agencies, for questionnaires were mailed out to all churches in the city. An amazingly high percentage of returns were secured: of 228 Sunday Schools, 200 returned the questionnaire; of 265 churches, 234 made returns. Figures were then extrapolated for the insitutions not heard from. Adequate allowance was made for the Catholics and the Jews, and on the basis of the Federal census reports, it was determined that 240,000 people in the city were either members of Protestant churches or had no relation to any religious institution. Not all these people were able to attend church or a Sunday School, even if they had wanted to, for the number included the sick, the infirm, those confined to institutions, infants, and the people who must, of necessity, work on Sunday.

Some studies had been made as to the percentage of a population kept from attending church for those reasons. The Society believed, on the basis of some spot checking done by the missionaries, that the conclusion reached in those studies was too high a percentage for Boston, so they used their own figures. Assuming that three-fifths of the non-Roman Catholic, non-Jewish population of Boston were "old enough, yet not too old, and well enough" to attend church services there should be in church on any one Sunday 144,000 individuals. The returns on the questionnaires, after making allowances for the various services of worship held morning, afternoon and evening, and the possibility that some individuals went to Sunday School and not to church, indicated that, at the most, 72,000 individuals attended a religious service of some kind on the Sunday when the survey was made. In addition to the information about church attendance, the questionnaire asked for the number of sittings available in each church. The returns showed that in the 265 churches in Boston, non-Roman Catholic and non-Jewish, there were accommodations for 165,000 people, more "than could possibly have gone to church if they had had the inclination to do so." Obviously the Protestant task in Boston was not to build more chapels or to start more religious meetings apart from the churches except as such might be preliminary to a church relationship, but to make better use, of the church equipment already available. Thus, one line of work which the Society had been doing came to an end; "The Society does not claim to be a church extension society in the usual acceptation of the term, but is a 'ministry at large' to the poor."[8] "The great need of the hour is not the provision of auditoriums. We have enough audience rooms provided for our Protestant population, more than all who are able to attend divine services."[9] "If the City Missionary Society stands for anything distinctive, it stands for house-to-house visitation. It is the bridge which spans the gulf between the rich and the poor, between the churches and the neglectors of public worship."[10]

The pages of the reports during the Waldron era have very little in them of what we would call, the theology of the work. The Society is "eminently practical" and the work "has been systemized." The contrast between this era and the earlier ones is marked in this respect.

Some of the missionaries who resigned or died during the Waldron era made enviable records. Earlier reference was made to Deacon Samuel C. Wilkins, who was with the Society from 1863 to 1896. For thirty-two years he made it a part of his work to visit the patients in the City Hospital. He "always received a cordial welcome from the superintendant and the nurses, as well as the patients . . . he put illustrated papers, leaflets and small books into the hands of those who could read . . . and repeated the invitations and promises of the Gospel to willing listeners." He was the father of Samuel F. Wilkins, the treasurer of the Society and the grandfather of Ernest H. Wilkins, former president of Oberlin College.

Laurin Bumpus was a missionary for twenty one years. He started a "social religious meeting" in the Fields Corner district which grew into the Central Church, Dorchester. It was said of him, "having been trained in the school of experience, he was eminently fitted for the ministry to the poor." His son became president of Tufts College. Lois Rice was born in Lincoln and graduated from Mt. Holyoke College. She joined the staff of the Society in 1865 and spent most of her years until her resignation in 1908 in the district around the Eliot and Walnut Avenue Churches. The pastor of the Eliot Church wrote, "when we think of the church, and of those who now compose our parish, we wonder where we should have been, or if we should have been anywhere now, if it had not been for Miss Rice." Harriet Carter was born in Boston. After graduation from high school she went to Concord, N.H., where she taught for a short time. She then went south and taught in Port Royal, South Carolina, going from there to work with refugees in Washington, D. C., and then to prison work in Richmond, Virginia. In Washington she was employed by the War Department and in Richmond by the Freedman's Bureau. In 1915 she died, after forty-four years of work, thirty-four of them as the missionary to the Chinese. "The last year of her life she made calls in 1051 places where Chinese men were employed and upon women and children in their homes." To this list of missionaries might be added Miss Clara Dyer, 32 years; Miss Helen Clark, 34 years; Miss Alice Winchester, 21 years, and who after four years of retirement was asked to return, and worked for four more years; and Miss Amelia Jaeger who at the close of the Waldron era had been with the Society 25 years.

Eighty-eight different individuals served as missionaries during the Waldron period. Nineteen of them were on the staff when he took charge and he left twenty-one for his successor. Of the nineteen who were there at the beginning, one remained throughout these years, three for twenty years or more, four from fifteen to nineteen years, and three more from ten to fourteen years. Of those who were employed during the era, thirteen remained for only one year and twenty-three more from two to four years. That gives an indication of a change in attitude toward missionary service between the earlier period and the era now under consideration. It may also indicate a change in purpose on the part of young women. Aside from those surmises, there are two things to be noted, one is that Waldron did not employ a man as a missionary. He inherited two from the previous regime. Both died within a few years and from that time on only women were on the staff. It may be, of course, that no men presented themselves for employment, or that the churches with which the missionaries were associated did not want men in that capacity, or that the budget would not stand the expense, but what ever the reason the fact remains. The second note is that Waldron, during the years he was in office, had to handle the employment of sixty-nine different individuals and the severance of about an equal number. That, in itself, is a fairly large piece of personnel work, involving many interveiws and taking up much time. And that does not say anything about the effect upon the churches which experienced such frequent changes of missionaries. Waldron must have had to spend some of his time explaining resignations to churches and winning their acceptance of new employees.

Waldron established a definite procedure for the employment of a missionary. When a vacancy occurred or an additional person was to be added to the staff, the candidate was proposed to the pastor of the church in the area where the person would be working, or if there were no pastor, to some person designated by the church. If the candidate was approved by the church official she was recommended to the Executive Committee, who then, officially, made the appointment. The records do not indicate that a church ever expressed dissatisfaction over a proposed candidate, but it can well be believed, that if a church had done so, the individual would not have gotten the job, for Waldron's great interest in serving the churches would have stood in the way. That process, carefully planned as it was, must have made the personnel task even more time consuming.

Each missionary worked in a well-defined area of the city. Since there was a great deal of movement among the population, it was encumbent upon the missionary to be alert to the changes that took place. In order to make sure that the missionary did so, Waldron instituted the practice of what he called "exploring calls." Occasionally a designated period of time was set aside when the missionary was required to restrict her regular calls as much as she could, in order to go from house to house in her area to discover the people who were living there. A missionary would know some of the families, for she would be working with them and her interest would lead her to concentrate upon those families; the "exploring calls" took her into places she had not been going in her regular work. For example, in November and December of 1892. Waldron called for a period of "exploring calls." In those months 10,330 visits were made, 3,704 of which were upon families that had not been called on before. Of that number 2,093 were Protestant families. The same kind of exploration was repeated in 1902. Then, of 6,923 visits made, 5,483 were upon families not before visited, of which 2,050 were Protestant. In 1908, during a stated period of time 11,950 exploring calls were made. "Of those families 857 were Jewish, 6,157 Roman Catholics and 4,576 Protestants. Among the latter only 246 children of school age were not already connected with some Protestant Sunday School."

Day-by-day visiting by the missionaries was the method upon which the Society depended, regular and systematic. The city was large, the number of missionaries was few, and the attack they waged was on a shifting population. The missionaries averaged over 19,000 calls a year during the era. The number was less at the beginning, but Waldron, believing thoroughly in the method, increased the number, and kept increasing it as he brought the work into a better state of efficiency. The missionaries went "into streets and alleys which would have been untouched by any Christian influence had it not been for the City Missionary Society . . . [they have met] unbelief, skepticism, Sabbath desecration, intemperance, gambling, poverty, ignorance." They found scenes "of suffering from poverty and sickness, of vice and degradation, of destitution of God's word and neglect of His house, of unbelief and impenitence."

Generalities may describe their experiences, but they do not transmit the personal element involved: the feelings of the heart and the thoughts in the mind of the missionary as she climbed the stairs in a tenement to find a mother of four children dying of consumption, her husband gone, where she does not know. Nor the feelings and thoughts of that mother as the missionary walked in. Nor can those generalities express the emotions of the missionary who, at the end of a difficult week of dealing with an almost overwhelming number of varied situations, was quietly resting in her room, reading, thinking and letting her mind turn on her own preparations for Sunday, when there came a knock at the door, a knock by a child, knowing no one else to whom she could go, to say that her mother had been found in the street outside their house and had been taken to the hospital, and that she and the other three children were cold and hungry; nor the joy in the hearts of all those involved when the missionary came upon a family newly arrived from across the sea, knowing little English, knowing no one, scarcely knowing how to get to the shops for food, and the missionary, able to speak their language and to help them on their way: to job, to school for the children, and to church for them all. Yet behind the generalities of the statistical tables, and the few cases given in the reports, are thousands of such episodes.

In the mass and the impersonality of the city the missionaries were like tiny leaves when they fall on the rushing torrent of a mountain stream, yet they were precisely the means by which life might be found and made over. The work of those missionaries seen against the crowded warrens of the slums and the uncaring realities of a growing industrialism was surely like pushing a heavy stone up a mountain side only to have it roll back again and again. But the work of those missionaries seen as person meeting with person in transactions that went on in spite of the world yet right in the midst of it, became a warfare, in which, though victory and defeat are strangely mixed, there was the greatness of victory. "Our missionaries walk in His steps" was true in very literal fashion.

> They have spoken His own words of comfort to the sorrowful; they have put His courage into the heart of some who were ready to commit suicide; they have shown the drunkard the only way to keep his pledge; they have taken little children in their arms and helped discouraged mothers; they have put the foreigner in the way to learn English, and led him to the house of prayer. The only efficient relief in the twentieth century as in the first, comes through Christian agencies, in personal living contact with men.[11]

We may use another illustration to make the same point, by taking figures and words from the 1908 report. In that year twenty-five missionaries were at work; they visited in that year 21,884 families; 272 individuals were introduced to churches and 781 children taken to Sunday School; jobs were found for 408 persons; 16 drinkers signed the pledge; 1,536 families were given "pecuniary aid"; and "hopefully" 112 persons were converted. That is not all the missionaries did, of course, for they taught Sunday School, led mothers' meetings, attended neighborhood gatherings, distributed Bibles and Testaments where they were lacking and wanted, found clothes for those who had none, and helped children, new to the city, to find their way to public school. Now let those figures become real with a section of a page taken from a missionary's diary; it is all in short phrases:

> went to court, and a few words with the judge secured the freedom of a woman arrested for shop lifting; her husband a temperate, industrious man; four little children; she must be insane. Went to the office of Commissioners of Penal Institutions to have a father sent back to Foxboro. Called on the undertaker to plan the funeral of a child; then to the mother to comfort and pray with her. Went to see a young man, separated from his wife, tried to point him to the One who could help him do right; called on the wife; talked to the pas-

tor about them should they go back to church. Went to see Mrs A.;
found her intoxicated; got her and the children to bed. Must see her
in the morning.

The missionaries did not attempt to duplicate or to assume the
work done by other agencies in the city. They tried to use the relief
money they were allotted, for emergencies only, except as the
family was a known church family deserving the help of the
Christian church. They did not gather up orphaned or deserted
children and arrange for each one themselves; they referred cases
to the appropriate organizations, unless, again, the child was of
Christian parents and thus had a claim upon the church. They
attempted to distinguish between Christian responsibilities for
other Christians and Christian service to all men, and then to
keep the work of Christians separate from the common responsibility of the body politic for the welfare of all citizens mediated
through the more general public and private instrumentalities.
They did not always succeed, but they were aware of what they
were about. They had predilections and prejudices which sometimes controlled their decisions and their actions, as for example,
a situation involving a Protestant-Catholic marriage, in which
they invariably threw their influence on the Protestant side. But
in general they went about their work serving people in behalf
of the church and seeking to draw people to the church and a
knowledge of Jesus Christ. Thus, they often turned for help to the
Howard Benevolent Society, of which Waldron was president,
to the various groups working with children, the Childrens'
Friend Society, the Temporary Home for Children, the Infant
Asylum, the Childrens' Mission to Children, and to other agencies which could be of help to those they found in their calling,
the Washington Home, the Provident Association, and the Overseers of the Poor. As far as the records indicate, the missionaries
established excellent relationships with all those agencies.

During the Waldron era, primary emphasis was placed on the
relationship between a missionary and a church. After the assignment of the missionary was made, Waldron paid careful attention to the judgment of the church on the work the missionary

did. The number of districts into which the city was divided for the purpose of missionary assignments was increased from eighteen, at the beginning of the era, to a high of twenty-four in 1907, dropping back to twenty-two by the end of the era. Nearly every Congregational church in Boston was involved in the plan. Some churches were responsible for two districts—Shawmut, Phillips, and Union churches—in which case two missionaries were assigned to each one. In other situations two or more churches were responsible for a single district—Second and Harvard Street churches, Dorchester, and Central, Trinity and Village churches, Dorchester—in which case a single missionary worked with both or with the three churches. Sometimes there were changes in the districts, but these were not often made.

The implementation of the church-missionary relationship varied a great deal. At one end of the scale it meant nothing more than the church providing the funds for the missionary's salary without in any way being involved in the work she was doing, unless she happened to bring a family to the church. At the other end of the scale, the missionary became, for all practical purposes, a pastor's assistant, teaching a Sunday School class, advising the young people's society, meeting with the women's society, calling in the homes at the minister's request. And there were variations in relationships all the way between the two extremes. But whatever the manner of the relationship the missionary knew that in her district she stood for a particular congregation and was the spokesman, not alone for God, but for a definite company of God's people.

A typical church-missionary relationship was that with the Mt. Vernon Church. "The Neighbourhood Women's Club was established at Mt. Vernon Church in 1905, under the supervision of Miss Mary A. Ballou, the minister's assistant and the City Missionary for this parish district." Among Miss Ballou's many activities was "making eight calls a day for six days each week upon the families in the district," many of whom were not members of the church. This calling from house to house and getting personally interested in the mothers of eight different nationalities was the beginning of the club. Then Miss Ballou goes on with the story.

In making those calls I met many women with children who had no connection with church or any organization. They just lived from day to day with no object in view but to make ends meet. The club met twice a month. There were no records kept and no formal ceremonies. Some of the women could not read very well but they liked to hear talks and to take part in discussions on family matters. The fathers and mothers who sent their children to Sunday School were interested in the church services for the evening and some came regularly to that service. One woman, who had never heard the Lord's Prayer learned it by its being repeated every Sunday evening.[12]

In their calling, the missionaries came upon immigrants from many countries. Statistics, both of the number of foreign born living in Boston, and the number of foreign born who "had been gathered into churches and chapels or Sunday Schools, or were under the care and instruction of the missionaries in their homes" are given in a number of reports during the era. In 1914, there were individuals, either adults or children, from twenty-seven different nationalities, who had been reached and brought into contact with church, Sunday School, or local Christians through the work of the missionaries. The government reports of that time give the figures for the number of different people from different areas of the world living in Boston. The figures for the number of immigrants reached by the missionaries given in the reports show variations from the total number of the immigrant population. One thing stands out. During the era the balance of the immigration swung from the Irish to the Southern Europeans, principally the Italians, and the Eastern Europeans, the Poles. The story of Christian work with those races is to be found in the pages of the history of the Roman Catholic Archdiocese. In the records of the Society there are accounts of missionaries finding and working with people from the Scandinavian and other northern European countries. Clearly, the difference in religious loyalties was recognized and accepted, and the efforts of the Society were directed to the newcomers who were Protestants.

In working with the immigrants the Society sought two things: first, to make them feel at home in the new land by providing missionaries who could speak their language and thus help to keep their religious faith alive during their period of adjustment; and then second, to guide them through a process of integration in which they might become part of a cosmopolitan community.

> The City Missionary Society does not strive to establish little Germanys, Swedens, Norways, Chinas, etc., [note the list], but its aim is to absorb persons of whatever nationality into our institutions of religion."[13]

> We are doing a full share in the work of Americanizing them [the children of foreign parentage]. They want to be Americanized, the problem is to do the work as it ought to be done, so as to give America the right sort of citizens when they grow up to voting age. . . .[14]

The missionaries believed that the end they sought could be realized only as the immigrants met and entered into relationships with the established citizens, and they tried to bring about those relationships through church and Sunday School. But they found, as the reports show, that the task in practice was not as easy as it sounded in theory.

Of special notice is the work with the Chinese. That had begun in the preceding era with Miss Harriet Carter as special worker for them and Mt. Vernon Church as the home for that activity. The work centered around a school conducted to teach the English language, and other subjects related to American history and life. Other activities, Sunday School, week-day group meetings and a good deal of personal visitation had developed. Waldron had a deep and abiding interest in the work; he never failed to report on it whenever the Board met, he defended it against its critics, and he did all he could to advance its interests. In 1892 when the era began, there were some 1,200 Chinese in and around Boston. There were seven Sunday Schools conducted by as many churches and religious institutions for their benefit. In general, all those schools had adopted the pattern of work that had evolved in the school of the Society. From the American point of view that situation was a typical piece of competitive activity which had arisen as people in various separate religious

Dr. Daniel Waldron and his staff of missionaries in the nineties

A group with Dr. Waldron at Rosemary Cottage, Eliot, Maine

Reverend Earl W. Douglas
Executive Secretary, 1942–1958

societies had gotten interested in work for the Chinese. The com-
petition came to be felt by those societies more keenly as the years
went by. From the Chinese point of view the situation created no
problems, for when they wanted to get together, even though
they were attending different schools, they did so, and in
the meanwhile they had a variety of locations and teachers to
choose from when they wanted to study. Through the work, some
of the Chinese made professions of faith in Christ and joined
churches in the city. A Chinese who had done so, reported after
he had returned from a visit to his home in China that "hard
words were spoken in his village of the missionary to the Chinese
in Boston because the people said she made them give up
worshipping idols."

A group of the Christian Chinese got together and arranged a
very simple home to which men out of work or sick (not sick
enough to be admitted to a hospital) could go. The Union Chinese Y.M.C.A. was organized early in the 1890's at the Berkeley
Temple, and as one of its activities took responsibility for the Chinese Christian Home.[15] When Mt. Vernon Church moved to its
new building at the corner of Beacon Street and Massachusetts
Avenue in 1895, the work of the Society was carried on in the
old Pilgrim Hall of Congregational House. That was not a particularly satisfactory place, but the school was maintained, enrolling ninety Chinese who were under the instruction of forty-
five teachers. In 1898 the school was transferred to the new
Pilgrim Hall. At about that time the experiment was tried of
enlisting Harvard students as teachers. The young men began
with great enthusiasm, but gradually the numbers decreased and
the numbers of excuses for absences increased until the earlier
plan under which church lay people did the teaching was rein-
stated.

A number of developments in this work are unusual. A Christian Endeavor Society was formed at the close of the century under the leadership of a young Chinese worker who came to Boston from California. That organization, which was Chinese-in-
spired and Chinese-directed, paid no attention to the separations
between the schools of the religious agencies in the city, but en-

rolled members from the entire Chinese community. In the report of the City Missionary Society, "it has seemed advisable to discontinue our Sunday evening school and prayer meeting. Our pupils have, thereby, the opportunity to attend the meeting of the Y.P.S.C.E." By the end of the Waldron era "more than fifty Chinese had united with Mt. Vernon Church," according to the annual report. The membership records of the church list sixty-six individuals whose names are Chinese. These people were but a small part of the fairly substantial Chinese Christian community which developed in Boston, "a people," so the report observes, "singularly apart from the main currents of our American life."

A close tie was built between the Chinese community in Boston and the villages and towns of South China. The Chinese in Boston and the Americans in South China moved back and forth with surprising freedom and regularity. Reports are replete with accounts of visits by Americans who had lived and worked in South China and who would be returning there, and of Chinese who had been back home and reported their experiences to their fellow countrymen here. Collections were taken in the Sunday Schools, the funds were sent to China and letters came back telling of the use made of the money. All those interchanges came to be linked with the work of the American Board of Commissioners for Foreign Missions, as the contributions of the Boston Chinese were passed to the officers of that Board to be used by them in their South China Mission.

In 1904, a meeting was held of the workers among the Chinese in New England. Over seventy people gathered in Worcester, coming from thirty-seven different schools to consider ways for improving their work. Among other things, that meeting resulted in the formation of the New England Chinese Sunday School Worker Union, which from that year on held an annual convention. The meetings alternated between Boston and some other city in New England where there were Chinese living—Hartford, Conn.; Haverhill, Lawrence, Pittsfield, Mass.; and Portland, Maine. By the end of the Waldron era there were fourteen Sunday Schools for the Chinese in Boston. As one of his parting recommendations Waldron urged the uniting of all those efforts into one Chinese church, the securing of a Chinese pastor, and the building of a home where men "worn out by overwork" might live. He quoted with approval from a paper prepared for a meeting of the Sunday School Union:

> We have asked them [the Chinese] to go to our missions tucked away here and there instead of leading them to one large Chinese mission and church presided over by an educated and spiritual Chinese pastor. We have each wanted to have charge of our own little work instead of joining together and forming one large aggressive church.

The Waldron era continued other programs which had been started earlier. Through the years special gifts of food were arranged for the needy at Thanksgiving. The Society thought of Thanksgiving as a time when church people who were able, could help those who otherwise would find the day no different from any other. The missionaries were aware of the danger in the activity and sought as best they could to avoid it. Provisions were taken only to families the missionaries knew, and as soon as a family which had received a Thanksgiving dinner was able to, they were led to share in providing a dinner for someone else. The Thanksgiving Day program was also an occasion for the introduction of families desiring guests in their homes, to families having no relatives or friends in the city, who would be both lonely and dependant on the kindness of others for their meal. In that way, personal relationships were engendered, at the same time the holiday was suitably kept.

The Christmas and Easter programs continued in much the same form as earlier. The work at Christmas appears not to have been very large, nor to have developed a clear purpose or structure. Only an occasional reference is found to it in the reports. When mention is made of it, the indication is that Christmas boxes were prepared, with gifts of clothing and toys in them, and taken to families known to the missionaries. The Easter activities consisted of greetings sent or taken to the inmates of the various homes in the city, the aged, the infirm, the cripples, and the orphans. Each year, a team of missionaries, often led by Waldron, visited as many of the homes as possible on Easter Day, conducting brief devotional services in each and distributing greeting cards personally. In 1909, individuals in forty-nine different institutions were remembered in that way; in 1914, the number of calls was over four thousand. The thought was that through the work, simple though it was, the people shut away from the regular life of society would know that they were thought of by Christian people and that the Easter message was for them in a very special way.

The "Fresh Air Fund" program was clarified and further systematized during the era. Its purpose was to provide for people living in the crowded sections of the city who could not otherwise do so, an expedition of a day, or longer period, away in different surroundings. Tickets were made available for street car rides to a park; all day picnics were arranged either at Franklin Park or Nantasket Beach, with transportation and lunch provided; and a limited number of mothers and children went to Rosemary Cottage in Eliot, Maine, for up to two weeks. For years, the West End Street Railway Company contributed a thousand dollars in tickets to the Society to help with this program, and special gifts were made by a substantial number of people. The total amount of gifts for this purpose exceeded $10,000 annually all through the era, and sometimes went as high as $15,000. This was said of the days at Franklin Park, "They are more than charitable.... People are provided with a good time ... Mothers are care free for the day ... Children amuse themselves without peril of automobiles or cars ... they [the picnics] furnish occasion for families to fraternize with those outside their own narrow circle of neighbours, or their own parish . . . Beyond all this is the international character of the Fresh Air Picnic."[16] "Thirty cents gives a mother or child, or an aged man or woman, a whole day of pleasure under the tent or the tree, with an appetizing luncheon at the right hour in the middle of it." Another report, after describing briefly Nantasket beach and the pleasure a child found in playing on the beach and in the ocean ended, "Thirty-two cents takes a child to that place and back."

Rosemary Cottage was open for eight weeks each summer. A staff of workers was secured. Mothers and their children were taken there for one or two weeks. The missionaries tried to choose those whom they knew needed such an opportunity in a special way. Here are some excerpts from a letter written by a little girl to her friend back in Boston:

> When we vacated the steam cars there were carriages to take us to the cottage. . . . The land around the cottage is covered with green grass and trees which are mostly apple trees . . . Miss Hull, who is a school teacher, is the matron; Miss Buck, a school teacher, is the assistant matron; Miss Small has just graduated from college and is going to be a teacher . . . I do not know the cook's name. . . . We have everything we want and we don't have to wait for anything. . . . We have singing every night . . . and a mug of milk before we go to bed . . . Our room is clean as wax . . . We went to church on Sunday.[17]

The cost to the Society for the operation of Rosemary was five dollars a week per person. The total outlay for that part of the program was covered by special contributions. Quite a number of church members endowed a bed for the summar ($32). Each year, between 220 and 250 different individuals had a holiday at Rosemary.

In the report for 1910, there is the first reference to a Daily Vacation Bible School. Mention of that was included because the school was held in the Highland Church, with which one of the missionaries was related. Each year after that, the reports describe these schools which at the time continued for six weeks each summer. They were under the supervision of Miss Dorothy Black, who was the New England secretary of the Daily Vacation Bible School Association. The number of schools held in Boston increased each year; and the number of churches with which the Society was related where schools were held, likewise increased. Teachers were recruited from the colleges, Wellesley and Mt. Holyoke, and from among the lay people of the churches. The Society saw in those schools another constructive summer enterprise. More than that, they were enterprises to which the missionaries could send or take the children of their families. There are no indications that at that time the Society took any direct responsibility for the schools.

The Centennial of the Society was observed from October 1916 to February 1917. There were four gatherings. On October 26, there was a surprise party for Mr. Waldron, planned and carried out by the missionaries. There was much reminiscing of days that were past, an act of memorial for the missionaries who had once served the Society, and a response by Mr. Waldron. He went around the room in which they were gathered and told the stories of the men whose pictures were on the walls. On January 28, 1917, the public celebration of the Anniversary was held at the Old South Church, "the spacious edifice was well filled for the occasion." Mr. Arthur Johnson, a member of the Old South, and president of the Society at the time, spoke first. After some gracious words about the work of the Society he announced the receipt of gifts and legacies to the Society of $96,000, and then he sat down. The Reverend Jason Noble Pierce, pastor of the Second Church, Dorchester, and the Reverend George A. Gordon, pastor of the Old South, followed, recalling other episodes in the history of the Society. Dr. Gordon made the point that the Society at its beginning had "organized the feeling of humanity that was abroad in society at the time." Mr. Waldron talked about the history of the Society.

The following evening, January 29th, the Boston Congregational Club entertained the officers and Board members of the Society, their wives and the missionaries at a dinner party in the Ford Building on Ashburton Place. The Reverend H. A. Bridgman, editor of *The Congregationalist,* and president of the club was the chairman. Arthur Johnson spoke, and in the course of his remarks announced another gift to the Society, this one of $10,-000. Mr. Waldron told bits of the past history of the Society. Then the Reverend Benjamin Wilmott, pastor of the Eliot Church, Roxbury, gave a thoughtful address on the future of "The religious heritage which makes through Jesus Christ a free way for every human being direct to the throne of the eternal." And he raised the question whether the form of the Christian faith can possibly survive in cities. He suggested that if the faith is to survive in cities, the city churches must be endowed, laymen living in the suburbs must belong to those churches and be willing to attend regularly, and churches must cease to be one-man shows.

On February 5th, there was a heavy snowfall, but the gathering planned by the Boston Ministers' Meeting was held even though a number of men were unable to get to Pilgrim Hall in the Congregational House. Arthur Johnson, Mr. Waldron, the Reverend H. Grant of Eliot Church, Newton, and the Reverend A. Z. Conrad, of Park Street Church, were the speakers. The affair closed with a pageant directed by Miss Jaeger, put on by thirty-three youngsters representing twenty-three nationalities, which portrayed the work of the Society.

The next morning Daniel Waldron was at his desk at the usual hour. He wrote the annual report for the year 1917. The work must go on in spite of such diversions as a one-hundredth birthday.

CHAPTER IX

Into a Turbulent Era 1918–1942

THE NEXT QUARTER OF A CENTURY was marked by a series of tumultuous events in our country and in the world, that wrought changes in the ways of society, and in the outlook and spirit of people. Yet these changes were really the determinative forces in the direction taken by history, and the determinative forces in the affairs of Boston and the organizations within it.

When this era started, the First World War was in progress; American men were overseas in a struggle that was stalemated and terribly brutal. The emotions of our people were deeply stirred. There was much hatred and vindictiveness toward the enemy. As the war came to a close, an epidemic of influenza swept across the country, becoming particularly severe in the Eastern states. Numbers of people died, the disruption of the economy caused by the war was accentuated, and fear took hold of many. Immediately after the war, as the men returned from Europe, unemployment rose. Then followed a struggle between employers and workers, the latter to gain higher wages and better working conditions, and the former to retain the power and wealth they possessed. Some serious strikes broke out which affected many people, especially those who, in the best of times, lived on the sheer edge of subsistence. In the middle twenties, the country was deeply disturbed by the activities of the Bolshevik government which had come to power in Russia. Fear of Communism grew, people were arrested, charged with being Communists, and deported. It began to seem as though citizens found Communists lurking around every corner and in every organization. This feeling was accentuated in Massachusetts by the Sacco-Vanzetti case, which while involving a number of different factors, was thought of as part of an undercover Communist plot undermining American institutions. The two men were finally put to death in 1927. This only added to the popular disturbance, for the defenders of the men were as vocal and as emotional as their detractors.

During the last part of the 1920's the country entered upon a period of uncontrolled speculation. The market value of investments rose rapidly to unprecedented and unjustified heights and enormous profits were made, at least on paper, by those who joined in the game. Many did so, not only the experienced investors, but large numbers of the general public as well. Money was easily come by and credit readily obtained. These years were times of high emotion. Restraints were off. Prohibition had been adopted, but people gaily broke its proscriptions. In government corruption was rife. Then came the crash. Banks closed their doors, the economy slowed almost to a halt, millions were thrown out of work, the wages of those who had jobs were cut, and there was widespread suffering as people tried to maintain themselves and their families without either a way to earn money or resources on which to fall back. The symbol of the thirties was a man of respectable background selling apples on a street corner in order to live.

The very order of society had broken down. Drastic remedies were set in motion by the government, but recovery was a slow process. People who had never been poor before knew poverty. As industry moved toward revival, another round of strikes occurred. That affected Boston as well as other parts of the country. As if to add further complications, Boston experienced an exodus of manufacturing to the Southern states which continued over the years. The country had not returned to normal when the Second World War broke out in Europe. Not directly involved immediately, many believed that America might keep out of the conflict. But the signs were all too clear that sooner or later the New World would be drawn in. Before the era ended, America was in the war, a war that changed all lives and the activities of all institutions in one way or another.

During this twenty-five-year stretch of time, the superintendent's office of the Society was occupied successively by two different individuals. But, with one major exception which will appear in its place, the program of the Society was continued along the same lines in this period as in the preceding one. Indeed, the one exception may not have been seen at the time as an exception, but only as an expansion of one part of the already existing program. Whatever the case may have been, the Society entered this era with three main types of activity: the general missionary work, the Fresh Air Program, and the services of relief for the needy. When the era ended, the Society was still conducting those same three types of activities.

In June 1917, Daniel Waldron was taken seriously ill, and early in December he died. He had continued actively to direct the Society for the first half of the year, and during his illness the missionaries and other workers continued to carry their accustomed responsibilities. But their work was unusually heavy, partly because the enlistment in the army of men in families under their care made greater demands upon their time and on their relief funds, as the main sources of families' support was removed. Also, the influenza epidemic created an unusually large amount of sickness in their families, again requiring much extra effort on their part. The record speaks of missionaries who found it necessary to clean and cook for some families in which every member of the household was stricken with the disease. The Fresh Air Programs, the days in the country, the picnics in the parks and the longer visits to Rosemary were maintained, but on a somewhat reduced scale, especially in the case of the picnics and the boat trips to Nantasket. The Chinese community became involved in the war effort and that necessitated some changes in program. During the year, the Chinese Y.M.C.A. moved to a new location on Tyler Street. Some of the contributions to the Society were reduced because of the war, but other givers helped and the affairs of the year 1918 were carried on with all bills paid, some money added to the investments, and the liquidation of a debt that had been carried over from the previous year. Mr. Arthur Johnson, the president of the Society, wrote the report for that year.

During the same year, the Executive Committee of the Board invited the Reverend Fletcher Douglass Parker to become superintendent and secretary of the Society, and Mr. Parker accepted. He was at the time the pastor of the Trinitarian Congregational church in New Bedford. Having spent two of his summers previously as an assistant at the Maverick Church in East Boston, he was not unacquainted with Boston and the Society. In his summer position he was associated with the Reverend Sidney Lovett, the pastor of the church, a relationship which subsequently had interesting results. The two men had built up a close friendship and a mutual respect for each other during the months they had worked together and they quickly renewed that partnership when Parker came to the Society, Lovett being a member of the Board at the time.

Fletcher Parker arrived in February 1919. Mr. Arthur Johnson had continued as president of the Society during the interim year at the request of the Board and he remained as president the first year of Parker's incumbency by agreement with him. At the end of that time, Mr. Johnson's resignation, all the while pending, was accepted. He had many responsibilities in business and the community which were most onerous during the war years and he felt that, of necessity, he had to put some things aside. Mr. William Ellison, a member of the Eliot Congregational Church of Newton, was elected to succeed him. Ellison was connected, not only with a church that for years had taken an active interest in, and made substantial contributions to, the work of the Society, but also with the Day family, members of which were deeply interested supporters. Mr. R. L. Day, was the one who, with his contribution specifically marked for the purpose, had started the Fresh Air Fund, and Mr. Frank Day had both served the Society on the Board and given to its support. Thus, the Society began this era with a new president and a new secretary-superintendent.

During 1919 the Society, under Parker's leadership made four important moves. First, the make-up of the Board of Managers was changed. This was done so that the churches in Greater Boston would be drawn into a responsible relationship to the Society. When Parker arrived, the Board was composed of forty-eight members, of whom twenty-four were clergymen. Those Board members came from the churches in the city and the two subur-

ban churches which for years had been interested in the Society
—Harvard Church, Brookline, and Eliot Church, Newton. At the
election following Parker's coming, fifty individuals were elected
to the Board. Fourteen were laymen re-elected from the previous
year and twenty-nine were new laymen; seven were clergymen, all
of whom were re-elected. Among the new members on the Board
were representatives from eighteen suburban churches: Arlington,
Melrose, West Medford, Wellesley Hills, Lexington, Winchester,
Wakefield, Cambridge, Newton, Melrose Highlands, and Wellesley Village.

The purpose in making the change was clear. Congregational
church members had moved out of the city into the surrounding
areas. Yet their business interests remained in the city and many
of them made the daily journey into Boston and home again.
While they were bound to become responsible for the suburban
churches which they joined, it was felt they still had a responsibility for the work of the churches in the city. Hence the Society
sought to establish a relationship with the suburban churches
through which that responsibility might be expressed. More than
that, it was really incumbent upon the churches of the metropolitan area, even though they were located in towns and cities that
were politically independent, to share in the missionary work of
the core city. One immediate result of this move was the receipt
by the Society of contributions from each of the newly represented
churches of up to $300 annually.

Second, the salaries of the missionaries were raised, an action
long overdue. The cost of living had risen, and the salaries of
workers in other agencies in the city had been increased, yet nothing had been done about the salaries of the missionaries. During
Parker's term of office three raises were granted the workers.
Moreover, the increased salaries were maintained during the financial slump of the early twenties. Third, repairs and improvements were made at Rosemary Cottage. Again, these had been
needed for some time. The property had been well and effectively
used since it had been given to the Society, but nothing by way of
upkeep had been done. At the very beginning of Parker's regime,
work was started, continuing during the following years.

Fourth, a summer camping program was started. It came about in this fashion: The Reverend Sidney Lovett, while the minister of Maverick church in East Boston, became convinced that the youngsters in his parish needed contact with the natural world and the experience of actually living in that world. He had turned his conviction into actuality. A member of the South Church, Congregational, in Andover, Mr. Frederick Foster, had given him the right to make use of a fairly large piece of land on the shore of Pomp's Pond as a campsite. Mr. Lovett had raised some money, built a small building on the property, secured some tents and other needed equipment, and had conducted a church camp.

Parker had shared in the camping enterprise with Lovett, had seen the possibilities in that program, and enjoyed the immediate and grateful response of the youngsters who attended the camp. The two men began to wonder why such a program should not be expanded, so that youngsters in other parts of the city might share in it. They invited three other members of the Board of the Society and two other interested individuals—the Reverend Benjamin Wilmott, the Reverend Ernest Guthrie, Mr. Albert Murdoch, a deacon of the Mt. Vernon Church, members of the Board, and Mr. Brooks, the boys' worker with Wilmott, and Mr. Witte, who had led the Maverick Church camp with Lovett—to join them in an informal conversation about their idea. That group agreed that the Society should begin a summer camping program as part of its work, and Lovett said that if the Board of the Society adopted that idea he was sure the Maverick Church would turn over to the Society its interest in the camp site at Pomp's Pond. The group talked further about the matter and worked out a series of proposals to be made to the Board for the conduct of such a camp. The whole matter was then presented to the Board, who at once adopted the plan. The camp was to be open for two months during the summer, one month for girls and the other for boys. The Society was to be responsible for the property and the program, including whatever leadership would be required, and the churches which sent the youngsters were to pay the camp fees.

Mr. Foster was pleased with the idea. He willingly agreed to the change in the management of the camp on his property, and suggested that for a modest sum he would deed the land to the Society. Not only that, but when some of the men in the Society, interested in the project, went to Andover to work on the property in preparation for the summer, Mr. Foster joined them. A few individuals made special gifts for buildings and equipment. In 1920 the camp opened. The arrangements were rough and primitive. Campers spent some of their time developing the camp site, otherwise, the program was typical of camping programs at the time, with set activities and awards for high standards of performance. The Board the Society thought of the camp as a means for accomplishing two ends: taking youngsters out of the city for part of the vacation period, and engaging those youngsters in a series of activities that would build both bodies and character.

For the first two or three years, the camp program was marked by a good deal of hard, back-breaking labor, done with a relatively small outlay of funds, as buildings were erected and improvements made on the property and the lake shore. Individuals who became interested in the program made generous gifts in its support. Church young people gave up part of their summers to act as leaders, doing so without remuneration. And the youngsters of the churches responded in numbers that kept the accommodations filled.

By the end of the summer of 1925, Mr. Parker and Mr. Lovett, having shared fully in the enterprise from its beginning, became keenly aware of the restrictions which limitations of time and equipment placed on the program. Only a small number of youngsters could attend Camp Andover, and there were so many in the churches who deserved and would benefit by the experience. With this sense of the situation in their minds the two men decided that one solution would be the establishing of a camp for boys, separate from the existing camp. If that were done, twice the number of youngsters could be cared for.

The two men set out to see what they could find. On Lake Winnisquam in New Hampshire, they came upon a most desirable piece of property which was for sale. They presented to the Board their idea for expanding the camping program and the advantages to be gained, and urged the purchase of the Winnisquam land. The Board agreed and took an option on the land. With the exception of a small area on which stood an ancient house, unlived in and unrepaired for years, the land was unimproved. Again came the task of getting a camp ready for use in a relatively short space of time. The old house, dilapidated though it was, served as headquarters with special financial contributions making possible the erection of a dining hall, two cabins, and the purchase of some boats. In 1926 Camp Waldron was opened. Much still needed to be done, but the campers helped and the program went on.

At that time, the values of summer camping were coming to be recognized by the general public, so there was manifest approval in the churches for the new development the Society had undertaken. The spirit of the time was one of disregard of confining traditions and a creative moving into new lines of activity. That spirit worked itself out in the lives of secularists and materialists as a disrespect for law, the gamble of the stock market, the excesses of the Great Gatsbys, and wild industrial expansion. But in the lives of those dedicated to a concern for the well-being of others, it produced such enterprises as Camps Andover and Waldron.

While this was taking place, certain leaders in the Negro community had opened a camp for their children at East Brookfield. They were in need of the same kind of assistance received by the Society at the start of their enterprise. Parker spent time with them about their project and then went to the Board with the recommendation that some financial help be made available. The Board voted their concurrence and for a number of years the Society made modest contributions to that work.

The other activities in the Fresh Air Program were continued during Parker's time. Additions and improvements were made at Rosemary: the accommodations were increased, the length of time the place was open each year was extended, and the staff was formally organized and put on salary. The Society continued to bear the entire cost of the operation, so that those who needed it most would be able to have the benefit of a country sojourn. The all-day picnics were planned and carried on much as in earlier days. Other organizations in the city were enlisted to help with that activity by sponsoring picnics with their own leadership and their own financing. The record speaks of the Y.M.C.A.'s of Boston and Newton, the Ladies Societies of various churches and other clubs taking poor families to parks or beaches in the neighborhood of Boston for a day. The trend was toward finding families to be served through the churches with which the missionaries were associated, rather than, indiscriminately, in the community at large.

The purpose of the general missionary work of the Society was stated with simple, straightforward clarity in the reports of those years. The missionaries and the work they did were the basic part of the Society's efforts. They were the fundamental reason for the Society's existence. Intimately related to the churches of the city, wherever they went and whatever they did, they represented the churches, speaking and acting for them. Parker sought to make the ties that existed between churches and missionaries stronger than before. On the other hand, the missionaries were closely in touch with the poor and the needy. They moved in and out of their homes, knew what the people were like and the problems they faced, and were aware of the evil in which people became involved. As Parker wrote on one occasion, "Our missionaries probably know more about the actual conditions of Boston than the representatives of any other social agency in the city . . . with the possible exception of the district nurses."[1] Yet they were neither social workers nor the givers of relief. Their task was to work with families by counselling and guidance so that lives would be changed. As that work of individual, personal guidance went on, families were drawn into the churches, and thus into the company of Christians.

The missionaries were at the center of the Society's program in more ways than one. The contributions which were made for the Thanksgiving and Christmas seasons came to be channeled through them and tied in with the family work which they were doing. So families and children whom they knew were benefited by the gifts that were made. They were the ones to recommend youngsters for camp, and mothers with their children, for Rosemary. They were the ones who recruited the individuals to go on the picnics. A diagram of the program of the Society, would put the missionaries in the center with a single line going out on one side to the poor of the city, and a number of lines going out on the other side to the various activities of the Society, for the missionaries were the connecting links between the poor and the program. Overhead would be a figure representing the principles of Jesus with lines flowing from Him to missionaries, churches, camps, Rosemary and all the rest.

During the years, two developments had taken place in the field of work with people. A great deal of knowledge of principles and methods had been accumulated, so unless workers kept abreast of that knowledge or had been trained in it, they were apt to be doing a less effective job than they should. Again, it had come to be accepted practice in similar agencies to assume more responsibility for the welfare of their workers than simply paying their salaries, even when those were adequate. To bring the workers of the Society up-to-date in the best practices of social work, Parker set up a staff training program. Under his leadership the workers met regularly for study and discussion. He also talked with Andover Theological Seminary about setting up a course of training for City Missionary workers in which college graduates might be enrolled.

Parker's training sessions continued for some time. The records do not indicate whether anything resulted from the conferences with Andover Theological Seminary. To bring the Society more in line with approved practices of institutional personnel management Parker recommended that a pension plan be set up for the workers. That was done. A capital fund was set aside to cover the annuities of the workers then employed, and a plan inaugurated under which the Society and the workers made annual payments to the fund. Pensions were to be paid to a worker when she retired, based on the conditions of her employment.

Two missionaries who served for brief periods during this era subsequently gained national, if not international reputations.

Miss Edna Baxter, who was a part-time worker of the Society related to the Union Congregational church, became dean of the School of Religious Education at Hartford Theological Seminary Foundation, and Miss Blanche Carrier, part-time worker with the Society related to the Central Church, became a noted author and teacher in religious education.

During this period mention is made of volunteer workers, recruited by and serving under the direction of one of the missionaries. For years the Society had depended upon paid, employed people to carry forward the work. The missionary assigned to the Maverick Church in East Boston saw that one way to multiply her efforts was to enlist the aid of church members. This she did. Thus, in the report for the year 1923 there are two names in the report listed under the rubric, "doing regular work without salary." This is worthy of note because of an expansion undertaken in the Society's program some years later.

Parker was so convinced of the centrality of the missionaries' work—he used to say that without this General Work, as he called it, there would be no Society,—that he urged a substantial enlargement of it. He pointed out that an agency calling itself a missionary society, and then trying to act out its name in a great urban area with a bare handful of workers, did appear to be using some strange kind of double-talk. He urged the Board to increase the number of workers. The Board agreed, and between the years 1924 and 1925 the number of missionaries was increased from seventeen to twenty-six. At the same time the Society had in its employ, besides the missionaries, twenty paid summer workers: the matron and six assistants at Rosemary, and two directors and eleven counsellors at the camps.

In 1920, the work among the Chinese was discontinued, and Miss Alexander, who had succeeded Miss Carter, left the employ of the Society. "Other agencies have taken up the work among the Chinese to such an extent that our work, which suffers from the distance between its headquarters [Mt. Vernon Church] and Chinatown, was discontinued."

Mr. Samuel F. Wilkins completed fifty years of service as the treasurer of the Society in 1925. He was honored on that occasion even though he did not retire. Reminiscing, he said that when he became treasurer, "the Society owned two $1000 bonds of the Jackson, Lansing, and Saginaw Railroad Company, a name which I think is indelibly fixed in my memory, paying eight per cent interest, the income to be used for the relief of the poor. . . . At the close of 1925, the Society held investments in the value of about $210,000." Increasing the number of missionaries, raising missionary salaries, providing a retirement program for missionaries, paying leadership personnel for Rosemary and the camps, together with increased relief needs because of the depression and the added workers, plus the rise in the cost of all operations, had required an increase in the Society's budget. In 1919, the income of the Society for all purposes was $41,276, of which $4,240 was in legacies, and $5,818 was from investment income and interest, the balance being from contributions. In 1927, the income was $83,205, of which $17,457 came from investment income, $9,984 from camp fees and $2,000 from free legacies. As nearly as can be determined, since the practice of itemizing the sources of contributions in the annual reports was discontinued at the time, the income from the churches remained about the same. There was a slight increase from $14,600 to $15,455. However, such a comparison is relatively meaningless, since the substantial gifts from individuals which accounted for the increase in total income over the years, came, without doubt, from church members.

This is not the whole of the financial story. In 1921, which is the first year after Parker's coming when figures are available, the invested funds of the Society totaled $188,213. In 1927 the total was $376,571, the assets of the Society having practically doubled in the space of a few years. Again, it is essential to remember that money was relatively free during those years and people were generous.

While Parker was with the Society, he made a number of interesting recommendations. As he looked at the city and the Society, he attempted to state what he thought to be the immediate needs which the Society should try to meet and the long-range developments for which the Society should begin to prepare.

These were the visions of a prophet and, whether right or wrong, should be recorded as the expression of one who as executive of the Society, sensed changes which ought to be taken into account. The visions, and Parker's suggestions for their implementation, came early in the time he spent with the Society. Later, the pressure of affairs and the responsibilities for the work occupied all his time and no more is heard about them. But they are in the record as the counsel of a person entering a new age and seeing that the Society and the churches it represented needed to make some adjustments and do some radical thinking in order to live in that age.

First, he noted that there were four agencies of the Congregational churches working at a missionary task. They were the Associations of the churches and their committees, the Massachusetts Home Missionary Society, the Congregational Church Union, and the City Missionary Society. He noted that there were also at work, only in a less general way, the Congregational Church Building Society and the "ever-generous" Old South Society. All four of the first mentioned organizations called on the same church laymen for leadership and service; all four went about among the same constituency for funds. While there was no criticism of the work each was doing, nor any indication they were competing with each other, there was the suggestion that one single Congregational agency in the city, raising funds for all missionary responsibilities of the churches, local, national and foreign, and conducting the mission task in Boston would be able to present a united approach to the people and eliminate the multiplicity of calls on their time and resources.

Second, he noted that some of the churches in the city were beginning to have difficulty maintaining themselves. Their members had moved to the suburbs, particularly those who had risen in the economic world sufficiently to enable them to do so. The people who had moved into the places they had vacated were either wholly uninterested in the claims of religion or, when interested, were so poor they could give little support to the church. Parker saw that if that development continued, the situation would grow more serious for the free churches until, fragmented as they were, they would no longer be able to make their witness to the city. Parker recommended that no financial support be given by the Society to any new attempt to establish a church, and that the existing churches unite their resources to form a great United Mother Church, with sufficient funds to provide adequate support for a well-conducted program of Christian activities. That Mother Church would have "splendid leadership, an adequate ministry, and chapels to meet neighborhood needs."[2]

The immediate situation about which Parker thought the Society should take action was described in this way:

> Our recreation equipment should be reinforced by a modest home with large grounds not far from Boston where a worn-out mother, a tired office girl, or some woman recovering from an operation and in need of a period of quiet and rest, could go, and where during the summer months recreation parties and picnics could make their headquarters.

At the end of August 1927, Fletcher Parker resigned to become the pastor of the Immanuel Congregational church in Hartford, Connecticut. The Reverend Ralph Rowse, pastor of the Broadway Community Church in Hartford, accepted the invitation to become the superintendent and secretary, arriving in April 1928 to take over the work. The program of the Society continued unchanged during the short interim. In the report for 1927, written by a member of the executive committee, there is a brief comment on the purpose of the Society. Evidently the subject had been raised in a meeting as someone had noticed the increase in the number of Societies working in the city for the benefit of the poor. The purpose of the Society, it was stated, was a unique one and there was no overlapping with the work done by other agencies in the fulfilling of that purpose. The Society sought to promote "the moral and spiritual welfare of the home as the unit of normal church life." All the work of the Society: the visiting and counselling done by the missionaries, the camps which served to train and develop character in boys and girls, the relief given, had that one aim in view. And there were no other agencies which did precisely that.

Shortly after Rowse came, the Board voted to nominate women

as members, and seventeen, representing the same number of churches were elected. Following that change the Board was composed of forty-two laymen, seventeen laywomen, and fifteen clergymen. The missionaries who began their work with the Society that year were trained people, three were graduates of the Boston University School of Religious Education, and two of the Schauffler Missionary Training School of Cleveland, Ohio. They were the first contingent of missionaries employed under a new policy which provided that, as far as possible, all workers of the Society should be trained persons. An associate for Rowse was employed and given a rather mixed portfolio: director of Camp Waldron, advisor during the winter months of the Waldron Boys Club, the membership of which was made up of campers; special worker for the relief cases which came to the office; and the planning for the next camping season. His salary was provided by a special gift. Then in the year 1929 there was added a review of the work of the Society.

No indication is given in the report of who made the review. From want of other evidence and by a linguistic comparison with other papers of known composition it may be concluded that Ralph Rowse did. Apparently he had an interest in that type of objective study, for in later reports there are summaries of other studies which he did. There were no recommendations made on the basis of the 1929 review; the document is simply descriptive.

It began with an analysis of the way missionaries spent their time. Each missionary was asked to keep an accurate record of a week's work and then prepare a summary tabulation. To that they were to add an analysis of the time given to the families for whom they were responsible. The report showed that the missionaries had dealt with between one and two hundred families, to whom they devoted considerable time, and between three and six hundred families on whom they called once or twice a year. Twenty-seven percent of a missionary's time was spent in general visitation, 21% in work with organizations, and 12% in work with individuals needing special help. Those figures were average with variations among the missionaries, but not specially marked. The general visitation was, in the main, with people who had a connection with a church, upon new families in a neighborhood, on children who were irregular in Sunday School attendance, and on the sick, the aged, and the crippled.

> This part of our work differs little from the pastoral visitation of a minister. It is carried on in fields where the work is more than a minister could do alone and where churches are unable financially to employ an assistant pastor or parish visitor.[3]

The surprising figure was the 21% of the missionary's time spent in group work. Missionaries were found serving as directors of religious education in churches, Sunday School superintendents and teachers, advisors to Christian Endeavor Societies, girls and boys clubs, mothers clubs, leaders of Junior choirs, and teachers in Week-day Religious Education classes. The review showed over four thousand different individuals were in the groups led or directed by the missionaries. The conclusion was that if the missionaries did not serve the churches in those ways, either the programs would have to be given up or the leadership jobs put on church members who were already carrying a great deal of church responsibility. In respect to the amount of time spent by the missionaries dealing with individuals, the review said that those

> . . . individuals and families are peculiarly ours. They belong to our churches either as regular attendants or members. When they get into difficulties which are too much for them . . . it is the privilege and the responsibility of the City Missionary Society to assume the leadership in the effort to help them get back on their feet.[4]

From that it appeared that 60% of the time of the missionaries was spent with the constituencies of the churches. There were exceptions. On occasion the missionaries did area visiting to discover new people, but that type of activity was given less and less time as the demands of the families under the care of the missionaries increased. The balance of the missionary's time was taken up with attendance at church meetings and services, conferences with pastors and officers of the Society, letter writing, telephoning, record keeping, and study.

The Review then went on to summarize statistically the Fresh

Air Program. Rosemary Cottage: nine leaders, 235 individuals in attendance for a total of 470 camp weeks, the Society paying the entire cost, except transportation from Boston to Eliot, Maine and return, which the guests had to find. Camp Andover for girls, then in its tenth season: eighteen counsellors, 200 individuals for a total of 518 camp weeks. Camp Waldron for boys: twenty-three counsellors, 176 individuals for a total of 521 camp weeks, with the boys and girls paying $10 a week toward the cost of their attendance. There were a few scholarships available. Thus, slightly over 600 different individuals took part in the Fresh Air activity. In general, the persons participating in the program were from the churches. In a separate report, it was stated that the program was being conducted at a deficit, and that invested funds were being used to make up the difference.

In 1930 a study was made of the boys attending Camp Waldron. Of the 174 boys present that year, sixty-six came from homes where one of the parents was missing, either through death, desertion, or divorce. The mothers of twenty-one of the boys worked; fourteen of the fathers had been out of work for part or all of the year. Twenty-three of the boys paid all their camp expenses.

But into this pleasant and useful round of activities came the depression, beginning in 1929, and growing increasingly worse through the early thirties, up to the closing of the banks in 1933, and the drastic steps that were taken to bring about recovery. The Society had to live through that period and deal with the situation both financially and through a changing program.

The report for 1929 indicates a recognition of impending trouble and a rather firm assurance that the Society would be well able to deal with whatever developed. The number of families who had to be helped financially that year increased by some 20% and the amount of money used in providing that assistance rose by about 30%. In addition the missionaries found it necessary to refer more of their families than before to other agencies in the city, which to both families and missionaries was a troublesome change. But having made the best provisions they could for those increases, the Society did not anticipate any great difficulty keeping its finances in order and its program fully operative. That

year about eight thousand dollars was spent refurbishing Rosemary, adding two bungalows, putting in electricity, adding some
modern equipment, a new water pump, a new refrigerator, better
toilets, and a truck. And the recommendation was made and
passed that the salaries of the missionaries be raised, although
there is no sign that the action was carried out.

By 1931, the report sounds a bit more tense and much more
concerned over the deterioration of affairs in the country. The
report opens with a statement of what the missionaries have been
doing:

> . . . to see that no family entrusted to our care suffers from lack of the
> necessities of life, to help children get the proper training in spite of
> depleted family resources, to foster among the jobless faith and hope,
> to bring love and light to the aged and sick, to attempt to build
> friendship in the face of circumstances which are often heartless,
> these are our tasks. . . .

Then Ralph Rowse, who wrote the report, launched into a discussion of the need for changing the economic system of the country in order that human values might be made primary. That was
a theme being bandied about rather widely in those days, and
Rowse echoed it. Then the report continued, "our missionaries
have not been decreased in number. Our camps have welcomed
from the poorer districts of the city the same number of mothers
and babies, boys and girls. Our grants for relief have increased."
The policy of the Society was to continue the program in the ex-
pectant hope that the abnormal conditions which had prevailed
would disappear. But the income of the Society had decreased,
and in order to carry out its policy the Society had sustained an
overdraft of $8,000, which was covered in part by taking from the
invested funds and in part by securing a bank loan.

In 1932, the Society continued its program, and made a special
effort to raise additional funds. The effort met with some success,
but the year ended with another deficit, which was covered by a
further draft on the invested funds. The cost of relief work had
gone up substantially. In 1933, it was clearly obvious that conditions in the country were more than a temporary maladjust-
ment, and equally obvious that the Society had to make immedi-

ate action to bring its affairs more nearly under control. At the same time, the Board hoped to be able to continue the program without any drastic change, so as to be in a position to move forward when times got better. Missionary salaries were cut, a flat amount taken equally from each individual, and other workers suffered a percentage cut. No missionary was asked to resign, but it was understood that should any of them withdraw from the work they would not be replaced. Camp Andover was opened for only four weeks instead of eight and the schedule at Camp Waldron was reduced by two weeks. Rosemary was operated for the usual eight weeks. Those reductions, however, did not save the day, for the Society had a deficit of nearly $9,500 at the close of the year, which had to be covered from invested funds and another loan at the bank. The Society told its supporters, in defense of those arrangements, that "we believe we have a responsibility to the individuals under the care of our missionaries which must be fulfilled if possible."

But the financial condition of the Society grew worse. One indication of the seriousness of the situation is a comparison between the giving of some of the churches to the Society before and during the depression. Seven of the churches which had been consistent and generous givers to the Society contributed $7,900 in 1917, and $8,000 in 1927. But in 1935 those same churches gave $3,170. And other church giving was reduced in relatively the same proportion.

In 1934, Camp Andover was moved to New Hampshire. The area in Andover had become crowded and the work of running two camps in two different places was proving to be very expensive. Some additional land was acquired contiguous with the property of Camp Waldron, so ample room was available for the joint operation. The buildings at Andover were taken down, transported to Lake Winnisquam, and erected there. During the summers of 1934 to 1936 only one camp was in operation, half the time for boys and half the time for girls. That resulted in a decreased operating expense for the camp program, although the increase in the cost of living offset to some extent the savings that were anticipated. The expense of moving Camp Andover was met by a few special gifts.

In 1937, the missionary staff was cut and the churches were asked to accept reduced service and at the same time to keep their contributions to the Society at the level of the previous year. However, there were clear indications that some serious rethinking had to be done about defining and carrying out the work of the Society. Instead of seeing the families who were in the care of the missionaries as being the responsibility of the Society for all their needs, the Board recognized its sheer inability to handle the required material relief. "Governmental agencies are providing the necessities of the people except for those little things which our own and other private relief funds are supplying." The job of the Society, then, was to "minister to the minds and souls of people." People caught by the breakdown of the social order need to know that someone cares about them, need to have words of encouragement brought them, need to be bolstered in their hope lest they fall prey to moral decay. While the government provided the minimum economic necessities of the people the Society must help "save the day for Boston in the matters of [the people's] social, moral and spiritual natures at a time when so much of merely material relief is being disbursed." That represented a considerable change in policy, forced on the Board of Managers by the circumstances of the time.

Behind the cold and unemotional words of the reports of those trying years must be seen the individuals who made up the Board, and especially the Executive Committee and the staff. They had to bear the anxieties of each day, the uncertainty that was rampant in the city, the fear of the unknown and immediate future, the complete inability to devise any workable solution to the Society's problems, and above all the heart-breaking task of facing day after day individuals who were suffering grievously in both body and spirit, and who had literally given up hope in life itself. The courage of those who did not give up the job they had taken upon themselves but remained faithful to the Society should be recognized. They carried within themselves the awful tension caused by their responsibility to the needy people in their care and their other responsibility of keeping the Society solvent and a creditable business operation. Theirs was an irresolvable dilemma, which imposed a heavy burden upon those who willingly carried it. No factual report should ever be allowed to dim the courage and the faith, as well as the uncertainty of spirit of those men and women who were then the Society.

There were changes in the officers of the Board during this era. William Ellison continued as president until 1937. He was followed by the Reverend Clarence Dunham, who has the distinction of being the first clergyman to occupy the office of president since the beginning when the Reverend Joshua Huntington was the president. Dunham had become a member of the Board of Managers in 1915, when he was the pastor of the Phillips church. In 1920 he left the Board when he joined the faculty of Gordon Bible College, serving first as professor and then as dean. He returned to the Board in 1926 when he became the pastor of the Pilgrim Church, Dorchester, and served as one of the two vice-presidents of the Board from 1935 until he became president. In 1941 Dunham resigned and Mr. Elliott V. Grabill, a member of the Highland Church, Roxbury, was elected. He had not been on the Board before taking the presidency, thus he came to the Society with a fresh vision of its possibilities. In 1943, the Reverend Robert W. Coe, of the Leyden Church, Brookline, became the president.

In the treasurer's office, Mr. Samuel F. Wilkins remained until 1927, retiring after fifty years service as treasurer. Mr. Elbert Harvey, of the Harvard Church, Brookline, was treasurer from 1927 to 1929; Mr. Philip Davis, also of the Harvard Church, from 1929 to 1938; Mr. S. W. Wilder of the First Church, Newton Center, from 1938 to 1940; Mr. Arthur W. Davis of the Union Church, Waban, served for one year; and in 1941 Mr. Charles Cummings of the Pilgrim Congregational Church, Dorchester, took the office, Of those men, Harvey and Cummings had been members of the Board before they became treasurer.

On October 9, 1941, the 125th Anniversary Birthday Party was held at the Harvard Church, Brookline. There were two outstanding features of the program. Birthday Candles were lighted in a "Candle Pageant." Some were "Memory Candles," standing for individuals who had served the Society in some capacity or other, and had passed on; others were "Honorary Candles," standing for individuals then living who had served the Society. The other outstanding feature was the presence of Dr. Ernest Wilkins, president of Oberlin College, son and grandson of men who had been active in Society affairs. He gave the address of the evening. On October 19th, a Vesper Service was held at the Old South Church to thank God for a century and a quarter of the Society's history and to seek His blessing for the future.

CHAPTER X

Large Dreams and New Enterprises 1942–1958

THE MILITARY FORCES OF JAPAN struck the Island outpost of Hawaii in December 1941. Early in 1942, Ralph Rowse presented his resignation to the Society and almost immediately left Boston. Mr. Elliott Grabill, who had assumed the presidency scarcely a year earlier, joined the armed forces. Two important positions in the Society were vacated at a most crucial hour. Almost at once, the Reverend Robert Wood Coe, pastor of the Leyden Church, Brookline, was asked to assume the office of president and, realizing the seriousness of the situation faced by the Society, acceded to the request. When he met with the other members of the executive committee, he had in mind the name of a man to recommend for the office of superintendent and presented the name of Earl Douglas.[1]

Douglas was born in Auburndale. After graduation from college he had attended theological schools in Greater Boston. During the years of his theological training he had served as pastor of the church in Orange, Massachusetts, and then, on his graduation had become the pastor of the Faneuil Church in Brighton. He was thoroughly familiar with the Boston area and conversant with the problems of the city. It is not known whether Earl Douglas had thought about the City Missionary Society and its work before he was invited to be an executive, but from subsequent developments it may well be that he had. Aside from such speculation, the fact is that Earl Douglas was asked to assume the post of superintendent of the Society, a title which he quickly changed into executive secretary, and, although he had been at the Brighton church hardly more than a year, he resigned to accept the proffered position.

When he began his work, the program of the Society consisted, in the main, of an organized effort in behalf of the needy and the poor in various areas of the city carried on by a staff of employed missionaries, and a number of summer enterprises for children, young people, and adults through camps and short time outings. The missionaries were related to the churches in the city in order to assist the churches in dealing with their constituencies and the populations in their areas, and also to draw the non-Christian individuals they found into the membership of the churches. For the summer activities, the Society owned camps in New Hampshire and Maine. Douglas defined all this shortly after he took office by saying that the program of the Society consisted of "Religious Social Work and Christian Youth Camps." He recommended that the Directors of the Society add that phrase to the seal that was used so that there would be no misunderstanding as to the purpose and aim of the Society. To this recommendation the Directors gave their assent and the seal bore that imprint.

At the very outset Douglas had to face and deal with the extraordinary and unprecedented conditions created by the war. Members of the Board of Directors of the Society joined the armed forces, ministers of the churches left to become chaplains, leaders of the various activities of the Society became increasingly hard to find, and the restrictions which the government placed on supplies and equipment made the job of conducting camps and recreation programs exceedingly difficult. While the program of the Society was well-defined when Douglas came, it was seriously upset by the demands which the nation placed upon all institutions and organizations in the body politic. There was a good reason why the new executive secretary took charge of the youth camps the summer after he began even though some of the Board members objected. No other person appeared readily available for the post.

But Douglas looked beyond the turmoil and the difficulties of the war. He had become the executive of an institution with a long and worthy history and a well-established life, and he believed that, serious though the contemporary circumstances were, they would not last forever. He saw that as soon as the war was over, the Society would still exist and be under obligation to serve the people of Boston. More than that, Douglas realized that even before the war, Boston had begun to undergo extensive changes. Perhaps he could not have given clear descriptions of what those changes were, but he knew they were taking place. And he realized that the war was bound to have far-reaching effects upon society, accentuating the trends which had already begun and creating new and unknown ones. In brief compass, Douglas sensed that a "New Boston" was already in the making. Because he was sure of that, he knew that an organization at work in the city had to remake itself to fit the new and unformed future or else become increasingly irrelevant.

Almost at once Douglas began to try to understand the real meaning that the work of the Society had for the ongoing life of Boston. And he set out to get the members and Directors of the Society to share in the search for that understanding with him. He raised two questions. He noted that there were many institutions and organizations at work in Boston, each of them with a particular purpose which it sought to fulfill. What, then, he asked, was the function of the City Missionary Society in the total life of the city? It was easy enough to pick out some statements made in previous years defining the work of the Society, but to do that in answering the question he raised would no longer serve, for the setting had changed. Government was taking over responsibilities previously carried by private agencies and the whole outlook of people had altered. The Society had to take all this into consideration.

The second question he asked was really involved in the first, yet for the sake of clarity it was raised separately. What, specifically, was the duty of a missionary? Again, it was agreed that she should call on the poor and help them handle their circumstances and problems. That was easily said, but it was much more difficult to spell out just what the words meant, especially when the complex of relationships in which a missionary was involved— church, Society, other organizations public and private—was taken into account. "Our work in contributing to the life of the community will be measured in spiritual terms. To be of real value, our program and methods must lend itself to a more vital religious experience."

Officers of the City Missionary Society, 1965–66

Left to right, front, Arthur V. Getchell, Stuart C. Haskins, James E. Gallagher; back, Reverend William A. Nicolas, Reverend F. Nelsen Schlegel (Executive Secretary), and S. Carlisle Crosby

Farrington Memorial, Lincoln, Massachusetts

Those were simple, quite obvious questions, yet they were absolutely fundamental, for unless they were answered carefully
and intelligently, the Society would be left to proceed on tradition, or at best, on tradition modified as changes were required by
the shifting forces in the body politic.

Such was the start of a period in which the work of the Society
was changed into a somewhat different form than it had taken previously. Thinking and planning and acting went on uninterrup-
tedly all the while. Doubtless some things took place which did not
work out. Certainly other things were well conceived efforts to
bring the Society into the very midst of the new world that was
coming to be. Douglas, through his awareness that the very foun-
dations of life were being shaken and his unwavering determination to lead the Society through the shaking to a new day,
changed the character of the Society in large measure while he was
the executive.

Actually, it can not be known what Douglas would have done
had it been necessary for him to lead the Society with the resources it possessed when he became the executive. Soon after he
took office, there came to the Society a bequest of over half a million dollars, left by Miss Elizabeth Garrett, who had been a member of the Old South Church. Douglas realized at once, both the
opportunities for increased service by the Society which that bequest made possible and the terrible danger in it, as churches and
individuals who had supported the Society might be tempted to
lower their giving, and thus their interest, when they learned of
the substantial endowment the Society had received. As he
pointed out the various pieces of work that might properly be
undertaken by the Society, he at the same time quoted an expert
in institutional financing who said that when a society depended
upon returns from investments for fifty per cent or more of its
annual income, the vitality and the effectiveness of its services
would be in jeopardy. Yet it was obvious to Douglas and to the
members of the Board that a bequest which more than doubled
the annual income from investments was bound to have a profound effect upon the Society and its future.

During the era a major change was made in the structure of

the Society. In 1948 new By-laws were written and put into effect. Under those new arrangements the Society became a self-perpetuating corporation of from sixty to seventy-five individuals, one third of whom were elected each year. No reference was made to any church relationship as necessarily involved in the selection of the corporation members. This did not mean that the connection between the Society and the churches was weakened. Theoretically, such was the case, but practically quite the opposite was true. The nominating committee was exceedingly careful to secure nominees for Board members from as many churches as possible. For example, in 1955 there were sixty-six different individuals on the Board of Directors from forty-three different churches. That year, seventy-four churches made contributions to the work of the Society so that while not all churches supporting the Society were represented on the Board, which would have been almost an impossibility, a majority of them were. The new Bylaws clearly defined the Society as a Corporation.

For the first time in its history the actual make-up of the Society was clear: the Society was the not more than seventy-five people who had been chosen to be the corporation. The corporation chose committees from among its membership. There have been changes in the names and functions of the committees through the years, but the principles of their choice and their responsibilities have remained much the same. The Board of Directors were the primary administrative and executive committee. The Board consisted of the officers, the chairmen of committees, and six other persons. The Board had "complete management of the affairs of the corporation, subject to the power of the corporation to determine matters of basic policy." There were seven standing committees: camp, religious education, Rosemary, missionary, investment, finance, and nominating—all but the last two having six members each. The duties of each committee were stated in considerable detail. In general, each committee was given full responsibility for the management of the particular part of the Society's work indicated by its name. Each committee was required to submit its budget to the finance committee, which determined the amount of money that would be allocated for its work. Bills of each committee were paid when they were within the budget allotment and after they had been approved by one of the corporation officers. The By-laws thus provided for a decentralization of program responsibilities and a centralization of over-all control. And a provision for the rotation of the membership of the corporation made possible, in theory at least, the enlisting of a large number of different individuals in the work of the Society.

Douglas was deeply interested in the missionary work of the Society and in the missionaries themselves, and he sought in a number of ways to strengthen that part of the Society's program. When he came there were thirteen missionaries on the staff, each one related to a church, and charged with the task of visiting among the poor to help alleviate their needs, to work with them personally for the resolution of their problems, and to draw them into the fellowship and life of the church. During his era sixty different individuals served as missionaries, some for short periods of time and others for longer periods. Mrs. Harriett Elliott joined the staff in 1944, continued through the Douglas era and remains active at the time of writing; Miss Mae Durkee came to the Society in 1949 and is still active; Mrs. Beatrice Nelson and Miss Helena Hanson served the Society for ten years each, the former from 1952 to 1963, and the latter beginning in 1953 and continuing on.

Special mention should be made of Miss Lucia Mikaelian. She began her connection with the Society in 1925. Her primary connection was with the Armenian people. For two years she worked out of the Shawmut Congregational Church; then she moved to the Cilician-Armenian Church of Boston, where she remained until her death in 1956. She was an officer in some of the Armenian organizations in the city, a trusted advisor to the older Armenian people who found difficulty adjusting to life in this country, a leader in the church, and to many, Aunt Lucia.

> She was not only a missionary commissioned to do a certain job, but also a friend, a sister, a mother, sharing with the family their burdens, their joys and sorrows, successes and failures, and leading them to the throne of God . . . she was superintendent of the church

school, president of the Women's Society, secretary of the church, church visitor, advisor to the young people, leader of the prayer meetings, and in the absence of a pastor, the preacher.[2]

Not all the missionaries were as deeply involved in the life of a church as was Miss Mikaelian, yet all were equally concerned for the welfare of the people with whom they came in contact.

A number of actions were taken during the era in respect to the missionary staff. Radical adjustments were made in their support and the perquisites provided. Salary raises were given on a number of occasions, but even then salaries remained relatively low compared with those of other agencies in the city. Almost at the end of the era, the Board of Directors learned that two of the missionaries were unable to carry out orders of their doctors for the benefit of their health because of insufficient funds. The salaries were extremely low at the beginning of the era, the cost of living rose rapidly, and the salary increases did not catch up fast enough. The pension plan which had been adopted by the Society years before was proving to be totally inadequate in the changed economic conditions and was discontinued. Missionaries who had made payments to the fund were reimbursed. They were then placed under Social Security, with the Society making its contributory share. That change, wise though it appeared to be when adopted, worked hardship on some of the individuals, for their salaries were scarcely large enough to stand a social security deduction without jeopardizing their financial position. The Society also made the missionaries participants in the Blue Cross-Blue Shield Plan. In 1954 a schedule for the classification and salaries of missionaries was adopted. At the time the maximum annual salary provided was $3000 for a well-educated worker with experience. By 1957 the minimum salary for all missionaries had been raised to $3000, after a "cost of living increase" of $500 had been granted. The Board was making a continuing effort to provide more adequate compensation for the missionary staff, an effort which, while unceasing, never quite managed to be wholly successful.

A number of opportunities were provided the missionaries for training in up-to-date social work practices. In 1944 they were urged to join the Massachusetts Conference of Social Work and take advantage of its meetings and lectures. The Director of the Home Nursing Service of the Red Cross gave that course for the missionaries in a special series of meetings. In 1948 an orientation program was adopted for all new missionaries. Beginning in a relatively simple way:

> Conferences are held in the Society's office to lay out specific assignments, during their first year, in the effort to help the worker know her community and those resources which have proved valuable over the years. Simultaneously, the new worker is identified with an older, experienced missionary to learn 'on the job' those valuable insights which can only be acquired through experience.[3]

By 1951, half the time of one of the missionaries was taken up with the orientation of new workers. Before the era ended that program was made a separate department of the Society's activities, along with other departments, and a director was appointed whose responsibilities included "field supervision and training."

One year the National Conference of Catholic Charities held its annual meeting in Worcester. As a part of the program of the conference there were a series of seminars, one of them on "Volunteer Personal Service," which was of particular interest to the Society's workers. At the invitation of Bishop Wright of the Worcester Diocese some of the missionaries attended. Beginning in 1952 the staff training program was given added emphasis. The child psychiatrist of the Metropolitan State Hospital gave a series of lectures to the missionaries. The following year the head supervisor of the Boston Public Welfare Department came for a series on modern public welfare programs. Another series dealt with various aspects of medical social work led by a group of leaders in the field. Then a start was made on a plan under which the missionaries might take courses at one of the Schools of Social Work in the city. That plan, as it developed, included both attendance at school while on the job and a leave of absence for study granted for a stated period of time. Each year after 1953, one or more of the missionaries were enrolled for courses or were on study leave.

A personnel policy was worked out and adopted. Typical of the time, it included the usual items: conditions of employment, salary, salary increments, perquisites, vacations, study leaves, and arrangements for retirement. For the older missionaries, those who had been with the Society for some time, the last item was particularly troublesome. Workers for the Society had, through the years, either retired when they decided they were no longer able to continue, or had died while on the job, as witness both Cushing and Waldron. To require a missionary to retire at a specific age seemed not only unjust but also the height of folly on the Society's part. As one of them wrote in a letter to the Board of the Society: ". . . armed with more resources than years ago, I am bedeviled with the threat of 'retirement' . . . there seems small reason for considering retirement as either imminent or inevitable. What is there about the age 65 that carries with it the need for suddenly retiring. . . . Some of the most useful and active persons I know are nearer 80 than 40." But the provision was included in the personnel policy and it was put into effect as specific cases arose.

Another development during the era was the addition to the staff of "specialists," that is, of individuals who had competence in particular parts of the work, or who were made responsible for some special enterprise. A number of such people were employed, some for short periods, others longer. Some were put in charge of departments and others of new enterprises. These specialists in the order of their appearance included a Consultant in Religious Education and Vacation Schools; Director of Camps; a Roving Missionary; Director of Public Relations and Finance; Director of Voluntarism; Clinical Psychologist; a hospital Chaplain; an Associate to the Executive; and, a Director of Personnel and Education.

The staff of the Society also was organized in a more systematic and detailed structure. Previously, the superintendent did just what his title implied, superintended the work. The staff members did different jobs, but all of them were directly responsible to the superintendent. Under Douglas' leadership the work of the Society was departmentalized, and a director for each department appointed. The directors then reported to the executive. In general, the departments were related to the committees of the Board, and the director of a department became a member of or an advisor to the committee. This was all carefully worked out in a "Table of Organization," presented to the Board in 1956 and adopted.

The work was also rearranged. Very shortly after Douglas came he pointed out the need for missionaries in Brighton and Chelsea and a bit later on he added Revere. By 1944 a worker had been assigned to Brighton, with which Allston was subsequently combined. In 1947 a piece of work was carried on in Chelsea. Juvenile delinquency had been on the increase there and an interested individual provided funds for an attempt to see what could be done. Under the direction of a college student who worked with the Central Congregational Church, a Boystown was organized. Enrollment soon went beyond three hundred. There was not much by way of equipment and leadership to help with the work, but through a diversified program the boys were led into wholesome activities. A pioneer project, it was neither followed up nor repeated. In 1947 a missionary was assigned to Revere, to work with the Trinity Congregational Church of Beachmont, but two years later the missionary resigned and no replacement was made.

Up to 1948 missionaries were appointed to work with and through churches, so that families with whom the missionaries dealt could be drawn into church relationships. In that year arrangements were changed. Missionaries were assigned to the Health and Welfare districts of Boston, and within those areas cooperated with designated churches. For example, two missionaries were assigned to the Jamaica Plain Health and Welfare district, one to work in cooperation with the Boylston Church and the other with the Central Church. The reason for this change appears to have been that since other agencies in the city dealing with people were organized under the Health and Welfare districts, it seemed best for the workers of the Society to be organized in the same way, since the missionaries had, very frequently, to relate their families to other agencies. In 1947 eighteen missionaries were assigned to seventeen churches, while in 1948 fifteen missionaries were assigned to seven Health and Welfare districts in cooperation with twelve churches.

A new area of work was in public housing projects. In 1953 one missionary was given responsibility for working in the new low-cost developments. She was to make door-to-door surveys of the new areas to learn the extent of the Protestant responsibility. Five years later, three missionaries and a part-time worker were involved in the task of keeping in touch with seventeen of the twenty-six public housing projects that had been built. Most of their time was spent in discovering Protestant families and relating them to churches. Occassionally Bible study programs and released-time classes were conducted in the projects themselves.

In 1952, Mr. Elliott Grabill, president of the Society, and then a member of the First Parish Church in Lincoln, a man who gave a great deal of time and thought to the responsibilities of his office, wrote in a report to the Corporation, "the initial and basic purpose of the Society is to intensify and improve the missionary program in the city. It is through the missionary service and as a supplement and corollary to the missionary service that many of the other programs of the Society exist. Thus, unless the missionary program be considered and developed as the most important thing the Society does, the other work of the Society can hardly stand on a firm footing." While those involved in other parts of the Society's program were bound to emphasize the significance of their enterprises, sometimes to the degree that all else was over-shadowed, there are good reasons to think that most members would have agreed with Mr. Grabill. The Society was what its name said it was, a missionary society. The only problem was, to define clearly the meaning of the words, and then conduct the missionary activity in such a way as to give the definition practical form. This problem became acute during the era under consideration. Granted that the missionary effort was the center of the entire enterprise, what precisely was that effort?

The missionaries called on families in their districts. As before, their interest and their responsibility were for the poor. But "in today's community the absolute, unrelieved poverty of those [early] days no longer exists." During the Douglas era missionaries did not speak of finding children starving or naked, or of opening a door to discover a dead body lying on the floor, as did the missionaries a century or more earlier. True, there were still many families living on a sub-standard basis, and many in quarters that were totally inadequate and ill-equipped; but there was not the awful, grinding, killing poverty, nor the filthy hovels of those earlier days. Public agencies were at work making it impossible for such conditions to exist and opening opportunities for better lives to those who would take them. Side by side with the public agencies were the many private ones, each extending aid to the needy in one form or another:

> Today's trend toward an expanding Social Service State with its great philanthropic enterprises must surely give rise to a re-orientation of much of our Christian charity. The present old age pension, unemployment insurance, day nurseries, school lunch programs, public year-round recreation, and the pending programs of public housing, extended medical care, and cooperative hospital service are but a few of the specific illustrations marking a trend which will surely restrict the scope of private charities.[4]

And that raised the whole question, theoretically at least, of the work the missionaries were to do.

In 1949, the work the missionaries were doing was described in this way: "Literally thousands of calls are made at all hours of the day and night to assist in meeting those tragic needs growing out of alcoholism, premature illness and accidents, divorce, desertion, delinquency and eviction." Four years later the work was defined a bit more carefully: "The resources of our government to meet bodily needs are quite adequate. Yet in the midst of plenty, one is aware of an ever growing sense of deep, personal, social and spiritual need." That statement was followed by a quotation from a recently published book, which was cited with approval, which described:

> a steadily enlarging mass of people whose basic normlessness and insecurity are tragically revealed in the indices of family disintegration and community apathy, in individual, emotional impoverishment, callousness and interpersonal hostility.[5]

What, then, was meant by the poor and needy? The Society, its executive and the missionaries were groping toward a definition of the "poor" that would be applicable to the new day. Since the old definition no longer served, a new one had to be found.

In 1955, the annual report carried another description of the work of the missionaries: they "look always for people who really need help ... going into the streets and alleys, highways and byways in the name of Jesus Christ to feed the hungry, to minister to the sick, to clothe the naked, and to visit those who are in prison." As if to emphasize that understanding of what the missionaries were about, the report for the following year featured, on the cover and inside in its account, "The Seven Corporal Works of Mercy." But that was Social Welfare work, or "Religious Social Work," and the question of the distinction between the service rendered by public agencies and the service rendered by a Christian agency was not answered.

Perhaps there was no distinction. Perhaps the "works of mercy" are "an integral part of the ministry of Jesus Christ, not an optional part of the program. ... In order for the church to be true to its role as the Body of Christ, it must manifest Christ's concern and compassionate action wherever there is human need."[6] Yet clarification of the role of the missionaries was needed. One part of the annual reports served to illuminate this. In 1956 there was a statistical report of the number and kind of calls the missionaries made that year. It is the only report of its kind during the era. Twelve missionaries made over thirteen thousand calls or ninety-one calls a month for each of the missionaries. One third of those calls were on "case work families," and a quarter were on the aged and the shut-ins. There were over a thousand calls on individuals in state and city institutions, and over a thousand calls on families in housing projects. The remainder of the calls were on new families who had moved into the missionaries' districts and on church school children. Compared with a similar statistical report forty years earlier, it is instructive to note the items left out of the more recent one: the number of Bibles given out; the number of persons induced to attend public worship; the number of chapel and neighborhood meetings held; the number of temperance pledges obtained; and, the number of persons hopefully converted. The difference in the items in the statistical reports of these two diverse years indicates a marked change in the understanding of the missionary task.

That change found expression again and again throughout the era in a number of ways. Often it was indistinct, but sometimes it stood out clearly, as for example, in a statement made by the supervisor of one of the Boston Family Work agencies. Of the missionaries she said:

> there are many things which we can do that you cannot; but there are some things you can do which we cannot . . . 1) you can help people directly to a faith in God which may be what they need most of all; 2) you stay with the family through its joys as well as its troubles; 3) you provide an environment in which people may be accepted and given a place regardless of the mistakes and the failures of their past.

That says nothing formally about the "Seven Works of Mercy," but it does define "the poor." For the "poor" become those people who lack the three things the supervisor listed, without which people fall into actions and conditions that are signs of social poverty.

The dilemma involved in this remained throughout the era. Perhaps it had to remain; its resolution only to be mediated through the lives of missionaries who in their own lives as they deal with their families, bring both interpretations of the word "poor" together, becoming the agents through whom the "poor" by God's grace become "rich." The answer to the dilemma, though not in any objective statement, was symbolized in the very arrangements the Society made for the work of the missionaries. For the missionaries were urged to treat their families as cases, and to use in their work all the best case work techniques available, relating their work to that done by other agencies in the city. But the missionaries were also to see their families as God's children, who needed above everything else to be led into a relationship with the church of Jesus Christ. On the one hand, missionaries were assigned to Health and Welfare districts—that was the case work side of their task. On the other hand, they were associated with churches—that was the religious side of their work. The two sides were brought together in the missionaries themselves, as they did all they could to help their families in every aspect of their need.

Camps Andover and Waldron were carried on throughout the era much as before. In 1946, the Board of Directors decided to employ a full-time director for the camp program. Mr. Waldo Stone was secured and when he resigned in 1948, William F. Young, Jr., took his place on a part-time basis. When the new By-laws were adopted in 1948, the camp director was related to the Camp Committee. These arrangements resulted in a more careful selection of leaders, a better organization of activities, and a continuing contact with the campers during the winter months. Improvements were made on the property. The lodge at Camp Andover collapsed in March of 1952, but with the help of many volunteers from the churches, the building was reconstructed in time for the opening of the camping season. A full-time caretaker was secured and housed in a building on the property. The number of individual campers was between 300 and 350 each summer, the majority coming from Congregational churches in Greater Boston, the remainder from other denominations.

In 1948 the Board of Directors spent considerable time discussing the appropriateness of the camping activity. To some members of the Board it seemed that summer camping was not a responsibility of a missionary society. Other agencies were in the field, with excellent equipment, expert leadership, and were charging relatively low fees to the campers. Furthermore, the camps of the Society had been a drain on the financial resources every year since they were started and there was no reason to believe they could ever become self-supporting. Instead, they threatened to become more costly each year as the buildings and equipment wore out and had to be repaired or replaced. These were added reasons why the Society should drop an activity which on grounds of principle had come to be viewed as foreign to the task of a missionary society. Discussion of this matter was carried on with considerable emotion for some time, and a wide circle of interested people in the churches became involved. Summer camping had an appeal and found a substantial number of supporters, particularly among those whose children would be affected, were the Society to stop its camp program. They saw the financial argument as totally specious and the argument from principle as idealistic. After the discussion had continued for a time, the Board voted to continue the program, and the decision was publicly announced. In 1951, the annual report contained a defense of "Church Camping." The statement was a copy of the "Philosophy and Objective for Church Camping," published by the International Council of Religious Education. In general, the statement set forth the idea that inherent in summer camping were a variety of opportunities for Christian experience and Christian learning.

During the era, the campers bore an increasingly large part of the cost of operating the camps, yet that department of the Society's activities did not become self-sustaining. In 1955 the deficit was about $7,500. In June 1958 there was "a recommendation for a study of the camps. The problem is that the City Missionary Society cannot afford to let the camps go on as they have been, in financial deficit. The camps are not being filled to capacity. Many churches have their own private camps and therefore refuse to support the C.M.S. camps. Voted, that a committee be appointed to study the camp situation."[7] There is no indication that a report was ever made by the committee that was named; the camps continued in operation to the end of the era.

The Rosemary program was moved in 1945, to the Farrington Memorial buildings in Lincoln. In 1943 Douglas discussed with the Board the problems connected with the continuing operation of the program at the cottage in Eliot, Maine. The property was badly run down and would need a large outlay of money for repairs in order to bring the equipment up to modern standards. The cost of conducting the program at such a distance from Boston had increased and was becoming almost prohibitive. Facilities that were occasionally needed in emergencies, hospital, doctors, etc., were not easily available. Douglas suggested that, "an alternative might be to find some nearer location where a building could be projected with the hope of making wider use of facilities. Conceivably our churches could find practical use for such property in seasons other than summer."[8] In 1944, "the providential discovery of Farrington Memorial more than fulfills the hope expressed in that [1943] report." That is the way the report reads. But actually the discovery of the nearby property and the vision of what could be done with it and the opening of negotiations to bring the vision into actuality were all the work of Earl Douglas. The story goes that one day he was driving up Route 2 when he happened to catch sight of the unused Farrington Memorial property. He stopped the car and got out to make inquiries. And there came to him then an idea of the way the property might be made more useful. Perhaps that story is apocryphal, but it need not be, for it is truly indicative of the keen creative perception and readiness to act which characterized Earl Douglas. Farrington Memorial had been established under the will of Col. Charles Farrington, a Boston merchant, which provided a trust fund to be used for the care of neglected city children. The buildings were opened in 1912 as "a vacation home for needy children and others." Trustees of the Foundation carried on a program from 1912 to 1941, when financial difficulties compelled the discontinuance of the program.

The property in Eliot, Maine was deeded to the Manchester, New Hampshire, Family Welfare Society which proposed to use it as a place to which children might be taken on outings. The Rosemary program continued with the same purpose at Farrington Memorial as in earlier years.

"The Dilemma of Our Aged. Among the problems your staff has always with it, none is more appealing or acute than the care of the aged." Thus began a page of the 1946 annual report, the words printed in large type. The same page was repeated in the report two years later. It is not known what Douglas had in mind as a way by which the Society might deal with the problem. The missionaries were continually calling on the aged, and were frequently asked to help them find suitable places to live, so it would appear they were doing everything that could be done by the Society. Then the Hyams Trust made a sizeable grant to Farrington Memorial. A farmhouse on the property was renovated and modernized; ladies from a number of the churches provided furnishings, put up pictures and curtains, and in other ways made the place delightfully livable. And a program named "Meadowcrest," directed by one of the missionaries, was started, through which elderly women were able to spend a holiday away from the city.

> Meadowcrest accommodates eight campers at a time, most of whom are in their sixties and seventies. Thirty-five women enjoyed the facilities this year. . . . To some Meadowcrest meant plenty of good food; to others, a change in environment; to others, it gave a much needed rest; and to most of them, it meant new friends. They have walked in the woods and on the grass. They have watched the sun paint the sky at eventide. They will have pleasant memories to brighten their sunset years. . . . The most popular activity was the daily rides. The ladies grew to love the station wagon.[9]

In 1956 Douglas discovered a cabin in the Blue Hills which was available to the Society if the Board would assume responsibility for it:

> The outlook is excellent, located on Ponkapoag Pond with approximately a 100 foot water frontage. It has the service of the Mounted Police several times a day. The cabin is structured in log cabin style and is in good condition. It has an outside fireplace and good basic equipment. It is an ideal spot for creative outdoor activities . . . there is no taxation and there would be no cost for the City Missionary Society.

The Board voted to assume the responsibility recommended, thus adding another bit of equipment to its outdoor program. For a time the cabin was much used by small groups from the city churches as a center for overnight camping and for day-time picnicing. But the upkeep of the property and the problems created by destructive marauders became too much for the Society to handle and the project was abandoned. The interest of the Society in the property was disposed of in 1960.

During the era, the Society restored two programs which it had dropped years before. In 1946 a missionary was appointed for work with the Chinese. At the time the Chinese Christian Church of New England was organized as an interdenominational fellowship. The missionary was assigned to work with that church. For most of the years which followed, the missionary appointees were women of Chinese ancestry. Then in 1943, Douglas proposed engaging in a summer program of religious education, on the grounds, a) that such was in line with the avowed purpose of the Society: "the moral and religious instruction of the poor"; b) that the Society had earlier participated in such a program; and c) that there was no comparable work being done through Congregational resources. Miss Lillian Moeschler was employed to develop the program, arrange training classes for leaders, hold conferences with the leaders during the course of the program, and carry on a schedule of visitation of the Vacation Church Schools which might be established. As this activity developed, a plan was worked out with Andover Newton Theological School under which students would be able to do their field work training in the schools with Miss Moeschler as advisor. This was called the Boston Summer Service Group. College students from various parts of the country enrolled in the program and were given an experience in religious education. It was hoped that the experience would lead to a vocational choice of religious work by some of those in the program, as indeed happened. There were twenty-four students in the program in 1952 from fourteen states, Puerto Rico, and Nova Scotia.

For a time, the number of Vacation Schools and the number of children enrolled increased each year. By 1949 there were forty schools in operation with over thirty-five hundred children participating:

> The Vacation Church School represents for some a cool, quiet place; . . . for some, opportunities to go places and see things; . . . for some, their only contact with the Christian Church; . . . for some, an introduction to a higher form of discipline; . . . children advance in attitudes toward and materials of worship; . . . children profit in increased knowledge and ability to use leisure time intelligently.[10]

But in 1953 the program was stopped:

> Today there are more recreational programs planned and supervised by city and local communities . . . new swimming and wading pools . . . more day camp type operations . . . mothers formerly available for service now seek employment . . . difficult to secure workers.

Miss Moeschler's responsibilities with the Society were, accordingly, changed.

In 1954 the Society entered into cooperative arrangements for the establishment of other new enterprises. The Society joined with the Massachusetts Congregational Conference and the Andover Newton Theological School in appointing and supporting a full-time chaplain at the Boston City Hospital. To the Society, the appointment meant a minister who would keep in continuing touch with individuals from families under the care of the missionaries when they were hospitalized. To the Conference, the appointment meant a person to visit Congregationalists who might not otherwise be reached by pastors of the churches. For the Theological School, the appointment fitted in with its clinical pastoral training program:

> And the same year: The Missionary Committee recommended that the Executive Secretary be authorized to enter into a joint relationship with the Old South Church and Andover Newton Theological School in the employment of a student to work in the South End. The cost of the project would be borne in equal amounts by the three agencies. The Board voted to approve this recommendation.[11]

In 1816, when the Society began, the work was done by church laymen who had been made aware of some serious needs in their town. No professional person was employed and no staff of experts recruited. All work was purely "voluntary." Douglas, in one of the reports he prepared for distribution among the members of the churches, wrote of the thousands of people, members of the one hundred fifty Congregational churches in the Metropolitan area, who could and should be actively at work giving expression to their Christian committment in active service for others. They represented an almost untouched resource of power and influence which should be used. The 'voluntary principle' on which the Society was founded and which is basic to the Christian faith needed restoring. That was the case Douglas made. However, he saw the possibilities in a limited way:

> What I have said [in the 1949 Report] concerning visits to the State Prison can be repeated over and over in relation to other state and city institutions located in Metropolitan Boston. Here one will

find many of the most pathetic of our forgotten people. They are
legion and their greatest need is for friendly interest. Put alongside
this observation the fact that our suburban churches have literally
hundreds of men and women with cars, good will and the desire for
worth-while service. The Christian obligation is clear and the possible ramifications in our Congregational fellowship are staggering.[12]

Although the vision was limited, Douglas saw it. He challenged
the Hancock Church in Lexington to support some plan that
would implement the vision. In consultation between the Society
and some of the church leaders, the latter proposed the establishment of what they called "Project Voluntarism," and they
pledged church support to underwrite the cost of such a program.
In June of 1955, the Reverend Gordon Heriot became the first
director of Project Voluntarism. A year later Mr. Horace M. Besecker, Jr., replaced Mr. Heriot. In 1957, "volunteers made 244
calls on elderly, lonely people in their homes and nursing homes
. . . individuals and groups in 52 churches made articles of clothing which was distributed by the missionaries . . . programs for
the men at Walpole State Prison were provided, men called on
the inmates . . . drivers transported families and individuals to
the camps, helped relatives visit the prisons, assisted people going
to the clinics . . . the camps benefited by work week-ends." Two
hundred ninety-two volunteers from seventy-seven churches were
involved in the program the following year.

Almost from the time he took office, Douglas spoke and wrote
of a possible United Protestant Strategy for the city of Boston.
He may well have hoped to see and take part in some such development. "The next logical step for Protestants in Boston is to
evolve a structure . . . looking toward a more united and inten-
sive Protestant city strategy." On one occasion he used as an illustration of what might be done the formation of St. John's
Church of East Boston, which was a federation of an Episcopal,
a Methodist and a Congregational church, none of which could
have survived alone. On occasion he connected the emphasis
with the formation of the World Council of Churches at Amsterdam in 1948. A united Protestantism in the city "would bring

Amsterdam to Boston" was the way he urged the matter. His reporting of the formation of St. John's Church was for the purpose of highlighting the death of the Union Church, a Congregational institution which, after a history of one hundred twenty-five years had closed its doors for lack of strength to maintain itself. But Douglas' interest in a united Protestantism had to reckon with denominational loyalties and interests, and he knew it. So although he continued to return to the subject on occasion, he directed his energies primarily into the Congregationalism of Boston, the denomination with which the Society had a direct relationship.

Very soon after his appointment he sought a friendly working relationship with the staff of the Massachusetts Congregational Conference and Missionary Society. Through the years he fostered and strengthened that relationship. When in 1951, the Society and the Conference, acting jointly, invited the four Boston Associations of Churches to meet and consider how they could be more closely associated in work in the city, doubtless Douglas had a great deal to do with the arrangements for that meeting. Dr. Ross Sanderson, Director of Field Research of the Congregational Board of Home Missions, at the time, spoke. Before the meeting adjourned, a committee was appointed to meet and consider the possibility of conducting a survey of the Boston area. The committee met, and after considerable discussion, decided to recommend the creation of a Survey Committee which would raise sufficient money and then employ Dr. Sanderson to make such a survey. The City Missionary Society was asked to be one of the sponsoring groups. The Board discussed the invitation and voted, "to defer at this time any action as to contributing toward the further employment of Dr. Sanderson." That was in 1952. Nothing more than that appears, either in the Minutes of the Board Meetings or the Annual Reports. But out of the various conferences and consultations came the creation of the Boston Area Congregational Committee. (The B.A.C.C.)

That committee, representing the four Boston Associations was to:

... work with the staff member [of the Massachusetts Congregational Conference] assigned to the Metropolitan Area of Boston to help in coordinating the resources of Congregationalism with the area and studying ways and means for promoting greater fellowship in the Metropolitan Area; whether through more frequent meetings of the four Associations, combining the various ministers' clubs, adjusting Association lines, developing public relations or whatever ways may seem to be the most desirable and effective.[13]

At that time the Board of the Society gave serious attention to the relationship which was proposed with the new area committee. Finally it was agreed that such a relationship should be maintained. In 1957 Mr. Carlisle Crosby was chosen to be the representative of the Society on the B.A.C.C.

In 1950 Earl Douglas had been elected by the Massachusetts Congregational Conference to be its Boston Area Secretary. In that position, which he held jointly with his position at the City Missionary Society, he had certain responsibilities for the life and well-being of the churches in the metropolitan area. As Douglas wrote when he assumed the Conference work, "I am able to consider the interests of both groups in the field of missionary extension, as those interests may appear in relation to the total inter-denominational Protestant strategy in the area."[14] When the Boston Area Congregational Committee was formed, Mr. Elliott Grabill was named the chairman. From the very start of the new committee the relationship with the Society was implemented by both the chairman and the executive officer.

Throughout the Douglas era the Society faced one continuing problem: finances. From the year of the Garrett bequest the Society operated under what may be called a paper deficit. Year after year the income of the Society for current expenses, that is income from invested funds, churches, individuals and the programs of the Society was less than the expenditures. Yet the Society remained completely solvent and ended each year with a balance. Mathematically and fiscally the performance was an impossibility but practically it was done. The explanation was that each year the Society received a number of legacies, some of which were unrestricted and undesignated and therefore available for whatever use the Directors might determine. For example, during the year 1952-53 the income of the Society was $131,-252. and the expenditures were $520 less, according to the financial report made by the treasurer. However, included in the income were over $25,000. received as legacies from five different estates. Of that amount $17,000 were added to the investments of the Society, the balance being used for current expenses. That procedure, completely correct, legal, and justifiable, enabled the Society to meet the demands caused by the increasing inflation in the contemporary economy and its own developing program.

Early in 1952 "Mr. Grabill ... pointed out that we have been running a deficit of $25,000 to $35,000 annually in recent years. He thought it was the consensus that, 1) we do not want to cut down the work of the Society, yet 2) we do not want to continue deficit financing of the work indefinitely; therefore, 3) we must broaden the base of our income from the churches. Various means were suggested."[15] A committee was appointed to make recommendations, but no report was ever made, and the Board went on approving budgets and making special appropriations without due regard for the deficits that appeared. Finally, in December 1954, the finance committee of the Board recommended that the firm of Marts and Lundy "be engaged to make a complete survey of the City Missionary Society, with the thought in mind of the practicality of a fund raising campaign to improve the Society's financial position." The Board so voted "it being understood that this was only a basic survey and was not a fund raising campaign."

Marts and Lundy sent one of their experts to Boston. He made a careful study of the Society's finances, the sources of its income, and presented a detailed report with recommendations. The report said that the Society should not consider a fund-raising campaign at the time, that the public relations of the Society were exceedingly poor with the result that large numbers of Congregational church members were completely ignorant of the Society, its work and their relationship to it. It recommended that the Society employ a Director of Public Relations and Finance to lead in a long-range continuing program of educating the con-

stituency of the churches and winning them to the support of the
Society. Following the reception of the report, the Board employed the recommended director and voted to continue deficit
financing for the time being.

The Reverend Reuben Coleman joined the staff of the Society
in 1956. Mr. Grabill, in his president's message for that year commented upon this:

> This last year will probably be looked back upon as the year in
> which the Society moved to come of age from a financial point of
> view and thus match its pre-eminent position in the field of service.
> It has been the year in which the officers and members of the Corpo-
> ration have faced the financial future and the problems of the So-
> ciety, and have taken steps to go forward, not by eliminating need for
> work, but rather to obtain reasonable backing from those for whom
> the Society works. . . . The work is being implemented and directed
> in devoted fashion by Reuben Coleman, himself a minister with wide
> experience in this kind of work.[16]

In 1957 a "Fair Share" program was launched. Churches were
asked to appropriate an amount equal to 2% of their current expense budget as their contribution to the work of the Society.
That program caused a bit of perturbation on the part of other
denominational missionary agencies who saw in it a threat, even
though a minor one, to their efforts to secure increasing missionary contributions from the churches. But the program was
launched and within a year twenty churches became "Fair Share
Churches." Over eighty other churches contributed to the work
of the Society although they did not meet the standard suggested
by the Fair Share Program. Even so, the expenditures of the Society for the year 1958 were $145,295 and the current program
income $108,635, the deficit being met, as before, by the use of
unrestricted funds.

The Society experienced some personnel changes. In 1947 Dr.
Coe left the presidency of the Society, but remained a member of
the Corporation. Mr. Elliott Grabill, who had by that time returned from military service went back to the office he left at the
outbreak of the war. In the interim he had moved to Lincoln and
transferred his membership to the First Parish Church. He re-

mained as president of the Society until 1957; then, the Reverend Charles Styron, pastor of the First Parish Church, Lincoln, was elected to the office.

But the more important change concerns Earl Douglas. During the years he was the executive of the Society he occupied a number of other very responsible positions. He appears to have taken those positions either because they were involved in the development of the Society's program or because they were implicated in the thrust he made in the direction of a united Congregationalism in the city. As with most men, he took his place on various boards and committees in the city such as, the Board of Directors of the Howard Benevolent Society, the Executive Committee of the Citizens Crime Commission, president of the Boston Congregational Club, and the Evaluation Committee of the Greater Boston Council for Youth. Those positions were normal ones for an individual interested and involved in community life.

But over and above those, and much more important and responsible, were the following: Executive Secretary of the Farrington Memorial Inc., Vice-president and then President of the Chinese Church of New England, the Boston Area Secretary for the Massachusetts Congregational Conference, and the President of the Boston Council of Churches. Each of those positions involved heavy responsibilities, yet each of them had a connection with the work of the Society. As Douglas wrote on one occasion, referring to only one of those positions, although the words would apply equally well to all of them, "The new relationship has enabled me to perform many new tasks which simply could not be done when the two agencies were working independently of one another." It is not known whether there were other conditions in the work of the Society which led to some of those appointments. The records give no indication. But purely from the point of view of the purposes of the Society, there was a certain logic to the fact that Douglas held those other offices. It might be concluded, in the absence of any record to the contrary, that the reorganization of the staff of the Society, with its departmentalization and decentralization, was necessary in order to free Douglas for those other positions. If that were the case, then the Society through the positions held by Douglas was literally making itself an agency which united other agencies and churches in service to Boston.

In September 1958 Earl Douglas was incapacitated by a serious illness. When the Board realized that their executive might be absent for a fairly lengthy period of time, an Executive Administrative Committee was appointed, consisting of the Reverend Charles Styron, Miss Lillian Moeschler, associate to the executive secretary, and Mr. Carlisle Crosby, the treasurer. The committee was asked to assume oversight of the ongoing work of the Society and to make such decisions as were required in the day by day activity. In May of the following year, Douglas, learning that his illness was far more serious than had earlier been suspected, presented his resignation to take effect on the first of September. The Board accepted the resignation with deep regret and made Douglas the Honorary President of the Society. Two months after the resignation became effective, Douglas died. Concerning his years of leadership the Board noted in its records, that "During this time the Society had tripled in size, activity and work load. A volume could be written on what was accomplished during the period."

CHAPTER XI

Into the Future 1958–

AFTER DOUGLAS' RESIGNATION had been received, the Board appointed a committee to seek out men who might be considered as possible candidates for the executive office. Recommendations were received and investigations made, and four months after they began their work, the committee proposed the name of the Reverend Sydney Menk, then in the employ of the Presbytery of New York City. Mr. Menk accepted the invitation extended to him and began his work with the Society in September 1959. On November 22, he was officially inducted into office at a service of worship held in the Mt. Vernon Church. He became the executive secretary of the Society and the Associate Minister of the Massachusetts Congregational Conference, filling the two offices which Douglas had held. In March 1961, Mr. Menk resigned from the Society to accept the pastorate of the Church of the Covenant in Boston. The months during which he held office were filled with routine matters and a number of emergency situations that had to be handled, such as the financing and building of the new dining hall at the camps and some rather serious personnel changes that had to be made. With his departure, responsibility for the administration of the Society's work was placed, once again, in the hands of an executive committee, the Reverend Charles Styron, Mr. Carlisle Crosby, and Mr. Horace Besecker, Jr. The latter was the Director of Social Services for the Society.

By December the Board had agreed upon a person for the executive position and extended an invitation to the Reverend Nelsen Schlegel, then the Field Secretary of the Council for Christian Social Action of the United Church of Christ. Mr. Schlegel had been a teacher in schools in the Near East and a pastor of churches in the States before assuming his position with the Council for Social Action. It was with a good deal of anticipation that the members of the Society looked forward to his coming. He arrived early in the year 1962 and was presented to a meeting of the Board on February 7th and to a large gathering of the Society and interested friends in May. For some time previously, consultations between representatives of the Society and the Massachusetts Congregational Conference had taken place concerning the relationship existing between the two organizations. The proposal for those consultations had come from the Conference, the officers of which were deeply interested in the strengthening of the work of the churches in the metropolitan area. The subject was one which had been brought into the center of attention during the Douglas era and had been dealt with at that time by making the executive of the Society the Conference minister for the Boston Area. The upshot of the consultations was the decision to stop the arrangement which had existed and proceed along other lines. Mr. Schlegel, therefore, when he took office was not asked to wear the two hats his predecessor had acquired.

Reviewing the work of the few years that have elapsed since the Douglas era closed, it is impressive to note the interest the Society has taken in its supporting constituency. Members of the corporation have been elected as provided in the By-laws and the Board of Directors chosen from among the members of the corporation. But there has been added a provision by which churches supporting the Society with gifts have chosen representatives who would attend meetings of the corporation. These representatives were named for one year, at the end of which time the supporting churches were invited to name their successors. Thus a much wider circle of people have been brought into direct contact with the work of the Society.

At the same time much more care has been exercised in the planning for and the conduct of the Quarterly Meetings of the corporation. All too often in the past these meetings were not held, or attendance was small and the program rather routine and hurriedly arranged. No agreement had been reached as to the most suitable time for holding the meetings, so that from one meeting to the next, the time was changed, shifting from the noon hour with lunch, to the late afternoon ending with supper, to the evening hours beginning with dinner. The programs of the meetings tended to consist of a report by the executive and a discussion of finances. During more recent years the Quarterly Meetings have been held regularly at a stated time. The place of meeting has rotated so that various supporting churches might entertain the Society and the church members hear of the work. The programs of the meetings have been designed to educate those in attendance about the program of the Society. There has been a marked increase in the number of individuals attending the Quarterly Meetings, some of this due without doubt to the greater number of people invited, but that does not appear to be the only reason for the growing interest in the meetings.

The camping program has continued, much as in previous years. The dining hall at Camp Andover burned in 1959 but special gifts were secured to add to the insurance money, and a new building erected to serve as a joint dining hall for both the camps. In 1960, the new structure was dedicated in honor of Earl Douglas. The farm building at Farrington Memorial burned in 1959, which necessitated a rearrangement of the Meadowcrest program for that summer. In 1960, a program called Family Camp was instituted at Farrington Memorial and has been continued with much acceptability since. In 1962 a new headquarters cabin was built at Camp Andover through a generous gift by Mrs. Willard Savage of Wellesley Hills. That same year the United Community Services appointed a committee to study and evaluate the properties and programs of New England camps. That committee recommended that certain changes be made in the kitchen and dining hall at the Society's camps. The changes were effected and the camps were given approved standing by the American Camping Association with an unusually high rating.

In 1963 the Missionary Committee of the Board raised the question of the place of the Christian mission in the work of a society which carries the word "missionary" in its title. That same year the annual report contained a rather extensive description of that one part of the Society's program:

> The major thrust of the Society's program in 1963 was, again, in the area of social welfare. Ten full time workers, and three part time workers, comprised our field staff. . . . All these missionary social workers are assigned to Boston Health and Welfare areas, and they are associated with churches in which they have their headquarters. They work with pastors in aiding needy people in their several neighbourhoods. They meet needs which are often material with emergency assistance. . . . But even more important at times is the aid they give to lonely and frustrated persons, and to families troubled with marital problems, illegitimacy, juvenille delinquency, alcoholism, desertion.

Perhaps the interesting difference in the titles of the work and the workers is an indication of the question that is being raised for the Society by the new age into which the world has moved and the lines along which the answers to the question are being sought. The program is now called "social welfare" and the workers "missionary social workers." Whether anything is really meant by the addition of the word "missionary" in the latter designation and what that meaning is, is an issue that is not settled. And it is the problem which became quite clear during the Douglas era, but which at the time was passed over as other matters claimed the attention of the Society.

In 1960 Mr. Horace Besccker, Jr. was made the Director of Social Services. In that position he was responsible for supervision of the employed missionaries and for a certain amount of social case work which he, personally, carried on. The following year there were eight full time missionaries on the staff. One had been with the Society for seventeen years, another for twelve years, another for nine, two more for eight years each, one for six years and one for four. That means, that of the eight missionaries, seven had joined the Society during the Douglas era. Since 1961 three of those missionaries have left the Society, one through retirement, another by resignation, and the third by death. Five of those missionaries remain. In 1962 the Board took note of the fact that four of them were nearing retirement.

In the meanwhile a number of persons have been added to the staff, and in the annual reports have been listed as having rela-

tionships with local churches in accordance with previous practice. It is noticeable, however, that the new employees have been,
without exception, either graduates of schools of social work, students in such schools, or have had some kind of graduate education that would prepare them for professional service with people. It is also noticeable that nearly all the new employees were
assigned to some specialized task or some new enterprise in which
they were asked to be responsible for certain well-defined work.
These new conditions would not necessarily interfere with a
church relationship, although they might, but certainly a more
specific direction appears to be indicated in the work of the Society by the type of people who have recently been employed.
This new trend appears in a statement approved for publication
by the Board of Directors in 1964:

> Today the Society expresses its purpose, still within this charter
> [of 1820, as modified in 1887] as ministering in the name and spirit
> of Christ to people with special needs in Metropolitan Boston, pro-
> viding not only material relief but also spiritual sustenance: new
> hope to the unfortunate and renewed faith to the discouraged. Al-
> ways it seeks to strengthen an appreciation of moral values and a
> sense of individual responsibility to enable persons to help them-
> selves to a better life.[1]

The Voluntarism Program has continued. In 1961 Mrs. Besecker was appointed interim director of the program when her
husband was made responsible for the Social Services and the
following year she was made a full-time permanent staff member. The number of individuals participating in this program
and the number of churches from which the volunteers have
come have increased each year. The original elements in the program—the calling in nursing homes, hospitals, and the Walpole
State Prison; the repair and upkeep work at the camps; the chauf-
feuring service for needy people—have continued. Training conferences for volunteers have been held. Through the kindness of
that institution's trustees, a headquarters for the work has been
established at the Farrington Memorial where the director has
her office, conferences are held, and gifts of food and clothing are
deposited. New lines of activity have opened: an adult literacy

program, and an after-school tutoring program in parts of the city where the percentage of school drop-outs is high.

A number of new enterprises have been launched. In 1961, Miss Moeschler, who quite clearly has been a most important member of the staff inasmuch as she has filled various positions, was asked to become for the second time the Consultant in Religious Education. In this re-assignment Miss Moeschler conducted church workers' training institutes and gave direct help to nearly twenty different churches. Under her guidance a program known as "Friendly Town" was promoted. The idea for this came from the church in Plympton. In 1960 families of that church invited children from the city to be their guests for a period of time during the summer months, thus providing the guests with a chance to get away into the country, and the hosts an opportunity to become acquainted with city youngsters. By 1964 churches in eighteen towns had enlisted in the program with ninety-nine families playing host to one hundred forty children.

In 1964 "Project Funmobile" was begun. A truck was donated by a church layman and equipped with play materials of all conceivable kinds. A worker was employed by the Society to have charge of the activity. Young people of suburban churches were asked to help. Forty-five different individuals gave one hundred seventy-four weeks of volunteer service. Each day, the truck, with its equipment and the workers, drove to the Columbia Point Housing area and led the youngsters living there in programs of activity. Over a thousand children participated each week. Said the policeman at the Point, "It's a Godsend."

The Blue Hill Protestant Parish had its inception with an enterprise launched by the Eliot Church in Roxbury in cooperation with Andover Newton Theological School. After a somewhat hesitant start there came a period of rapid development until the program became indigenous to the Blue Hill district. Shortly after its beginning, the Society began to aid in the work. Staff members, who were in some cases students at the theological school, came under the supervision of Mr. Besecker, until a full-time director for the Parish was hired. Some staff members were employed jointly by the Society and the Parish, and the responsibilities of the workers divided between the programs of the two agencies.

In 1963, the missionary societies or interested committees of six Protestant denominations, Baptist, Congregational, Episcopal, Methodist, Unitarian Universalist, Presbyterian, united in the employment of a Protestant chaplain for the Columbia Point Housing Project. Nearly 7,000 people live in the project, among whom are 274 families with Protestant backgrounds. In those families are nearly eight hundred children. The nearest Protestant church is about a mile away. The Society has had missionaries visiting regularly in the project for some time. The participation of the Society in the support of the chaplain is but an extension of an interest taken much earlier.

During the Douglas era the Society established relationships with other agencies and institutions in the city, and through those relationships entered into jointly-conducted tasks. The practice of engaging in cooperative enterprises has continued. In 1962 the Society entered into an agreement with the Boston University School of Social Work by which the Society became one of the agencies providing field work opportunities for students of the school and supervision for the students' work. There is no way of knowing how many of these new enterprises will become permanent parts of the program of the Society. They are lines along which the Society has moved as it has sought to take its place in the life of the new age.

With the Washington Park urban renewal project, another opportunity for service was presented to the Society. By the early months of 1963 more than six hundred families living in the Washington Park area had been notified by the Boston Redevelopment Authority that they would have to move. While the cost of moving is met in large part by the authority, the very fact of having to move created a wide variety of personal problems for the individuals who were involved. The government workers responsible for the renewal program were quite unable, because they were so few and their time was fully occupied by the task in hand, to deal with the personal problems and needs. As one outcome the Society secured a trained person to direct and supervise volunteers from the churches who are willing to serve as advisors to such displaced families wanting help. Volunteers have appeared; families to be relocated have sought counsel and advice; and Voluntarism has added another task to its list of opportunities for service. The basic purpose of Voluntarism, the relating of Christian people to the needs of the city, has grown clearer through the years. But it must be said that the program will be useful and challenging only as meaningful needs are discovered and when Christian people realize that their commitment calls them to give answer to those needs.

When Mr. Schlegel became the executive secretary of the Society he was asked to serve in only one of the dual roles Douglas held. The Congregational Conference had other plans. Those plans, however, involved the Society, so that the change in the responsibilities of the executive did not indicate a drawing apart of the two organizations. Since the day the Boston Congregational Committee had been formed, conversations had continued, with lapses, about the future possibilities of that committee. The Conference had secured the Reverend Allen Hackett, pastor of the Pilgrim Church in St. Louis, as the Greater Boston area minister. That helped to set the stage for the developments which followed in rapid succession.

In 1961 the Society appointed a special committee to work with representatives of the four Congregational Associations in Greater Boston in a study of the structure of Congregationalism in the urban area. Early in 1962, the Reverend Albert Penner, minister of the Congregational Conference, spoke to the Board of the Society about the proposed Metropolitan Boston Association of the United Church of Christ. Subsequently, the Reverend Frederick Meek, the Reverend Charles Styron, and the executives of the Society were asked to represent the Society in a meeting of the four Boston Associations to work out a detailed plan for the new structure. In the constitution of the Metropolitan Boston Association, prepared by that committee and presented for study to the constituent organizations, was the following provision:

> The City Missionary Society is one of the constituting bodies which comprise the Metropolitan Boston Association. It shall be a

recognized instrumentality of the Metropolitan Boston Association, with voting privileges and the relationships as specified in the Constitution and the By-laws.

The Board of the Society approached this proposal with due caution, as befitted an organization with a history of a century and a half behind it. In March 1963 the Board said in its Minutes, "The City Missionary Society desires to become in a large measure the instrumentality of the Metropolitan Boston Association in furthering the churches' mission in Boston." The following September, a resolution was presented at a meeting of the corporation and adopted:

> The City Missionary Society, while eager to retain its historic autonomy, endorses the formation of the Metropolitan Association, pledges its support to efforts which may lead to further commitment to Christian mission among the people of our churches in Metropolitan Boston, and offers the services of its officers and staff toward the development of plans and programs which may lead to more effective Christian services to people with great social and religious needs.

Having given voice to its feeling about the united development, the Society took its place in the new Association. The Reverend Charles Styron became the first chairman of the M.B.A. Council, and the Reverend Allen Hackett became a member of the Board of the Society. And as if to give testimony to the union that had come about, when the M.B.A. voted to establish a Department of Housing and Public Education and to employ a trained person to head that department, the vote carried with it the stipulation that the director, when secured, be on the staff of the City Missionary Society.

At this point the story stops, but doesn't really end. A new day has dawned for Greater Boston and no one can guess what the future holds in store. The City Missionary Society moves into that unknown future carrying with it the accumulated experiences of the past, the courage born of numerous victories over strange and difficult circumstances, and the willingness to venture into new enterprises granted it by the faith of its members in the Living Christ of the Church.

EPILOGUE

To Speed the Day

T HE CITY MISSIONARY SOCIETY has completed one hundred and fifty years of service to its community. The story began with a group of men who were moved by the dynamics of their faith to bring it to those of their contemporaries who were denied its blessings by ignorance and poverty. Their beliefs about their responsibilities for others led them to clothe that faith in activities defined by the needs they discovered. The purpose of the Society was clear, and the means that were used for gaining that purpose were relevant to the conditions existing at the time.

The same principles are just as discernible in the next period of the Society's history. As the years passed, the character of Boston altered profoundly. The homogeneity of the population was broken by the vast influx of alien people who came to the city out of their own dire need; the customs and standards by which people had lived were no longer widely held, not only through the impact of the newcomers but also because many of the citizens who had their homes in Boston moved into the suburbs, choosing to live away from the turmoil of the city while maintaining their offices or places of business in it; and the face of the city had been transformed, as the older sections became more and more dilapidated and over-crowded, and as extensive public and private works added to the land area and provided easier movement in and out of the city.

Along with this the understanding which members of the Society had of their religious faith had undergone a significant modification growing out of their pietistic heritage and the evangelistic emphasis of the period. The city was literally crowded with poor, ignorant, and, as the Society believed, heathen people who were utterly lost, and the Society set out to rescue as many as they could, going to them with the faith it held and the beliefs by which its members expressed that faith. The work took new and different forms in the latter time, a sign that the Society had adjusted its ways to a changed world and a changed understanding of the Christian faith.

There is a significance not to be overlooked in the hiatus between the early period and the later. The men who made up the Society were quite sure that God had some use for their organization, but they did not know what that use was. They had gone through periods of doubt and uncertainty as they finally decided to give up the two main pieces of work they had been doing, turning them over to other more inclusive and effective agencies than theirs. The move seemed to them to be the right one to make for the best interests of those for whom they had deep concern, but it left them with practically nothing to do. Some in the Society wished they had never relinquished those activities; others suggested starting some parallel activities to at least be busy, but second thoughts showed the futility of that. So they waited. There were those who fell away believing that doing nothing was rather a useless business. Those who remained kept themselves united in faith and commitment, trusting that a way would open to them if such were to be their future.

Members of the Society now, as they look back on those earlier years from the vantage point of a broadened understanding and richer experience, are bound to have mixed feelings about the work that was done. There must be the recognition of the courageous faith with which those forefathers labored and a measure of pleasurable pride in their achievements. But mixed in with those feelings there is bound to be some criticism, even stern judgment. There is much that is wrong in what they did, seriously wrong. Yet it is only men of the present who can see that. Those who lived and worked a century and more ago did what to them, given their faith and the circumstances of their time, were the right things for them to do.

The past has gone. The people who lived and the work they did have been gathered up into the heritage of the past and turned into printed lines on the pages of history.

The City Missionary Society, along with all other institutions and organizations of mankind, is being carried into the future. The city of Boston is changing, some changes wrought consciously and deliberately by the citizens, others coming out of human reactions to the world-wide complex of events that mark each day. The churches of the Metropolitan area are changing, now much more rapidly than in the past, partly consumed by the struggle within them between the conservative members who would maintain things as they are and the liberal people who would stop all that is being done to launch out with new untried programs. The organizational patterns which have bound church to church, and the churches to their agencies, are being changed and in the process are being badly shaken as various groups within them seek to preserve their interests. The era is stamped with change, and the future is unknown.

The problem the Society faces is that of discovering the tasks which peculiarly and properly are its own. Some of the activities which the Society is carrying on are now being done by other agencies, sometimes more effectively than the Society can hope to do them. Other activities which were started to express some new insight into the significance of the Christian faith a few years ago have solidified into forms which may well turn out to be inadequate and irrelevant. And the structure of the Society and its procedures, inherited as they are from earlier years, may not be fitted either to discover what the Society should be doing or to do what it discovers. The present rapidly changing era has in it both a great challenge and a terrible danger.

Those who direct the affairs of an institution may, in their fear of an unknown future or their desire to preserve security for themselves, insist on maintaining the work as it is being done. They can foresee, in small measure at least, the trouble and the pain that will come if changes are made and they choose to continue what *is*, instead of responding creatively and constructively to the new circumstances that have come to be. The City Missionary Society is now, at the end of one hundred and fifty years, in precisely such a position of danger.

But the Society has been in such a position before, and the Society knows from its own past that precisely because there is danger there is also challenge. Surely, the faith which enabled the Society to change itself in those earlier days will suffice to guide the present. The Society has been bequeathed wealth and tradition and the loyalty of many people, but this will not be enough to preserve it as it is. However, it will be more than sustained, if it enters fully, and with faith, into the uncertainties of this changing age.

The spirit of the Society through these one hundred and fifty years has been well-expressed in this prayer by Walter Rauschenbush:

"Grant us a vision of our city, fair as she might be; a city of justice, where none shall prey on others; a city of plenty, where vice and poverty shall cease to fester; a city of brotherhood, where all success shall be founded on service, and honor shall be given to nobleness alone; a city of peace, where order shall not rest on force, but on the love of all for the city, the great mother of the common life and weal. Hear thou, O Lord, the silent prayer of all our hearts as we each pledge our time and strength and thought to speed the day of her coming beauty and righteousness."

Presidents of the Society
(with their Church connection)

1816–1819	Reverend Joshua Huntington	Old South Church
1820–1823	Josiah Salisbury	Old South Church
1824–1832	Samuel Hubbard	Park Street Church
1833	John Tappan	Union (Essex Street) Church
1834–1835	Pliny Cutler	Old South Church
1836–1840	John C. Proctor	Park Street Church
1841–1843	Julius A. Palmer	Park Street Church (charter member Mt. Vernon Church)
1844–1845	Philip Greeley Jr.	Bowdoin St. Church
1846	William T. Eustis	Park Street Church
1847–1849	Ezra Farnsworth	Park Street Church
1850–1855	Daniel Safford	Park Street Church (charter member Mt. Vernon Church)
1856–1862	Charles Scudder	Old South Church (transfered to Union Church)
1863–1869	Edward S. Tobey	Mt. Vernon Church
1870–1872	Charles G. Nazro	Mt. Vernon Church
1873–1874	Amos W. Stetson	Union Church
1875–1885	James White	Salem Street Church
1886–1891	Arthur W. Tufts	Walnut Ave. Church
1892–1907	Richard H. Stearns	Old South Church
1908–1915	Jacob P. Bates	Harvard Church, Brookline
1916–1920	Arthur S. Johnson	Old South Church
1920–1936	William Ellison	Eliot Church, Newton
1937–1940	Reverend Charles Dunham	Pilgrim Church, Dorchester
1941	Elliott V. Grabill	Highland Church, Roxbury
1942–1947	Reverend Robert Wood Coe	Leyden Church, Brookline

1948–1957	Elliott V. Grabill	First Parish Church, Lincoln
1957–1962	Reverend Charles M. Styron	First Parish Church, Lincoln
1962–1965	James E. Gallagher	Hancock Church, Lexington
1966	Reverend Stuart C. Haskins	Pleasant St. Congregational Church, Arlington

APPENDIX B

Executives of the Society

During the early years there was some confusion about the employed personnel of the Society. Choice has been made in terms of the responsibility carried by the persons involved.

1818–1833	Reverend William Jenks	Secretary and minister to seamen
1833–1834	Reverend Isaac Barbour	General Agent
1841–1846	Reverend A. A. Phelps	General Agent
1846–1850	Reverend George A. Oviatt	Secretary and General Agent
1842–1892	Mr. Andrew Cushing	1842–1850 missionary 1850–1856 assistant to the president 1856–1892 secretary
1873–1918	Reverend Daniel W. Waldron	1873–1892 clerical missionary 1892–1918 secretary
1919–1927	Reverend Fletcher D. Parker	Secretary
1928–1942	Reverend Ralph H. Rowse	Secretary
1942–1958	Reverend Earl W. Douglas	Executive Secretary
1959–1961	Reverend Sidney G. Menk	Executive Secretary
1962–	Reverend F. Nelsen Schlegel	Executive Secretary

APPENDIX C

Offices of the Society

"In the early years of its history the meetings of the Board of Directors were held at Park Street and Old South Churches, and sometimes at private residences."

—Annual Report 1898, page 7

1841–1846	96 Washington Street, upstairs.
1846–1847	Joy's Building, upstairs. Entrance, 81 Washington St.
1847–1852	21 Cornhill, upstairs.
1852–1857	96 Washington St.
1857–1872	Tremont Temple
1872–1899	19 Congregational House, 7A Beacon St.
1899–	Congregational House, 14 Beacon St.

APPENDIX D

Names of the Society

At its organization October 9, 1816,
  THE BOSTON SOCIETY FOR THE MORAL AND
  RELIGIOUS INSTRUCTION OF THE POOR

At the time of incorporation, February 21, 1820,
  THE BOSTON SOCIETY FOR THE RELIGIOUS AND
  MORAL INSTRUCTION OF THE POOR

The General Court of the Commonwealth of Massachusetts adopted an Act to change the name of the Society, February 27, 1841,
  CITY MISSIONARY SOCIETY

Notes

CHAPTER I

1. Justin Winsor, *The Memorial History of Boston* (Boston: James R. Osgood & Co., 1881), IV, p. 153.
2. M. A. DeWolfe Howe, *Boston, The Place and the People* (New York: The Macmillan Co.), p. 151.
3. Oscar Handlin, *Boston Immigrants* (Cambridge: Harvard University Press, 1959).
4. Winsor, *op. cit.*, IV, p. 28.
5. Howe, *op. cit.*, pp. 193-194.
6. H. Shelton Smith, Robert T. Handy, Lefferts A. Leotachler, *American Christianity* (New York: Charles Scribners & Sons, 1960), p. 537.
7. Joseph S. Clark, *Historical Sketch of the Congregational Churches in Massachusetts* (Boston: Congregational Board of Publication, 1858), p. 229.
8. *Ibid.*, p. 243.
9. Quoted by James Truslow Adams in *New England in the Republic* (Boston: Little Brown & Co., 1926), p. 353.

CHAPTER II

1. Hamilton Andrews Hill, *History of the Old South Church* (Boston: Houghton Mifflin, 1889), II, p. 362.
2. *Ibid.*, p. 431.
3. *Boston Recorder*, October 15, 1841.
4. Hill, *op. cit.*, II, p. 342.
5. Winsor, *op. cit.*, IV, p. 104.
6. Adams, *op. cit.*, p. 198.
7. Hill, *op. cit.*, II, p. 419.
8. Annual Report 1817, p. 2.
9. *Ibid.*, p. 6.
10. Winsor, *op. cit.*, IV, p. 652.
11. Hill, *op. cit.*, II, p. 207.
12. Josiah Quincy, *A Municipal History of the Town and City of Boston* (Boston: Charles Little and James Brown, 1852), p. 20.
13. Winsor, *op. cit.*, IV, p. 246.
14. Hill, *op. cit.*, II, p. 403.
15. Annual Report 1817, p. 6.

CHAPTER III

1. Annual Report 1818, p. 1.
2. Isaac Smith Homans, *Sketches of Boston* (Boston: Phillips, Sampson and Co., 1851), p. 205.
3. Annual Report 1819, p. 22.
4. Hill, *op. cit.*, II, p. 467.
5. *Ibid.*, p. 413.
6. *Ibid.*, p. 412. Quoted from the *Daily Advertiser.*
7. Annual Report 1819, p. 16.
8. Annual Report 1818, p. 4.
9. *Ibid.*, p. 3.
10. Third Annual Report, p. 6.
11. *Ibid.*, p. 8.
12. Annual Report 1819, p. 15.

CHAPTER IV

1. Quincy, *op. cit.*, p. 303.
2. Seventh Annual Report, p. 31, 32.
3. Quincy, *op. cit.*, p. 109.
4. Mary Caroline Crawford, *Romantic Days in Old Boston* (Boston: Little, Brown & Co.), p. 95.
5. Adams, *op. cit.*, p. 403.
6. Homans, *op. cit.*, p. 215.
7. Robert H. Lord, John E. Sexton, and Edward T. Harrington, *History of the Archdiocese of Boston* (New York: Sheed and Ward, 1944) I, p. 695.
8. Adams, *op. cit.*, p. 334.
9. Lord, Sexton, Harrington, *op. cit.*, II, p. 193-194.
10. *Ibid.*, II, 199, as quoted from *The Jesuit*, October 31, 1829.
11. *Ibid.*, II, 196, as quoted.
12. Adams, *op. cit.*, p. 328 f.
13. Annual Report 1820, p. 4.
14. Annual Report 1822, p. 17.
15. Annual Report 1828, pp. 9ff.
16. Annual Report 1826, p. 16.
17. Taken from various Annual Reports 1824 to 1828.
18. Annual Report 1825, p. 4.
19. Annual Report 1828, p. 22.
20. Annual Report 1822, p. 17.
21. Annual Report 1821, p. 7.
22. Annual Report 1824, p. 7.
23. Annual Report 1822, p. 5.
24. Annual Report 1827, p. 16.
25. Annual Report 1828, p. 10.
26. *Ibid.*, p. 7.
27. Annual Report 1826, p. 13.
28. Annual Report 1824, p. 15.
29. Annual Report 1822, p. 42.

30. The *Recorder*, August 17, 1822.
31. Annual Report 1830, p. 1.

CHAPTER V

1. The History of the Old South Church says that Kimball was a member of that congregation, II, 482. The minutes of the B.S.R.M.I.P. for June 10, 1840, say that he was a member of the Pine Street Church.
2. Annual Report 1830, p. 17.

CHAPTER VI

1. Walter Muir Whitehill, *Boston: A Topographical History* (Cambridge: Harvard University Press, 1959), See Chapter V for changes of this period. This delightful and urbane book describes the changing topography of Boston through more than 300 years.
2. Winsor., Justin, *op. cit.*, IV, p. 35.
3. Samuel B. Warner., *Streetcar Suburbs* (Cambridge: Harvard University Press, 1962), p. 14.
4. Adams, *op. cit.*, p. 332.
5. Annual Report 1842, p. 13.
6. Annual Report 1847, p. 6.
7. Annual Report 1848, pp. 4-6.
8. Minutes of the Board Meeting, December 26, 1840.
9. Annual Report 1849, p. 1.
10. Annual Report 1845, p. 10.
11. *Ibid.* 1845, p. 1.
12. Lord, Sexton, Harrington, *op. cit.*, II, p. 652.
13. *Ibid.*, p. 199.
14. Directions to Tract Distributors No. 14.
15. Lord, Sexton, Harrington, *op. cit.*, II, p. 650.
16. Annual Report 1847, p. 4.
17. Annual Report 1844, p. 25.
18. *Ibid.* 1844, p. 5.
19. Minutes of the Board Meeting. October 1, 1849.
20. *Ibid.*, October 9, 1849.
21. Annual Report 1849, p. 6.

CHAPTER VII

1. Annual Report 1891, p. 7.
2. Minutes of the Board Meeting, February 14, 1842.
3. Annual Report 1891, p. 9.
4. Sermon, "In Memory of Andrew Cushing," preached at Mt. Vernon Church, December 4, 1892, by the Rev. Samuel E. Herrick. Pamphlet.
5. *Saturday Review*, July 10, 1965, p. 18.
6. Annual Report 1847, p. 6.
7. Annual Report 1848, p. 5.

8. Lord, Sexton, Harrington, *op. cit.*, II, p. 460.
9. Warner, *op. cit.*, p. 6.
10. Roy A. Bellington, *The Protestant Crusade 1800-1860* (New York: The Macmillan Company, 1938), p. 240.
11. Lord, Sexton, Harrington, *op. cit.* II, pp. 453-454.
12. Handlin, *op. cit.*, p. 109.
13. Winsor, *op. cit.*, III, p. 546.
14. For Bishop Williams' comment, see Lord, Sexton, Harrington, *op. cit.*, III, p. 40.
15. Annual Report 1876, p. 10.
16. Annual Report 1844, p. 21.
17. Annual Report 1848, p. 20.
18. Minutes of the Board Meeting, February 18, 1850.
19. Minutes of the Annual Meeting of the Society, March 5, 1866.
20. Minutes of the Board Meeting, September 20, 1858.
21. Minutes of the Meeting of the Executive Committee, June 27, 1859.
22. Annual Report 1850, p. 6.
23. Annual Report 1860, p. 44.
24. Annual Report 1850, p. 5.
25. Annual Report 1855, p. 9.
26. Annual Report 1865, p. 9.
27. Annual Report 1866, pp. 19-20.
28. Annual Report 1858, pp. 5-7.
29. Annual Report 1862, p. 8.
30. Annual Report 1867, p. 6.
31. Annual Report 1878, p. 11.
32. Annual Report 1879, p. 8.
33. Annual Report 1872, p. 8.
34. Annual Report 1864, p. 5f.
35. Annual Report 1865, p. 19.
36. Annual Report 1904, p. 22.
37. Miss Sidney Moore, *The Heart of a Woman* (Boston: Y.W.C.A., 1966), p. 6.
38. Massachusetts Missionary Society, Annual Report 1839.
39. Annual Report 1881, p. 21.
40. Annual Report 1850, p. 9.
41. Executive Committee Minutes, March 19, 1888.
42. *Ibid.*, May 14, 1888.
43. Annual Report 1883, p. 10.
44. Annual Report 1871, p. 10.

CHAPTER VIII

1. Pamphlet, *Centennial Anniversary*, Published by the City Missionary Society, October 16, 1916, p. 50.
2. *Ibid.*, p. 42.
3. Pamphlet, *Our Centennial*, published by the City Missionary Society, October 16, 1916, p. 27.
4. Hill, *op. cit.*, II, p. 413.
5. Annual Report 1895, p. 11.

6. *Centennial Anniversary*, p. 10, from a paper read by Miss Mary Ballou, one of the missionaries.
7. Annual Report 1903, p. 8.
8. Annual Report 1902, p. 33.
9. Annual Report 1906, p. 28.
10. Annual Report 1911, p. 48.
11. Annual Report 1910, p. 46.
12. Pauline Holmes, *One Hundred Years of Mount Vernon Church* (Brattleboro, Vt.: Vermont Printing Co., 1942), pp. 80-81.
13. Annual Report 1906, p. 32.
14. Annual Report 1913, p. 40.
15. Annual Report 1896, p. 17.
16. Annual Report 1911, p. 30.
17. Annual Report 1910, p. 20.

CHAPTER IX

1. Annual Report 1919, p. 8.
2. Annual Report 1920, p. 10.
3. Survey of the Work of the City Missionary Society, 1930, p. 4.
4. *Ibid.*, p. 5.

CHAPTER X

1. The way Dr. Coe came by that idea is worth relating. In 1941, the Board of the Society had appointed a committee consisting of Dr. Robert Wood Coe, the Reverend Andrew Richards of the Second Church, Dorchester, and Mrs. Ashly Leavitt of Harvard Church, Brookline, to make a survey of the Brighton-Allston district to see if a missionary should be appointed to work there. The committee decided to interview all the ministers in the area. In the course of the interviews they were so impressed by the knowledge and enthusiasm of one man, that when Ralph Rouse presented his resignation they knew precisely who should be his successor. When Dr. Coe spoke to the Reverend Clarence Dunham of the Pilgrim Church, Dorchester, who had been named the chairman of the committee to look for a new executive, he voiced the unanimous opinion of the committee which he had led.
2. Memorial Testimonial prepared on the occasion of Miss Mikaelian's death in 1956 by members of the Cilician-Armenian Church.
3. Annual Report 1948, p. 11.
4. Annual Report 1947, p. 5.
5. Annual Report 1953, p. 5.
6. Annual Report 1957, p. 4.
7. Minutes of the Meeting of the Board of Directors, June 13, 1958.
8. Annual Report 1943, p. 9.
9. Annual Report 1954, p. 8.
10. Annual Report 1947, p. 14.
11. Minutes of the Meeting of the Board of Directors, October 8, 1954.
12. Annual Report 1954, p. 6.

13. Annual Report 1953, p. 7.
14. Annual Report 1952, p. 8.
15. Minutes of the Meeting of the Board of Directors, February 8, 1952.
16. Annual Report 1956, p. 3.

CHAPTER XI

1. C.M.S. Mission, April 1964, p. 3.

Index

Eliot Church, Roxbury, 272
Elliott, Mrs. Harriet, 245
Ellison, William, 221, 238
Embargo Act of 1807, 4
Essex Street Church, 26, 28
Evangelical Union Church, 167

Fair Share Program, 264
Farmer, H. T., 181
Farrar, Miss Cynthia, 55
Farrington Memorial, 255–256, 265, 271
Federal Street Church, 22
Federalists, 4
Female Bible Society, 56
Female Missionary Society, 26, 66
Fenwick, Reverend Benedict, 46
Field, Mrs. Lorena, 147
Finances of the Society, 23, 36, 50–51, 70, 75–76, 79–80, 103, 124, 143–146, 191–193, 229, 235, 262–263
Fire of Boston (1872), 131, 187
First Church in Dorchester, 22
Fisher, Mrs. Ann, 70
Foreign Mission Society of Boston, 13
Foster, Frederick, 223
Freeman, James, 7
Fresh Air Fund Program, 179–180, 214, 220, 225, 233–234
Friendly Town, 272

Gale, Samuel, 70, 75
Garden Street Church, 117
Garrett, Miss Elizabeth, 243
Garrison, William Lloyd, 44
General Agent of the Society, 76, 97
German immigrants, 172–173
Gibbs, Miss Armeda, 149, 167
Gordon, Reverend George A., 190, 216
Government Relief Agencies, 237
Grabill, Elliott V., 238, 240, 250, 263, 264
Grant, Reverend H., 217
Greenleaf, Reverend Jonathan, 63
Gulliver, John, 53

Hackett, Reverend Allen, 275
Hale, David, Jr., 53
Hale, Moses, 82
Hanover Street Church, 47, 78
Hanson, Miss Helena, 245
Harry's Hall, 26–27
Harvard College, 7, 9
Haskell, Ezra, 53
Hawkins Street Sabbath School, 31
Heriot, Reverend Gordon, 260
Herrick, Reverend Samuel, 128, 195
Highland Church, Roxbury, 196
Hobart, Albert, 50
Hollis Chair of Divinity, 7
Home visitation by missionaries, 67, 157–160, 201, 204
Homes, Henry, 14, 22
Hopkins, John, 22, 23, 24
House Meetings, see Social Religious Meetings
House of Correction, 39
House of Industry, 39
Howard Benevolent Society, 207, 265
Hoyt, Henry, 143
Huntington, Reverend Joshua, 12, 13, 15, 21, 50
Hubbard, Samuel, 50, 97

Immigrants, 43–44, 89, 138, 209
Incorporation of the Society, 50
Infant School Society, 82
Institution visiting by the missionaries, 68, 176
Irish famine, 89
Irish immigration, 94, 131–133
Italians, 138

Jaeger, Miss Amelia, 202, 217
Jenkins, Colonel Joseph, 53, 71
Jenks, Reverend William, 28, 29, 50, 62
Jesuit, The, 47
Jewish work, 173
Johnson, Arthur, 189, 190, 216, 220, 221
Jones, Reverend David, 175

Index

293